Garden RAILROADING

Getting Started in the Hobby

Selected by Kent Johnson

KALMBACH BOOKS

 Published by Kalmbach Publishing Co., 21027 Crossroads Circle, Waukesha, WI 53187.

Printed in Canada

02 03 04 05 06 07 08 09 10 11   10 9 8 7 6 5 4 3 2 1

Visit our website at
http://kalmbachbooks.com
Secure online ordering available

Publisher's Cataloging-in-Publication
(Provided by Quality Books, Inc.)

Garden railroading : getting started in the hobby / selected by Kent Johnson. — 1st ed.
p. cm.
ISBN 0-89024-369-7

1. Railroads—Models. I. Johnson, Kent J., 1968-

TF197.G37 2002   625.1'9
QBI02-200009

Art director: Kristi Ludwig
Book design: Mark Watson

Cover photo by Joel Hayward

The material in this book has previously appeared as articles in *Garden Railroading* magazine.

Contents

SECTION 1

Railroading in the great outdoors

Jim Forbes

Do you enjoy gardening? Great! You can combine that interest with large trains. It's called garden railroading. The lush greens of the trees, graceful curves of the track, and persistent rumbling of a train work in harmony to form a slice of everyday life in miniature.

The difference between a traditional indoor model railroad and a garden railway is the difference between realism and reality. An indoor layout creates the illusion of reality by using artificial materials—mountains are made of plaster or foam, and rivers are created using plastic resin. A garden railroad brings everything outdoors. Mountains are made of dirt, rivers are real water, and rocks are actual stone.

While this hobby may be new to you, it has been around for more than a century, primarily in Great Britain. In the United States, garden railroading achieved some popularity in the 1920s and '30s, but nearly died out by the end of World War II. Its resurgence was due in large part to the advent of colorful LGB trains from Germany in the late 1960s. As the company introduced more American-style trains, people took notice and garden railways began to spring up all over the country. Since then, numerous other manufacturers of large-scale trains have entered the market.

Fun in the sun

Part of the fun in this hobby is following the practices of a full-size railroad and working with the landscape. You need to consider the topography of your land and any existing gardens, trees, or other obstacles when planning your railway. If your backyard is sloped, you might build wood or metal trestles or raise the line on earthworks and use timber or stone retaining walls. The choice is strictly up to you. After all, it's your railroad!

You may think that garden railroading is a hobby strictly for gardeners or people who like trains. The truth is that anyone who loves being outdoors can be a garden railroader. Your railroad can reflect those interests. If you enjoy electrical challenges, for instance, you can build a line with a complex track plan. If you have some carpentry skills, you can make buildings from scratch and model a city. And if you like to work with machines, try building and operating a live-steam locomotive.

The railway garden

The "garden" part of garden railroading is another fascinating aspect of this hobby. Many nurseries and specialty plant growers sell dwarf and miniature versions of all types of plants. These specimens are ideal for garden railroads since they fit with the scale of the trains by having smaller features and a slower growth rate than their full-size cousins.

Don't think you have a green thumb? Many beautiful railway gardens have been created by people who claim not to be gardeners. There are plenty of resources available to help get you started. You can start by visiting a local nursery or landscaping center. Employees there will be happy to answer your questions.

Garden railroading is a deep and exceptionally rewarding hobby anyone can enjoy. It might be the best hobby for your family, because increasing numbers of women, children, and families are enjoying it together. Give it a try.

Marc Horovitz

‹ A garden railroad is a fascinating addition to any landscape and is a great way for the whole family to enjoy model railroading.

^ Notice how the train looks natural in its surroundings. Garden railroaders are adept at using the dwarf varieties of plants to accent the trains without dominating them.

Ruth Strong

Getting started in the hobby

Kevin Strong

^ **The author laying track on his own East Broad Top Railroad in New York during the summer of 1997. Forty yards of dirt have been brought in to augment the landscape and a few scale trees have already been planted.**

If you're like many folks, you have a train sitting in a box and a small circle of track to run it on. You've seen trains running outside, either in pictures or in person, but you're not sure how to get to that point, or even where to start. Before you run headfirst into the yard, shovel in one hand, track in the other, a firm foundation is needed. This is where you can draw on the experience of others.

Start at the beginning; that is, talk to the folks at the store where you bought your first train set. Really get to know the folks at the local train store, and tell them what you want to do. They are your first line of attack when it comes to questions. If they can't answer them, they will probably know someone who can.

That brings us to perhaps the most valuable resource any beginner can ever hope for—other modelers. If there are other like-minded individuals in your area, then the folks at the hobby shop should know how to put you in touch with them.

In all likelihood, there is also a garden railway society somewhere near you. (See the "Club directory" published in *Garden Railways* magazine.) Probably the best thing you could do for yourself is get involved with your local club. Each group is a collection of knowledge. The members have "been there, done that," and probably have the T-shirt, or at least the bruises, to prove it.

Once you get involved with a group, it's important to remember one old lesson: "There is no such thing as a stupid question." I have yet to meet anyone who is reluctant to share knowledge about trains and gardens. When you're just starting out, there are so many things you have to try to understand and keep straight that it gets confusing. We've all been there before. I've had my share of "learning experiences." If I can keep someone from having to experience the same thing, I will. That way you won't get frustrated and take up underwater basket weaving instead.

While the club is the best source of firsthand knowledge, there are other sources of information. Train shows and conventions are great ways to meet others and see the products available for the hobby. Conventions offer you a chance to go on "railroad

Marc Horovitz

tours," where you can see other enthusiasts' railroads. This is a great opportunity to try to figure out what works for you and what doesn't. You can get a feel for the look of a railroad, and how you are able to interact with it. Take lots of pictures, and steal all the ideas you can. (Your local club or neighboring groups may offer similar tours during the summer, too.) There are also clinics at the conventions. Here you can receive in-depth lessons on any number of topics from some of the foremost experts in the field. Then, there are other specialized conventions like the National Small Scale Steam up, for live-steam enthusiasts, or the Narrow Gauge Convention, just to name a few.

You can find out about these and other gatherings in the many magazines available to the hobbyist. *Garden Railways* is just the tip of the iceberg when it comes to potential sources for literature for garden railroaders. A good hobby shop or newsstand will have a ready line-up of diverse titles available. Don't just stick to railroading magazines, though. Some of your best help may come from gardening magazines, particularly if there is one that caters to your particular climate. There are also a number of related books and videos, many of which are advertised in *Garden Railways* magazine.

Garden railroading is keeping up with the information age, too. There are a large and growing number of Web sites and chat groups devoted to this hobby. Just pull up your favorite search engine, and surf away. You can spend an entire evening on just one or two sites if you're not careful. We train nuts love to share information.

That, I suggest, is the key. The best thing you can do as a newcomer is to find folks with similar interests. Nothing makes this hobby more enjoyable than sharing it with others. The friends you meet along the way will be friends for life. it doesn't matter where you live, or how often you move. These people will always be there to answer your most basic question, or just to have you over for a cold drink and an afternoon of running trains. There's just something neat about that.

Just do it

Kevin Strong

All photos by Kevin Strong

You now have a train and it looks pretty neat running in a circle around the living-room floor. You've been looking at the magazines, surfing the Net, and talking to folks in your garden-railway society. Yet, your backyard still sits barren. There are a lot of things to think about and directions you can go. "Just how am I going to decide what I want to do?" you may ask.

<< Move the circle of track from your living room out to the backyard, hook up the power, and see what happens. There's something magical about blades of grass that a pile carpet just can't equal.

^ Existing gardens are great places to start thinking about locating your railroad. Move the track to various locations in your yard to see what strikes your fancy. Here, a grape arbor provides a pleasant backdrop for the beginnings of a dog-bone trackplan, while a dry rock garden might be an ideal setting for a railroad.

The short answer is that you don't have to decide. This, perhaps, is the largest stumbling block to new garden railroaders. There are so many choices available to today's hobbyists that starting down a particular path can be overwhelming to the point of inaction. That variety, however, is the hobby's strongest asset. Embrace it and get ready to explore the many different roads you can travel.

Now's not the time to decide what you're going to model. Don't worry about scale, narrow gauge vs. standard gauge, or any other choices like that. You'll have plenty of time to figure that out later. Your focus should be on the first step—getting trains running outside. Everything else will come in time. And getting them running outside is really simple. Remember the loop of track you have set up in your living room? Pick it up and move it to the backyard. (Disassemble it first—it goes through the door easier.)

"Where should I move it?"

It doesn't matter, really. Find a place where you think you may want to build the railroad, and put the track there. Hook up the power to the trains, grab a chair and a cool beverage of your choice, and sit back. If you don't like it where it is, pick it up and move it again. Experiment. Run the track through the trees, under the bushes, along the deck, or just out in the middle of the yard. There's something magical about just getting the trains outside in the open. They become real, not toys. Sometimes the mere act of bringing the trains outside can ignite the imagination. Once they start moving around, you're well on your way.

"Well on my way to where?"

Again, don't worry. You're headed in the right direction. Garden railroads evolve over time (and thyme evolves over garden railroads). As you watch your train running amongst the petunias, you will doubtless start to see a vast railroad empire running over the yard. Your heart will beat faster. Your adrenaline will rise. Guess what, though—it's time to put on the brakes. It's okay to have a vision of what you think your railroad may look like years down the road. Just don't try to do it all in one step. Great railroads don't spring up overnight. They take planning, or you will just wind up frustrated.

The key is to start small. You have your big plan in mind. Now, divide it up into little projects or "phases." Since you're just starting in this, you really have no feeling for how much time and energy you have to devote to the railroad, or how much the railroad is going to require. Unfortunately, that's not something anyone can help you with, either. It's all dependent on what you have going on in your own life. Starting with a small line allows you to get your feet wet with an operating railroad, then expand outward as time and energy permit.

There is another reason for starting small. Again, it harkens back to just starting out. You're going to make mistakes, and it's a lot easier (and cheaper) to replace 100 feet of track than 1,000 feet.

Most things come in threes, and there is a third reason to start small. Remember all those choices I told you not to worry about? Well, once you get the trains running on the railroad, you're going to start making some of those choices. That may involve changing a few things on the railroad. Again, it's cheaper and easier to fix this on a small railway than to rip out a vast backyard empire.

"Okay, I think I want the train to go here. Should I rent a backhoe yet?"

No. There's still a lot to think about before you go tearing up the sod. Most of these issues center around how the railroad will fit into the landscape and how you will be able to interact with it. We'll go into a lot of this in more detail in the following chapters.

Perhaps the biggest "mistake" beginners make is that they spend so much time planning, they never get out to enjoy what they've planned. Think of this hobby as a buffet. There are a lot of different choices. Grab your plate and sample a little of each. Then go back for the dishes that you liked the best. The key is to step up to the bar in the first place. Get the trains outside and off of the living-room rug.

All photos by Marc Horovitz

Temporary garden railroading

Jim Hudson

The local railbus waits by a small station on this non-permanent railway. A temporary garden line can be built relatively quickly using the shortcuts outlined in this article. But don't mistake a temporary line for the real thing. It is just a stopgap so you can get something up and running while you plan and build your real garden railway properly.

By building a temporary garden railway, you can have a modest but real, operating garden railway. Once you've accomplished this, you can take the time to do a proper job of selecting a location for a permanent railway, surveying the site, working out a concept, and turning that into a realistic plan for construction.

A temporary garden railway may also be for you if you can't construct anything too permanent where you are living right now. You may be able to get the OK if your railroad can be torn out in a day or so, with no harm done, when moving time comes.

For your first attempt, I recommend keeping things very simple. Your goal should be just getting your feet wet with something that can be completed in a few weekends. The term "temporary" doesn't imply poor-quality or sloppy work. In fact, one main purpose here is to learn how to do a good job through hands-on experience.

Building a temporary garden railway

This brief article certainly won't cover everything you should or shouldn't do, but here are a few thoughts to get you started.

You can have a tight oval of track with a couple of sidings in a space only 5 x 10 feet or so. Remember to keep the plan small and simple. You may already have a starter set. For this purpose, that small locomotive and cars and those pieces of sharply curved sectional track from the set are just fine. The idea here is not to create an intricate track plan or even a highly realistic garden railroad, but to learn and get a train running outdoors. I suggest avoiding bridges and tunnels completely for now. The more effort you put into this railroad, the harder it will be when demolition time comes—and remember, it will come.

You don't need to do much prep work for this railroad—just clear a space on the ground. It's easier if the space you have to

1 To get started, "crunch" the track into the dirt to leave a footprint. This will give you an outline of the track's route.

2 Dig a shallow trench, lay in an inch or so of ballast; level, and then set the track in place.

3 Add more ballast on top of the track up to tie level; dust off the track with an old paintbrush and then water the track.

4 Add some rocks, plants, and structures, and your line Is complete. Between the rocks is a tiny sedum, *Sedum dasyphyllum,* the tree, still in its pot, is a young *Pinus contorta* 'Spaan's Dwarf.'

work with is level, but you can push some dirt around to even out this small area if needed.

Real railroads use a bed of crushed-rock ballast to support their tracks. This method is easy and works well for a garden railway in just about any climate. The crushed rock locks together lightly to hold the track, yet it can also move a bit to accommodate the track's tendency to expand in summer sun and contract in winter cold.

You should be able find to what is called "crusher fines," "1/4" and smaller" (or "1/4" minus"), or "crusher dust" at your local rock yard or quarry. Whatever you use, make sure it is crushed rock, not smooth, rounded river rock like pea gravel or squeegee.

Be sure to use a dielectric paste (LGB offers this as no. 51010 Conductive Paste) in the rail joiners as you assemble the sections of track to maintain good electrical contact over time. Also use track clips or wire ties to keep the sections together

Identify any bumps and dips. After you've test-run a train or two, consider adding some plants, a few appropriate rocks, and some small buildings to bring your new railroad to life. Some low-growing groundcover like sedum, hardy junipers, and maybe a few colorful, small-leafed annual flowers will go a long way.

By now your little garden-railway experiment should look pretty good. You should also have gained a much better feel for what interests you and where your talents he. If you find you've made some mistakes along the way, great! That's part of the exercise. Ask lots of questions and don't be afraid to tear out and rebuild part or all of what you've done so far. If you have trains running through a real garden scene, you've already accomplished more than many armchair garden railroaders do in years. Step back and enjoy your handiwork, give yourself a pat on the back, and start planning your permanent garden railway!

SECTION 2

Railway concept
and site selection

Jim Hudson

Marc Horovitz

The great American architect Frank Lloyd Wright insisted that his apprentices work around the grounds of his Taliesin school commune. Each took a turn as a farmer, cook, laborer, mason, or carpenter. Not only did this help to keep expenses down, it provided these aspiring designers with something invaluable—practical experience. Wright's belief was that his students couldn't begin to understand design until they had gained a firsthand understanding of how things worked in the world around them, which makes sense.

Jack DiSarro

« Larry Rose's Rio Verde Western Railroad closely follows Colorado narrow-gauge practice in both equipment and operation. This is an example of adhering closely to a specific theme.

‹ Jack DiSarro scratchbuilt his sugar-cane train. The sugar-cane theme is only loosely followed on his railway, and most emphasis is placed on the engines and rolling stock.

If you've started building a small, temporary garden railway, you've gained some practical experience. Now you're ready to start thinking about planning a permanent railway. Your mind may already be racing ahead to visions of completed scenes. I'd like to suggest that you try to fight off that temptation a bit longer. Take some time to study and consider all your options.

You might think that the first place to start on planning your garden railway is with its location. Well, that's certainly one of the things to consider, but I think you'll do yourself a disservice if you first pick a spot, then try to fit a railroad into it. The best approach is one where you merge a number of elements: your own concepts of style and theme, the space you have to work with, and the amounts of time and money you can invest, to name a few. Work at one aspect for a little while, then approach it from another angle, then another, until you finally blend it all together. I think you'll find evidence of this kind of thought in most of the "great" garden railways. Even if you aren't planning a "great" garden railway, the project will still require a good chunk of your creative energies over an extended time, so it is worth some deep thought.

There are no rules saying what you have to do next, but my suggestion is to start by considering the type and style of garden railway you want to build. Try to identify a theme that will help direct how and what you build.

Prototype modeling

Does your main interest lie in replicating a particular railroad or a specific time and place? This can be as general as "something with an Old West feel," or a bit more specific, such as "turn-of-the-century Colorado narrow-gauge railroads," or as specific as "Silverton, Colorado, in the spring of 1898." Each of these themes represents a different level of involvement and a different emphasis on model (locomotives, rolling stock, structures) accuracy.

Less immediately obvious, but probably more significant, are the effects each approach will have on how you plan your railroad. In the first example, just building rugged mountains with some track on spindly wood trestles will accomplish the task. For the last example, you'd need to say, "Okay, the mountain with the strange rock outcropping goes here, the track must curve around past the depot just so, the river goes there, and we need to build a bunch of buildings from scratch." There are dramatic differences in the levels of effort involved in the various approaches.

Forget prototypes, let's have fun

Maybe you don't know or care all that much about a particular railroad, but you're just after a certain feeling. There's nothing wrong with that, either, especially in garden railroading, which has evolved as a less fussy pursuit than smaller-scale, indoor model railroading.

Perhaps the type of plants and the general style of the trains is more important to you. Buildings and other accessories may be few, if any. I think it's safe to say that most of your neighbors and friends will be less impressed by the historical accuracy of your railroad than by the composition and interplay of trains and landscape.

Maybe you seek an escape from life's realities with something offbeat and whimsical. Doghouses on rails, old musical instruments made into locomotives, buildings painted in a cacophony of colors, plants that look like they belong on another planet. This isn't for everyone, but it's proof that garden railroading can be an art form where self-expression is the objective.

Location, location, location . . .

It's true in retail and real estate that location is everything. Maybe this also applies to garden railroading. Before you narrow down your style or theme too far, you need to start identifying the pros and cons of possible sites for your railway, In the process, allow your theme to be modified a bit to fit your site. Try to work with your site instead of against. it. For example, if your yard is dead flat and you have it in mind to model the Rhaetian Railway of the Swiss Alps, it's still possible; but realize that you'll have to move a lot of dirt and rocks to build up those mountains.

Try to consider the practical factors as well in your site selection. If your yard

Marc Horovitz

The theme of Samuel Addison Muncy's railroad is pure fantasy. His railroad contains not one piece of straight track and all structures and rolling stock (like the engine pictured here) are straight out of his imagination.

floods when it rains, you probably shouldn't build a railway at the low point.

Statistically speaking, the most likely site for a garden railway is the backyard. But that still leaves quite a few decisions to make, like what kind and how much impact you want your railroad to have. Should it dominate the view out the family room window or be almost hidden at first glance? And how will you relate to the railroad? You might walk alongside it, all around it, or into the middle of it. The experience is different in each case. Visit as many garden railways as possible to develop a feeling for what you do or don't want.

Weigh your subjective considerations against more solid, practical things. For example, you may be planning a circle or loop. Does a particular site have the physical space to accommodate a good-sized turn? No matter if it has the feeling you want, if your trains won't go around the curves, you won't have much fun running them. You may realize that you don't have the space to fulfill your foremost garden railway desires. Here's when you get back to the idea of working with the space you have and maybe coming up with a theme you like almost as much—in other words, Plan B.

Suppose your first choice would be to model the Denver & Rio Grande Western Railroad in the 1920s. That implies some pretty good-sized locomotives and cars requiring big curves and room to stretch their legs. But if you don't have the space to build a whole railway based on this theme, what can you do? Shift your focus a bit. Maybe you do have room for those trains to run through the scene on a simple loop. The track might emerge from a tunnel, branch out on a short siding at a station, then disappear again around a bend. Then, perhaps, the main theme of your, garden railway could be the small mining railroads that fed the bigger system. It's still the same scenery, the same era, and the same buildings, and you'd still get to see those big locomotives run occasionally. You've just put your emphasis on a different part of the overall scene.

Even if you have a large garden railway, it's good to divide things into several small scenes or vignettes. For example, you might create scenes in two or three corners of your yard. You don't need to connect them with one solid mass of garden railway. A single track can leave one scene, slink along the back fence on a plain, gardenless right-of-way, then arrive at the next corner scene. You'll actually have a heightened sense of the train going somewhere without your garden railway taking over the yard.

Putting it all together

By now, you should be developing some ideas about your theme and site location. Before you go too far, though, temper those ideas with a strong dose of reality. Consider your potential investment in achieving your goals, not just in financial terms, but, more significantly, in terms of time, energy, and overall effect on your lifestyle. Now is a good time to ask yourself if your garden railway will be an accent to your house or a dominant element. How much time will you spend building and maintaining your railway?

It's easy to let your dreams get away from you. I don't mean to discourage you from building a garden railway. I just think you'll get more enjoyment from making visible progress on something achievable than working for years on something overwhelming. If you do this, the worst—no, the best—that can happen is that you'll take your first garden railway to a nice level of completion and then be planning an expansion before long.

SECTION 2

Surveying your site

Jim Hudson

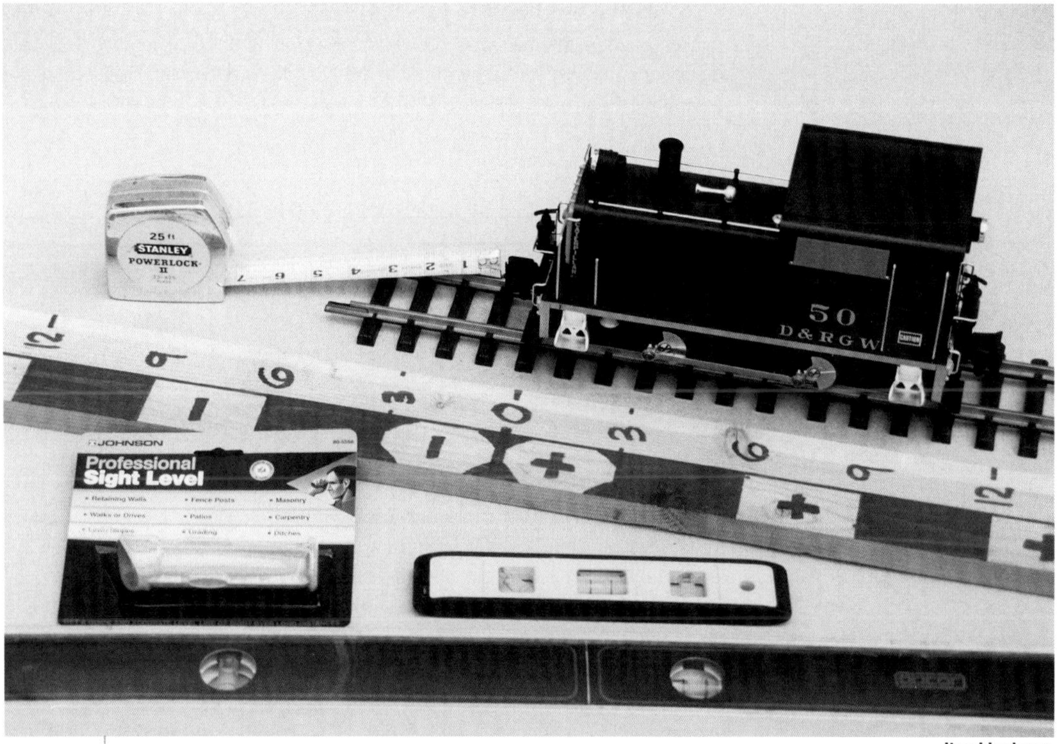

Jim Hudson

Surveying the site for your garden railway can be fun and painless with a few simple tools. Counterclockwise from the top they are: a tape measure, a home-made surveyor's pole, an inexpensive sight level, a long carpenter's level, and a small level.

At work recently we had our annual company picnic. As I was driving home, it occurred to me that a great event and a great garden railroad have one thing in common: planning. For the picnic to be a success, someone had to pick a date and a place, organize games and activities, arrange food for a small army of people, and, finally, follow through to make sure it all came off smoothly. For your garden railway, you'll need to pick a location, organize a concept and a plan, arrange for appropriate materials and equipment, and, finally, follow through to make sure that it turns into something real.

Note: The numbers **above** the zero mark indicate that the pole rests on ground **below** where the figure is standing.

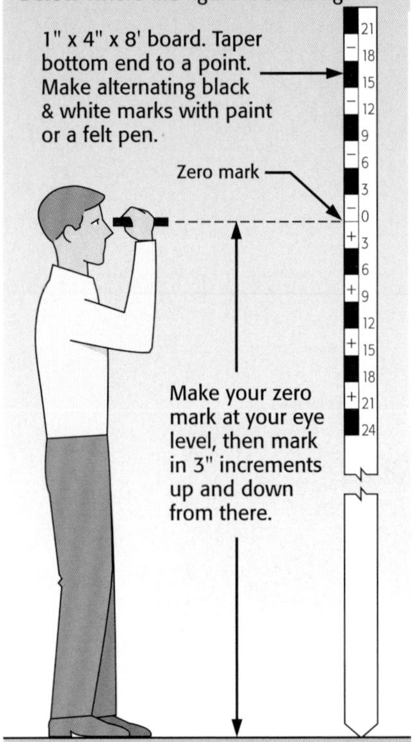

Note: The numbers **below** the zero mark indicate that the pole rests on ground **above** where the figure is standing.

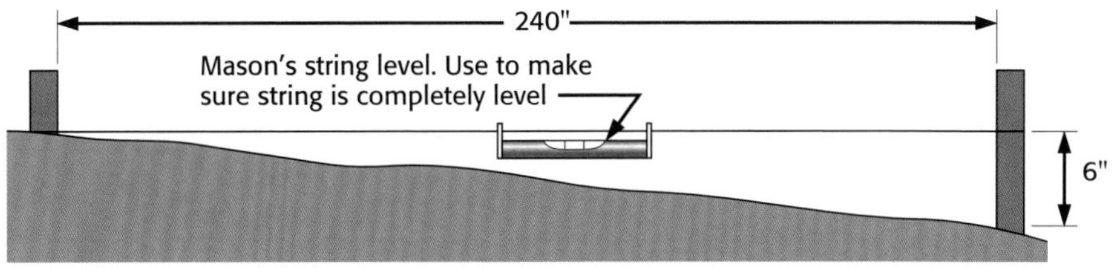

Determining grade using a string level

In the illustration, there are 240" between the stakes and a 6" difference in elevation between the upper and lower stake, measured at the ground. To determine grade, divide the difference in elevation (6") by the distance (240"): 6 ÷ 240 = .025, or 2.5% grade.

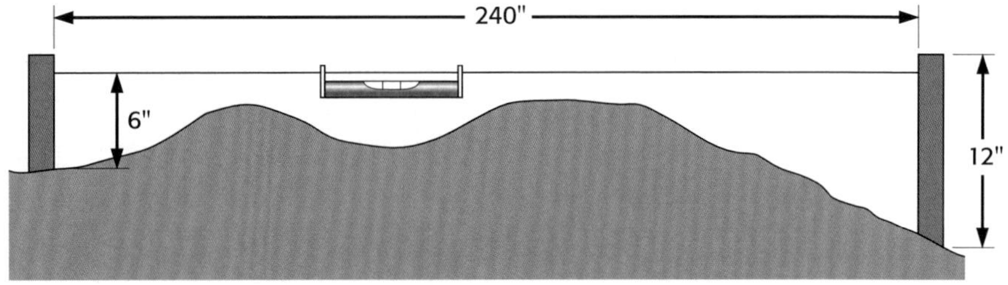

Determining ultimate grade over uneven ground

When working with uneven ground, the string must be raised to clear obstacles. Compute the actual elevation difference by subtracting the lesser from the greater. In this example, the elevation difference is 6". Figure the grade the same way as mentioned above.

Perhaps by now you've developed some conceptual thoughts about what your permanent garden railway should be. It's time to start combining those ideas with the practical experience you gained while building a small temporary garden railway. The next step is to gather some cold, hard facts about the space you have to work with. in other words, it's time to do some surveying. Don't worry—you don't have to be a civil engineer. You don't. even have to own an orange safety vest. A few simple tools and techniques will suffice to help you assemble all the information you need.

If you really want to do a professional job, you can contact a local land title company, for a plat map of your property. This should be free or cost just a few dollars at most. It will show you the basic dimensions of your lot. If you think your railroad will go anywhere near your property lines, this is a very good idea.

Even better would be an old site plan of your lot, perhaps from when your home was built or remodeled. It would also be a good idea at this point to check with your local building authorities about any easements, or setbacks. This could help avoid having to tear up your railroad for access to underground utilities, or chopping the top off your mountain because it violates a height restriction. These may seem like remote possibilities, but stranger things have happened. A few minutes on the phone now might save you big headaches later.

Simple surveying

Time to venture out into the wilds of the backyard. Arm yourself with a measuring tape (the longer the better), an inexpensive hand-held sight level (under $20 at your local home-improvement center), a simple surveyor's pole (homemade is just fine), and a pad and pencil. You might also benefit from taking along an assistant to help hold the tape and the pole.

The horizontal measuring part is fairly obvious. How long and wide is your space? What obstacles are there? Try to be thorough. Maybe bulldozing the yard is an option for you, but more than likely you'll be working around such relatively immovable objects as large rocks, trees, structures, and the neighbor's fence. Try not to make too many judgments at this point. What seems like an obstacle might be a scenic opportunity in disguise. Also, avoid making assumptions, such as thinking that your seemingly square building corners and property lines really are so. You might end up having to force your railroad's tracks into a tight curve where you thought you had plenty of room.

If you do a proper job of this whole process, you'll likely discover a few things about your own backyard. Don't be too surprised if you find yourself saying something like "Hmm, that dimension is only 20′ but it takes at least 30′ for a track to climb up and over itself comfortably." That's the purpose of doing all this measuring.

Just as important as "how long and how wide" is "how high." You probably don't have a surveyor's pole, but you can easily mark off an 8-foot board in 3″ increments. If you want it to look official, use alternating black and white paint marks. If you will be the only one looking through the sights at the pole, you can make a "Zero" mark on the pole right at your eye level. This will save you having to add and subtract dimensions to figure the difference in elevation between two different points. If your eye level in your normal garden-railroad work shoes is 5′6″ above the floor, you would make your Zero mark 5′6″ from the bottom end of the pole. When you look through the sight level, the marks below the Zero mark on the pole represent elevations above you. Marks above the Zero mark represent elevations below you.

For example, suppose your assistant takes the surveyor's pole across the yard to a spot that is a foot higher than the spot where you are standing. If you look through the sight level at the pole, the crosshairs in the level should line up a foot below the Zero mark. This works backwards from what you might expect, but you'll become accustomed to it pretty quickly. Just be sure you always stand up straight and wear shoes with similar height heels, so your eye height is always the same as when you first marked it on the pole.

The degree of accuracy decreases considerably over distance, but for most backyard purposes this method should be good enough. If you have some truly large areas to cover, or you just feel you'd like to be more precise, conventional surveyor's gear is an option. It is expensive but you may be able to rent it locally. Better yet would be to have a surveyor or civil engineer as a friend.

Pick some logical object in your yard (something that won't be moving anytime soon) to use as a benchmark and call that height 0″ elevation. Everything else is just so many inches above or below that mark; i.e., + 6″ or -3″. You'll want to periodically measure elevations at spots all around your space. Definitely measure elevations wherever there is a noticeable change, such as at the top and bottom of a slope, the top and bottom of a retaining wall, and so forth. Mark each spot with something durable—a stake in the ground or a dab of paint—and measure and record its location in the yard. As Hansel and Gretel learned, bread crumbs don't make good markers.

You can feel free to adjust the precision of your measurements according to the materials involved. A concrete block wall is hard to change, so you might measure it to within a 1″ tolerance. Dirt can be moved easily, so a 3″ tolerance may be plenty accurate. A 2- or 4-foot-long carpenter's level will be more useful than the sight level and pole for more precise measurements in small spaces. Perhaps even more than horizontal measurements, a vertical survey will surprise you and help you later in planning. What you thought was fairly level ground might have resulted in your train struggling up a five percent grade.

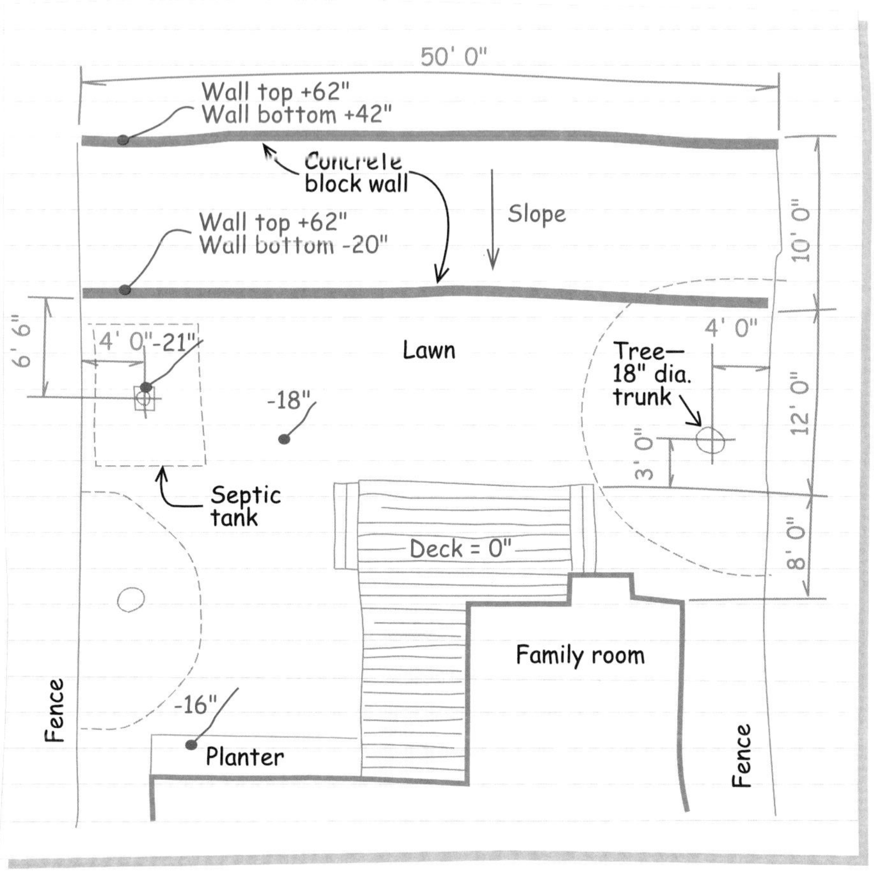

Sample site-plan sketch

A rough sketch is all you need to get started. On this one, features are labeled in black, elevations in red, and dimensions in blue.

SECTION 3

Drawing the plan for the site

Jim Hudson

Jim Hudson

Back to the drawing board. Even if you have no experience as a draftsman, you can take all the information you've collected (as outlined in the previous chapter) and record it on some type of scale drawing. You can find some grid paper (graph paper) at your local art or drafting-supply store, if that will help you keep everything square and in scale.

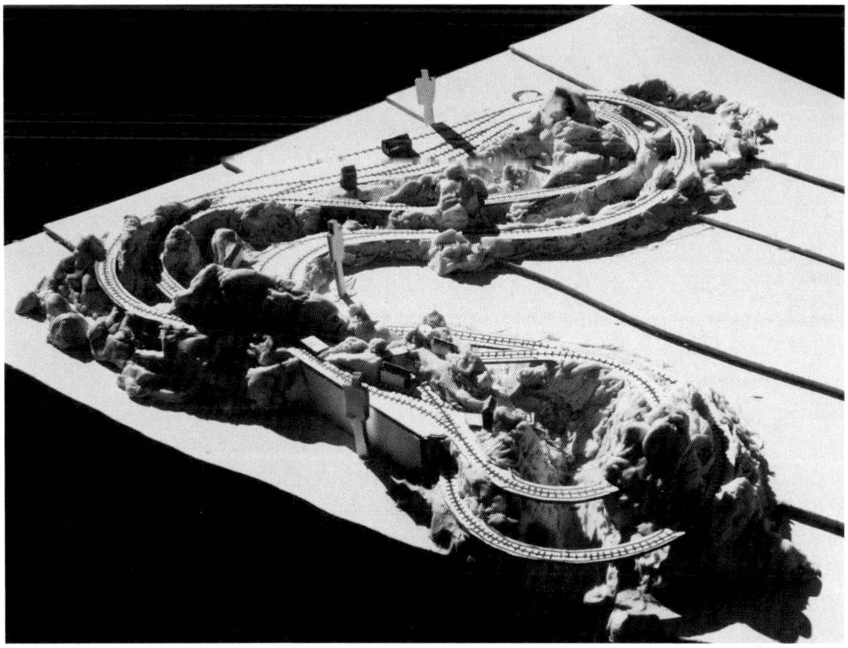

Bob Treat

To draw your plan, pick the largest scale that will allow you to fit your proposed railway on a manageable size sheet. For this purpose, you'll probably be using a scale like 1/4″ = 1′0″. This means that each 1/4″ on your plan stands for 1 foot out in your yard. It doesn't take long to figure out that if your yard is 100 feet wide and you choose a scale of 1″ to the foot, you'll need a piece of paper 100″, or nearly 9 feet, wide. That's not too practical, so you might consider dividing your plan up onto several sheets if you want to work in this large a scale.

You can impress your architect and engineer friends by buying what looks like a six-sided ruler and calling it by its proper name—a "scale." Architects use scales marked for the dimensions that represent a foot on the real thing, such as 1/8″, 1/2″, or 3/4″ = 1′0″. Engineer's scales are marked in 10ths, 20ths, 30ths, and so forth. A 1/10″ mark can stand for a real 1″ or 1′0″; it's your choice. Your decision on which scale to buy may be affected by whether or not you buy one of the track-planning templates on the market. LGB makes one that is 1/10 actual size, so you'd want an engineer's scale for use with that one. CTT, Inc. makes one that is 1/12 actual size, or 1″ = 1′0″ scale, so an architect's scale would be more appropriate for this template.

You may at first think a template is necessary. I encourage you to use one if it helps, but I've noticed a tendency for people to design railroads with lots of straight track and rigid corners when using a template. Breaking out of the square mold of the template with a more freehand approach can result in a track plan with graceful flowing curves, like the prototype. This can be done with a template, but you have to fight the almost subconscious urge to make things too rectangular, like a toy-train layout.

To round out your basic drafting-tool kit, throw in a good, sharp pencil, an adjustable triangle, and a compass. One more important item is a big eraser!

If you are into computers, you may want to skip the "hard copy" and do all your planning with some kind of computer-aided drafting (CAD) program. Several good CAD track-planning programs have been introduced in the past few years. You'd probably want one that already has a library of standard large-scale track components, instead of having to create it from scratch.

There are a couple of good reasons for going to all the trouble of making scale plans for your garden railway. The first is simply to help you avoid technical mistakes, such as mathematical errors or wrong measurements—sort of a system of checks and balances. If you think at first that you measured something correctly, you may find it doesn't all work out when you put it down in its proper scale relationship on paper. Don't feel bad. It happens to the best surveyors, too. It's much better to remeasure and erase now than to try to move a big chunk of half-built garden railroad later.

Second, it's just far more practical to move things around on paper at a small scale than in the real, full-size world. It's possible that you will come up with a nearly ideal plan right off the bat, but it's much more likely that you will want to try several major design concepts and perhaps hundreds of different detail variations.

« Here is a selection of drafting tools from which you might choose to draw a scale plan of your line. Counterclockwise from under the locomotive, they are: grid (graph) paper; a large 45° triangle; an engineer's scale; an architect's scale; an adjustable triangle; a parallel rule (the black bar on which the other tools are sitting); a metal erasing shield; a small 30°-60° triangle; a calculator; an eraser; a small 45° triangle; a compass that holds a pencil; two different track-planning templates; some low-tack drafting tape for holding your drawings to the table; and a roll of sketch paper.

‹ A model of your model railway can help you visualize what the final product will be like. This one was built by Bob Treat in San Diego for his G-scale Snow Creek Railroad. The mockup was made of modeling clay and illustration board.

A model of your model railroad?

You may find that you have some difficulty visualizing what your two-dimensional plan will look like in three dimensions. In that case, you may want to build a model of part of your garden railroad, probably in the same scale as your plan, using bits of cardboard, paper, and styrofoam.

You still may not be seeing much visible progress out in the backyard thus far. Don't worry. Rome wasn't built in a day. You may just be laying the all-important groundwork for one of great garden railways of the future!

Track plan types

Jack Verducci

There are two broad categories of track plans commonly in use: continuous running and point-to-point. The drawings below show various permutations of each.

Continuous running is preferred by operators who favor the Observer (a person who sits along the line, watching the trains go by) philosophy, since the trains for the most part follow a single route and require no special operation to run. These track plans include the loop, the dogbone, the folded dogbone, and the figure-eight, over-and-under.

Point-to-point is a line on which the trains run to the end, then return by backing up; or the engine runs around the train via a passing siding; or the locomotive is turned on a turntable or a wye. This probably provides the most realistic operation and would be as well suited to the Engineer (a person who runs the train, either following it with a remote control unit or running it from a fixed point) as it would be unsuited to the Observer.

Loop-to-loop is similar to point-to-point, except that the entire train turns around on a reversing loop. Reversing loops require some electronics to prevent a short circuit.

A switching railroad is one in which the primary goal of the operator is the shunting of cars. Sidings are used to store cars and to allow a switch engine to maneuver. A switching railroad can be a railroad in itself, or it can be a feature on any of the previously mentioned railroad types.

Basic continuous-run track plans

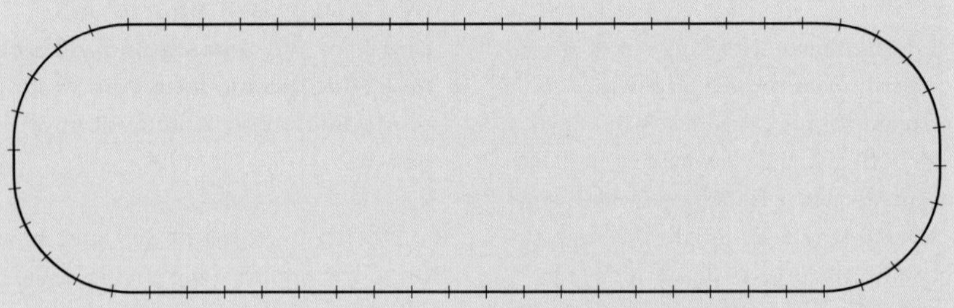

The loop is the most basic of track plans for continuous running, and it can be any shape. What makes a loop attractive is the fact that the train can run forever without coming to the end of the track. The loop can be expanded and made more interesting by the addition of passing sidings, spurs, and branch lines. With the addition of landscaping, the basic loop can be further enhanced.

The dogbone is similar to the basic loop. Between the loops the train runs on what appears to be a double track. This plan works well in flower beds where there may not be enough room for turns in the center areas.

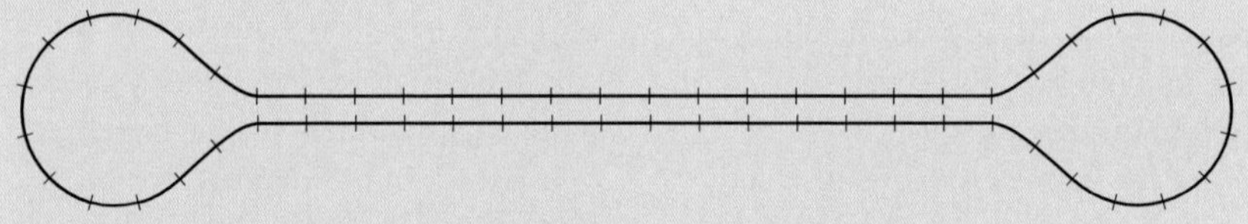

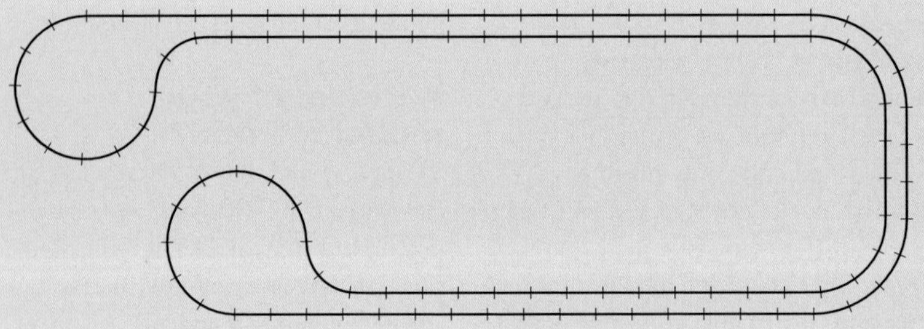

The folded dogbone is the same as the dogbone, but the track is arranged to fit into a specific area. Dogbones can also be folded and twisted to create situations where the train passes over and under itself. We will see this versatile plan used in the future.

The figure-eight, over-and-under is a favorite for small areas. A basic figure-eight can also be built on a single level by using a crossing track. However, a more interesting figure-eight is one that goes over and under itself. With this plan, when you include a bridge and a tunnel, the train will appear to be running on two levels.

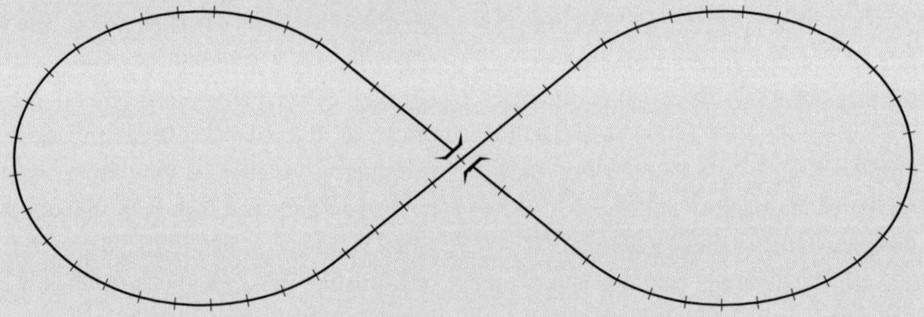

Point-to-point track plans

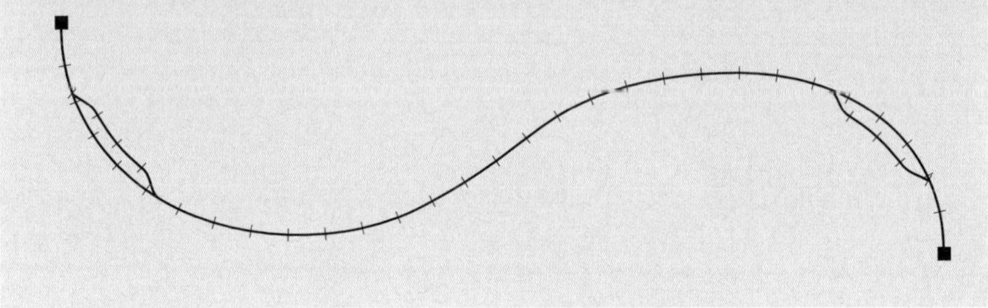

The point-to-point, in its basic form, runs from one end of the line to the other without the locomotive turning around. This plan can be improved by adding a passing siding at each end.

The Engineer can park the cars on the mainline (at a station), then bring the locomotive around the train and couple it to the other end for the return trip.

Larger railroads could incorporate a turntable or a wye to turn the engine. Space permitting, an entire train can be turned on a wye, as is sometimes done in prototype operation. The drawback is that this is an operator's railroad. You must be willing to do the switching at each end. This is for people who like the Engineer philosophy of operation.

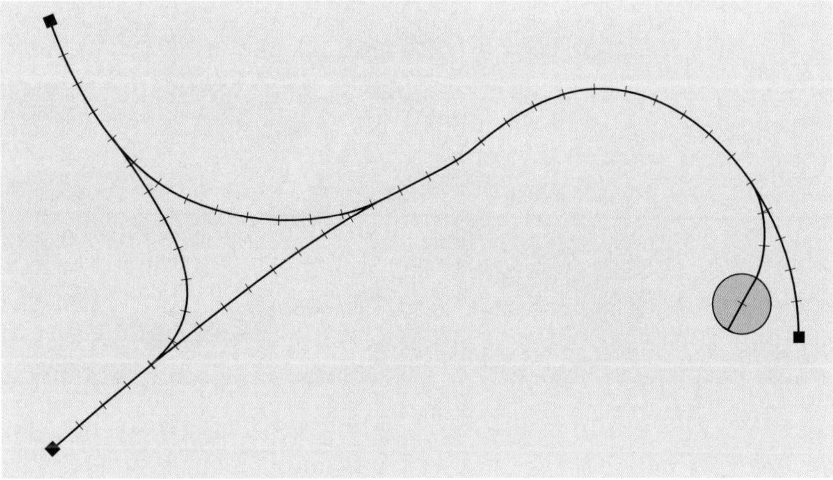

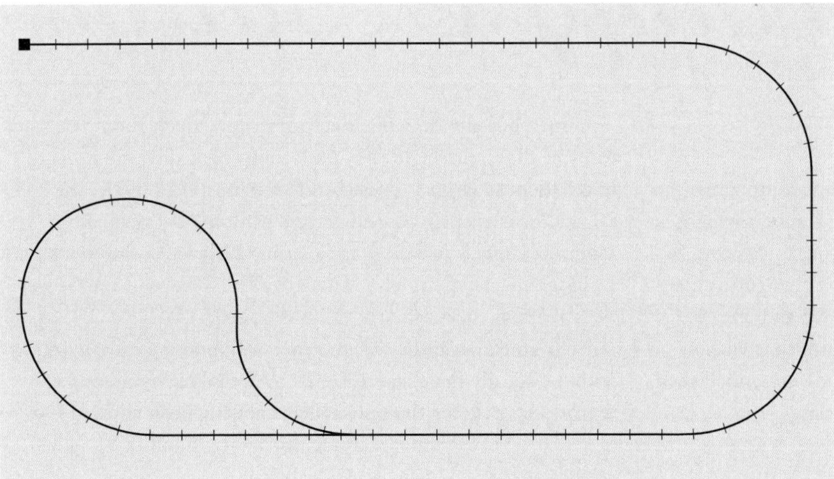

The point-to-loop plan allows a train to go from one point to another on a single track, then to turn around for the return trip without a switching maneuver. At the "point" end (the end without the loop), the train could again be turned on a turntable or wye. This plan could be used in an area where you have room to turn at one end of the line but not at the other. Using the Engineer concept of operation, you could have a switch yard at the "point" end, where cars could be made up into a train that would then be sent out to the loop end, where it would be turned for the return trip.

The loop-to-loop track plan allows a train to travel from one place to another on a single track and turn at both ends without switching maneuvers. Reverse loops require special electrical considerations to prevent short circuits and should be used only if absolutely necessary.

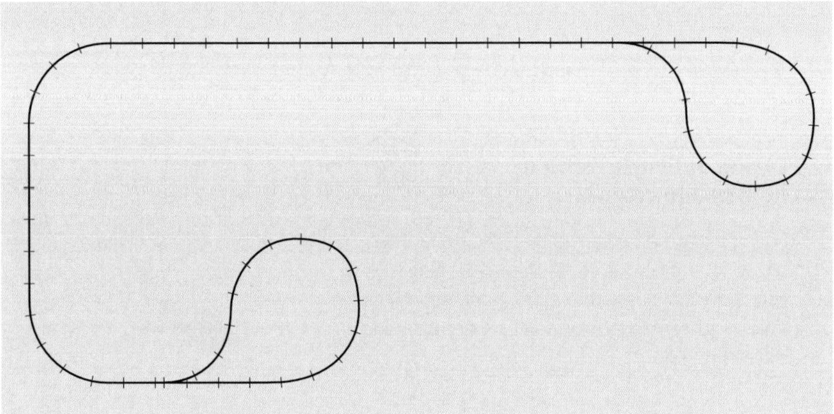

Marc Horovitz

Incorporating elevation

Jack Verducci

Unless you are building a flatland railroad, you will probably want to incorporate elevation and landscaping through which your railroad can ran. You will find it challenging to create a landscape that rises and falls, giving the illusion that your train is travelling through a miniature world. A simple and effective way to accomplish this in a relatively small, flat area is with a figure-eight track plan. This plan can be altered and embellished in many ways, but for now we'll stick to the basics.

Using your site drawing, determine how much room you have to fit in the figure eight. My philosophy regarding curves is to make them as large as possible. If your area is 20′ wide, use a 10′-radius curve. If you only have 8′, still make the turning radius as large as will fit. I am a strong believer in flex-track and wouldn't use anything else. This gives the freedom to make gentle, sweeping curves to any radius required.

Let's go through the design process. Suppose we are working with a basically flat space 10′ x 20′. We must assume that a theme and style for the railway have already been chosen. For this example, we want a mountain, a small lake, and a waterfall.

A figure eight that is completely exposed looks toylike. To create the illusion that the train is travelling somewhere, plan a tunnel at one end of the railway. This will disguise the turn and block the train from view as it comes around the curve, which will add to the illusion that the train is changing direction or reentering the scene from somewhere else. Tunnels add mystery to the railroad. It's fun to watch the train disappear and reappear. Two tunnels on a railroad this small may be too much, but a cutting of built-up rock formations could be used to partially hide the curve at the other end.

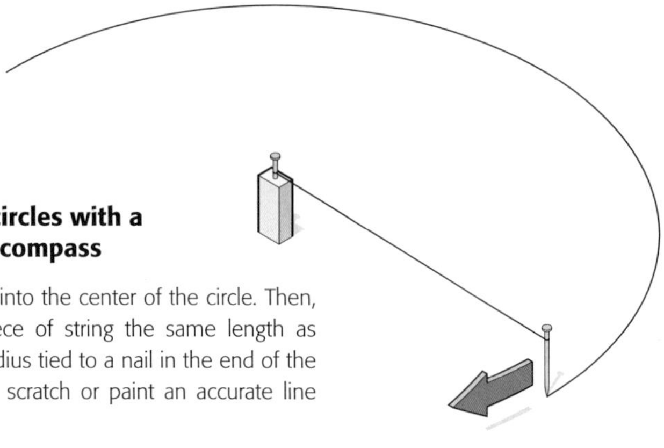

Laying out circles with a homemade compass

Pound a stake into the center of the circle. Then, by using a piece of string the same length as your curve's radius tied to a nail in the end of the stake, you can scratch or paint an accurate line on the ground.

1

We first raise the area by installing a row of boulders around the perimeter to bring the lowest point up by 12″. Some space will be lost in doing this, so a 12″ margin will be designed in around the area. The boulders may not actually fill the margin, but we will use the space inside it for the purposes of track planning. If we find that there is room left over, we can always expand the curves a little to fill in the available space.

What remains is a space 8′ wide, so this will be the diameter of our curves. On the site plan, draw in two 2″-diameter (8 scale feet) circles with a compass to represent the curves. To complete the figure eight, connect the circles with two lines that cross in the middle. This is our simple working plan. The principles are the same no matter how large the railroad is to be.

The next step is to determine what the track grade will be. In order for the track to cross over itself, a rise of 10.5″ will be required to allow clearance beneath the bridge. (Since this is a small railroad, small equipment will be used. On a larger line with bigger stock, more clearance may be required, but you would have more room to make the climb.) An easy way to figure out the grade and clearance is to use π (3.1416).

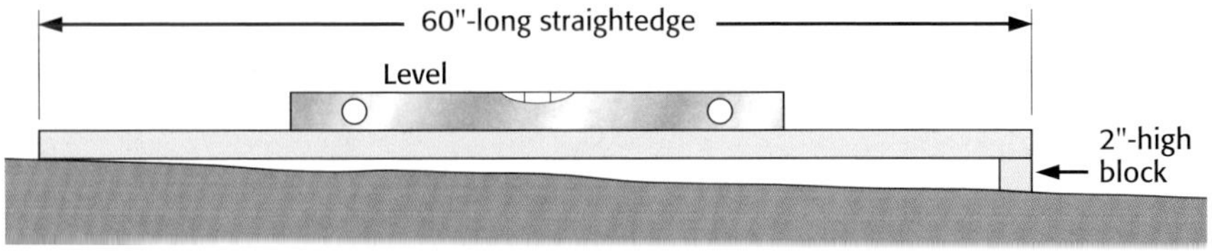

Using a level to set specific grades

This example uses the same 60" that was used in the text. Use a 60"-long level, or a straightedge of that length, and place a shorter level on top of it. We have already calculated that a 2" rise over 60" will give us approximately a 3.5% grade, so place a 2" block under the low end of the straightedge. When the bubble shows level, the grade will be 3.5%.

2

Calculate the circumference of the 8′-diameter circle using the formula $C = \pi d$, where C is the circumference and d is the diameter. Thus, $C = 3.1416 \times 8 = 25.12'$. Convert this to inches by multiplying by 12, which comes to 301.44″. We know that we need a rise of 10.5″, so we divide this number by 301.44, giving us the result of .03483, or about 3.5%, which win be the grade required to bring the track up. This percentage of grade is a little steep, but it is workable with small equipment. We now know that our basic design will work.

The next step requires transferring this information from paper to site. I like to mark the future roadbed directly on the ground with marking paint. Special cans of spray paint that are intended to be used upside down are available where landscape materials are sold.

Drive a stake into the center of the circle and use a string the length of the circle's radius, tied to the paint can, to make the circle (see fig. 1).

The next step is to set the grade. To do this, you will need some wooden stakes about 24″ long, some marker flags, marker paint, and a transit or string level. A carpenter's level that has been rigged to read level at 3.5% can also be used (see fig. 2).

To lay out the 3.5% grade, drive wooden stakes into the ground along the proposed route, spaced 60″ apart (fig. 3).

Laying out a grade with grade stakes

1. Using marking paint, lay out the trackplan on the ground. A center stake and string can be used as a compass (see fig. 1).

2. Starting at the lowest point, drive a stake into the ground far enough that it is firmly planted. Measure 60" along the route and drive in the next stake. Repeat this every 60". Don't worry if the last stake is not 60" from the first.

3. Starting at the ground-level stake (0"), and using a transit or carpenter's level, mark the next stake at a point 2" higher than the ground-level stake. Continue around to the summit, marking each stake 2" higher than the last. When you reach the summit, repeat the process in reverse until you arrive back at ground level.

4. When all stakes are marked, cut each at its mark. Paint the stakes a bright color. These will serve as benchmarks when installing the roadbed. Since the stakes will (in most cases) end up at ground level, they might easily disappear below the grade during construction. So that you don't lose your stakes, mark each one with a flag.

Except in areas that suffer from frost heave, these stakes can stay in the ground forever unless they need to be removed to make way for a bridge or trestle. They indicate the path of the railroad and the grade it will follow. The stakes would have to be closely followed on the small example below. On a larger line, the track could move to one side or the other of the stakes.

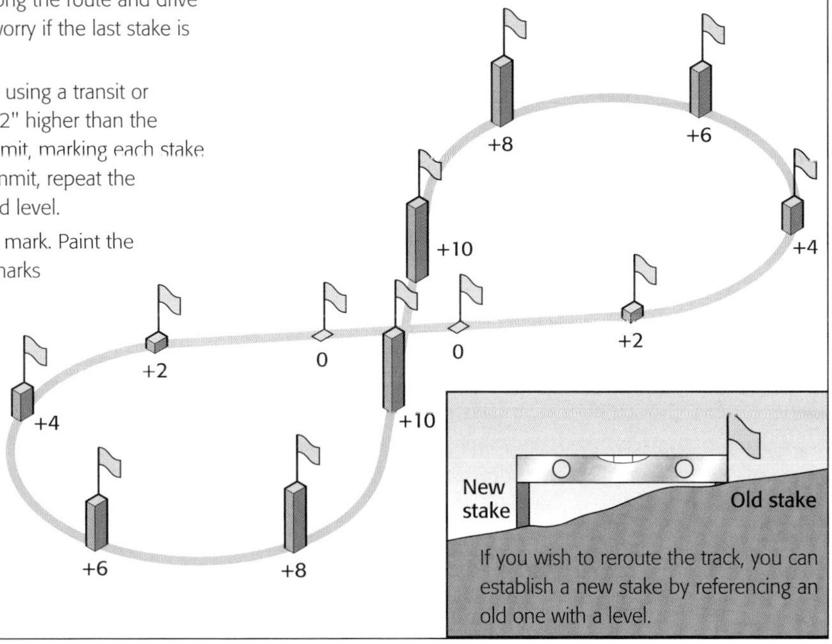

If you wish to reroute the track, you can establish a new stake by referencing an old one with a level.

3

Marc Horovitz

A versatile figure-eight

Jack Verducci

The folded-dogbone track plan was used on Kent Kirkorian's railroad, and the layered effect is apparent. The train is on an ascending track. Its next stop will be the high-level yard at the back of the railroad (not visible in this photo).

The figure-eight is a versatile design that can be used to create great depth. In fact, when working with a small area, this may be the only practical track plan that can accomplish this. In a larger area, however, a single figure-eight may look a little spartan. Even though I prefer less track over more, there still needs to be enough main line to keep things interesting. I have used similar track plans, all variations of the folded dogbone, on several railroads that were built on flat ground.

This folded dogbone (fig. 1) offers a lot of landscaping possibilities. The track passes over and under itself at two or more places, which helps achieve the three-dimensional or layered look when viewed from scale eye level. There can be two large turning loops at each end, since the loops overlap. For example, in a space that is 12′ wide you could have two overlapping turning loops that are each 10′ in diameter (fig. 2). The train will travel from right to left twice and from left to right twice, each time on a different track, which adds interest to the line.

The folded dogbone is a simple plan and the main line flows nicely. Through the creative use of landscaping and a few track plan variations, you can really keep your guests wondering where the train is going next or exactly where it is when it goes out of sight. To add more interest to this basic design, a series of sidings and towns can be incorporated to give the railroad purpose. Space permitting, a smaller, separate point-to-point mining, logging, or other industrial railroad could be incorporated into the line as well. A minimum of two tunnels and two bridges are usually required to make this design work visually, though you could add many more. The actual roadbed can be moved in a variety of ways to create interest (fig. 3) and the railroad can be elevated above grade in several places if you wish to incorporate a lot of trestle work.

Another track plan that allows the railroad to climb over itself to create interest is a simple loop or dogbone that includes a climbing loop at each end of the line. This plan may be better suited for an area that is too narrow to fit in the four lines encompassed in the folded-dogbone plan (fig. 4). Towns and villages can be built within or around these loops.

Remember, the basic philosophy is to take a simple track plan and make the landscaping complex; both of these plans allows you to do this.

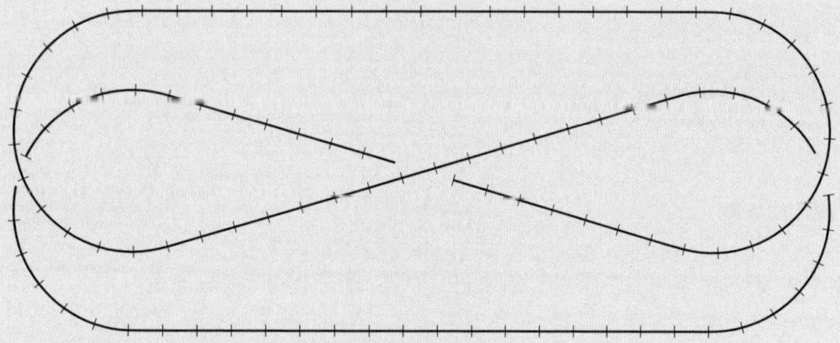

The folded dogbone trackplan

The folded dogbone is a deceptively simple trackplan. The track passes over and under itself several times in a complete circuit of the line, presenting many landscaping opportunities.

1

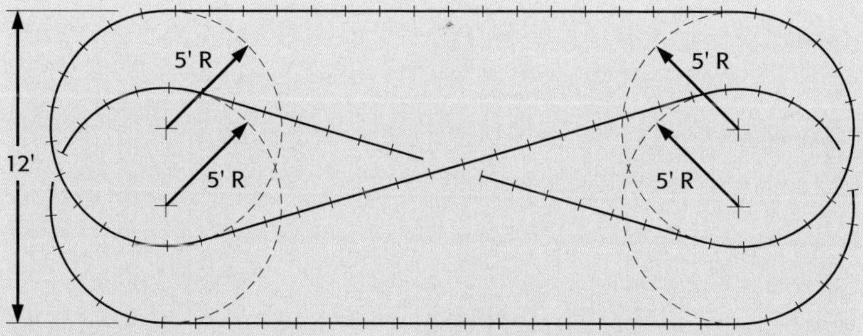

A space saver

The folded dogbone is also a space saver. You can have two relatively large turning loops at each end in just a little more than the space it would take for one loop. For example, you could have two 5'-radius turns in a space as little as twelve feet wide. Bear in mind it takes a space ten feet wide to have one five-foot-radius turning loop.

2

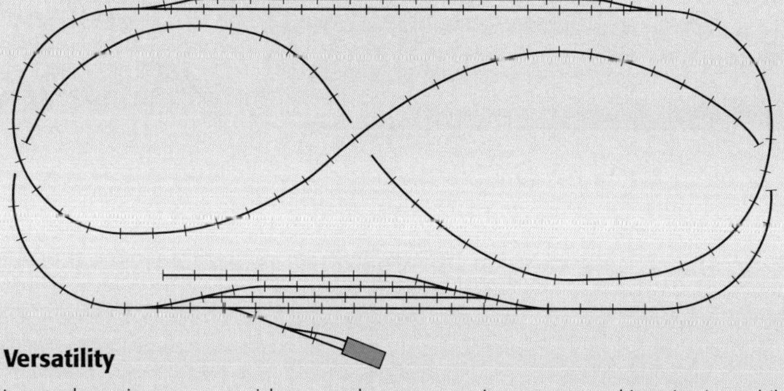

Versatility

In actual practice you may wish to vary the route to suit your taste and imagination, while still maintaining the basic plan. A series of passing and/or spurs can be added to the line to make prototypical operation possible. If space permits, a small point-to-point railroad could also be added.

3

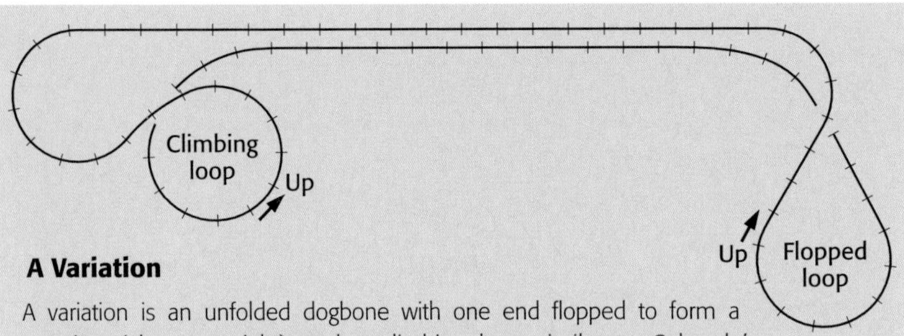

A Variation

A variation is an unfolded dogbone with one end flopped to form a crossing (above at right) and a climbing loop similar to Colorado's Georgetown Loop added to the other end. These could be reversed or you could have the same type of loop at both ends—it does not matter. The main idea is to incorporate changes in elevation into the railroad. In this plan, only two apparent lines travel east and west as opposed to four apparent lines in the folded dogbone. This plan could be used in an area where there is room at the two ends, but limited space in the middle, such as a flower bed.

4

Marc Horovitz

A town can be built on a flat area or on a hillside. By taking advantage of a hillside in a garden railway, the town can be elevated to make the structures more visible. Hundreds of examples of real towns built just like this one can be found in the Rocky Mountains of Colorado and in the gold mountains of California.

Design hints for working with flat ground

If at all possible, raise the entire area in which the railway is contained. Build the lowest rail line 12″ to 18″ higher than the pathway or ground level. Use the grade-stake method to lay out your track plan and grade.

If you would like a relatively flat track for live-steam operation, a way to obtain the illusion that the train is changing elevations is, again, to raise the entire line off the ground. In this case, though, you would not have an over-and-under track plan but rather a simple loop. The next step would be to vary the landscaping around the line. Mountains can climb above the level of the track, and valleys would fall below, while the train stays on a constant, level grade.

Varying the distance of landscape features from the track can also enhance grades or make them look steeper. An optical illusion can be created if the landscape rock and terrain are made to descend as the track ascends. This causes the eye to see a steeper grade than actually exists.

Plan your railroad so that, from the normal viewing point, the terrain in the background is at the highest point and the foreground is at the lowest. The area in between can be variable. This will give the illusion of greater distance. If the entire railroad is raised, some of the landscaping can actually be below track level, as in a dry wash or canyon, for example. If you are building at grade (in other words, at ground level—not elevated above the natural grade of the land) you will have to provide drainage if the landscape goes below grade, or you may end up with a lake.

Consider building towns or villages in a place where some of the landscape is higher than the town and some is lower. This will frame the scene, providing a backdrop for the town and making it look like it is set in the mountains.

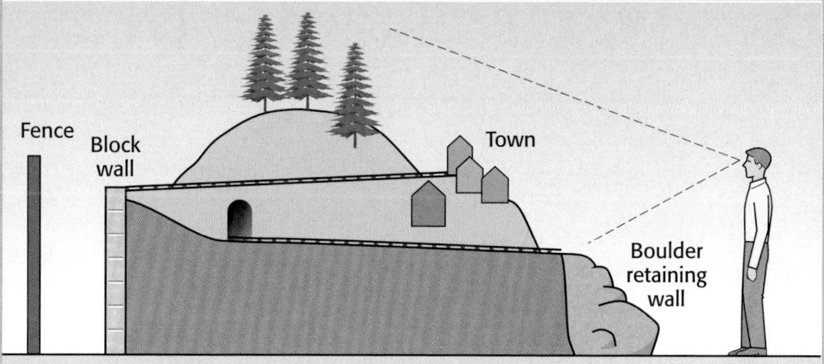

Elevating the line

Track in the foreground should be at the lowest point on the railway and the track at the back should be at the highest. This allows the viewer to see more of the railroad. Scenery that varies in height adds to the realism of the scene.

Different methods can be used to raise the railroad. If you want a natural look, use boulders to form a retaining wall in the foreground, then blend in the landscaping. If you want a more formal setting, can use bricks or concrete blocks to make a retaining wall. This will provide a sharp rise and actually give you more railroad real estate, since the wall does not angle back as boulders used as retainers would. Using a formal wall is like forming a picture.

Since the backside of the railroad is the highest point, it is almost always better to use a formal retaining wall to make a sharp rise. This is especially true if you are working in a confined space where the back of the line may be up against a fence.

Note: If you are building a retaining wall along a fence line, be sure to leave enough space to install a new fence when the time comes. It is a good idea to replace an old fence before building your railroad.

Integrating the railroad into the landscape

Jack Verducci

Jack Verducci

There are two basic garden-railroad settings. In one, the garden railroad has its own place and is an island unto itself. The railroad is set in place and no attempt is made to integrate it into the surrounding landscape. This is not to say, though, that the railroad itself is not landscaped. A good example of this type of railroad is one that is built in a large, raised planter box surrounded by a concrete walkway. Although the cement work blends into other cement features in the yard, the railroad's space is clearly defined.

Jack Verducci

<< At one end of the garden on Don and Sue Watters' Tahoe & Truckee Railroad in Los Altos, California, there is a pond and waterfall. The formal brick-lined pond and bottom half of the waterfall existed before the railroad. The area behind the existing waterfall was built up and the waterfall was extended all the way up the hill to form a new stream.

< The railroad used to be at ground level on the lawn. The grass is now free of track and the new Tahoe & Truckee runs in its own area. A boulder retaining wall blends the lawn with the railroad. Baby's tears were planted in the cracks to soften the look and tie the lawn in with the wall.

Other examples of railroads with their own places are the elevated lines commonly used for running live-steam locomotives. These are primarily running tracks and, in many cases, are not landscaped at all. In both of these examples, integrating the railroad with the surrounding landscape is not a priority.

The second type of garden-railroad setting is the integrated railroad, This is a railroad that runs in either a preexisting landscape or in a landscape that was built for the railroad. In this type of garden railroad, the idea is to blend, or integrate, the railroad with its surroundings.

Integrating the railroad

One of my favorite garden railroads is Don and Sue Watters' Tahoe & Truckee Line. Don had started his railroad several years ago as a line that ran on his lawn. He contacted me about designing and building a larger, improved railroad that would meet his true desires. The Watters' backyard landscaping, a peaceful setting that offers the feel of forested mountains, was professionally designed. One of our goals was to integrate the railroad into this existing landscape.

The old railroad had to go. It was anything but integrated. Being on the grass, it limited the use of the lawn and created mowing problems. In carefully examining the site, we realized that there was a space between the lawn and the fence in which a railroad could be built. This turned out to be a larger space than we realized when we started removing plants and clearing the area for construction.

Since Don's first railroad was on the ground, it was not hard to convince him that an elevated line would be much more fun to operate. After surveying the area, the decision was made to go ahead with the raised railroad. First, a block retaining wall was built along the fence line, about 18″ away from the fence, to allow limited access to the railroad and working room to build a new fence when needed. Next, fill dirt was brought in to raise the railroad's area to the desired height. In some places, the railroad landscaping is over six feet high and, at the lowest level, is about 18″ from the ground. The basic construction method was to raise the back side of the area with a retaining wall and to make a front wall using natural materials, in this case boulders.

Blending railroad and landscape

Then came the fun part. Blending the railroad with the existing landscape was fairly easy, since it was built along the fence. The railroad became a natural backdrop for the full-size landscaping. Some areas are so well blended you cannot tell where the full-size landscape ends and the railroad begins.

There was an existing brick mowing strip that became a border between the railroad and the lawn. Large landscape boulders were used to form the front retaining wall. Once it was built up, trees were added to the wall to make it look less like a stone wall and more like the beginning of a mountain area with a forest. Baby's tears were planted between the boulders to soften their lines and to blend the lawn with the wall.

Rock color was also an important consideration. We used brownish-gray rocks with some reddish tones. These are relatively neutral in color and do not contrast with the existing landscape. If one wanted to show a clear line of demarcation between the railroad and the full-size landscape, contrasting colors could be used. For example, gray granite or red cinder would be striking if placed next to a green lawn.

Concealed observation areas

The Watters' yard had an existing brick patio with several built-in benches, along with freestanding patio chairs and tables. The railroad was built so that parts of it could be viewed while sitting in this area. The railroad is elevated, but the viewer, when seated, is even lower, which affords an even better view of the trains.

Observation areas can more easily be built into the railroad when you are starting from scratch. Sometimes this might just be a bench placed somewhere within the railroad area. With a little imagination, you can come up with some well concealed—or, I should say, well integrated—seating areas for observation. Rocks, stumps, or logs placed a certain way can be part of the landscape, but can also double as seating areas.

The main idea behind integration is to make your garden railroad part of your yard, rather than a separate thing that is placed in it.

Other ways to integrate the garden railroad

The author's Crystal Springs Railroad, in San Mateo, California

Jack Verducci

1 On my railroad, the gazebo and deck are integrated into the scene by softening their edges. On the right, dwarf Alberta spruce blends the deck into the railroad, while, on the left, a cryptomeria hides the end post of the gazebo's railing. The gazebo predates the railroad, so the railroad has grown around it.

Jack Verducci

2 An unsightly control box is partially hidden by the addition of a rock formation and trees. The rocks hold the soil in place. Drippers water the trees, so there is little runoff. Notice how the rock formation leads you into the railroad area beyond. There are no trains in this area, but the landscaping is similar to the garden railroad's, which prepares you to see more as you walk along.

Anne and Otto Graf's Santa Fe & Kitchen Corner Railroad, Newark, California

3 The railroad of Anne Graf and her late husband Otto is unique in that it has a variety of railroad settings in one railroad. The backyard, seen here, is fully landscaped in miniature.

Marc Horovitz

Marc Horovitz

Marc Horovitz

4 The front yard is exposed to a lot of pedestrian traffic, so a method for protecting the railroad was devised. What the casual observer sees is a nice front yard with a white picket fence around it. But on weekends, down comes the fence to reveal the railroad!

Marc Horovitz

5 The side yard is an elevated line built on 44 posts, similar to the live-steam railroads mentioned in this chapter. This section connects the front and backyards.

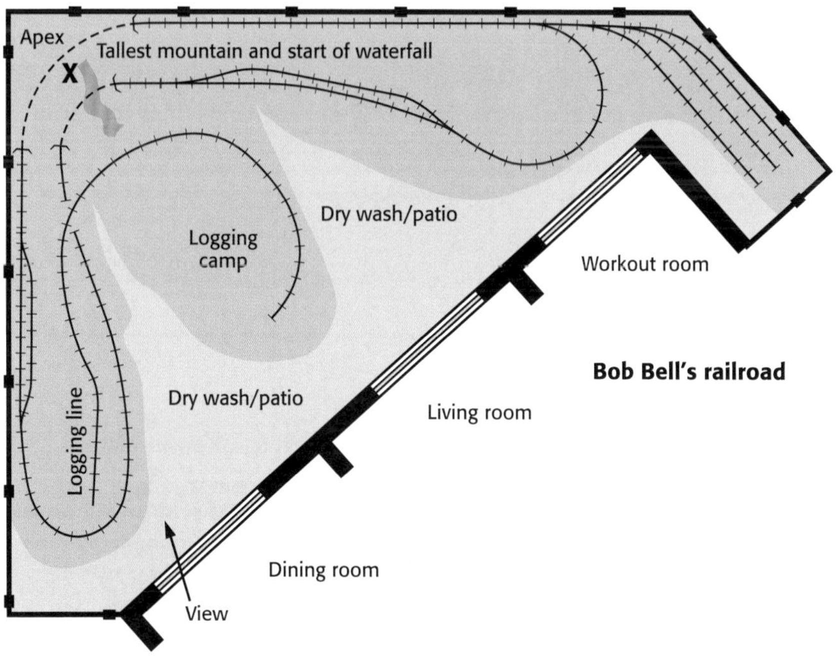

Bob Bell's railroad

Using perspective for more depth

Jack Verducci

I made a discovery in my own front yard. For many years we had the normal (a relative term) San Mateo front yard, which included some sort of small tree and a lawn. In the early 1990s we experienced a drought. The lawn was not watered, and it looked pretty bad when the drought was finally over. Instead of replanting it, my wife Pauline and I decided run the railroad out into this area. No thought was given at the time to the view from the window.

We installed the landscaping and built the railway. Then, while sitting in the living room one day, I noticed all of a sudden that we had a really neat view. Now, instead of looking at the neighbor's house we could look out on a miniature world. Yes, we can still see the neighbor's house in the background, but we can mentally block it out. This is what made me come to the realization that a garden railroad could be used to create a view where one does not exist.

Jack Verducci

The large picture window in Bob Bell's dining room was treated as if it were a picture frame and the railroad landscape was approached as one would approach a painting. Balance and perspective were taken into account. The dry wash, here in the form of a concrete walkway, is tapered as it recedes from the house, leading the eye to the high mountains in the distance.

A gentle S-curve can lead the eye into the scene. This works for highways, waterways, dry washes, and track. The waterway (or roadway) curves around the bend, helping to create the illusion that it goes on and on.

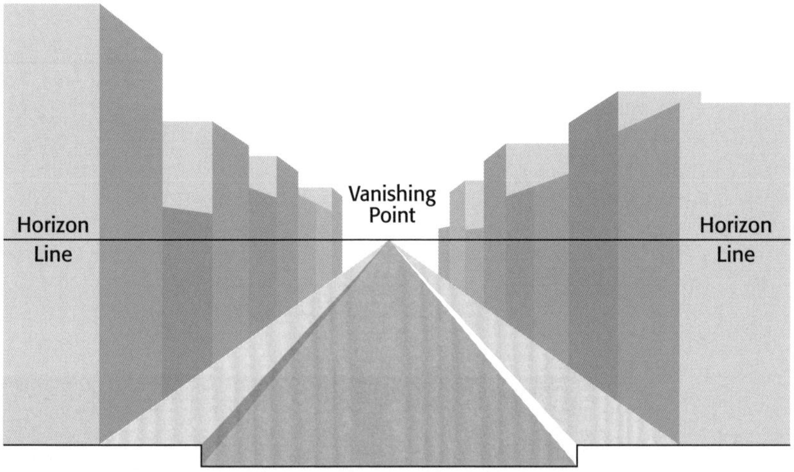

The sketch is an optical illusion. As the buildings, shown here as simple masses, are drawn smaller, the eye perceives them as vanishing in the distance. Your eye is directed to the point where the street disappears altogether—the vanishing point. The same principle can be used in three dimensions in the garden.

Perspective and vanishing points

It is beyond the scope of this book to go into a detailed explanation of vanishing points and perspective. Basic art books are available that explain these principles in detail. Here is an abridged version.

As things are seen by the eye, they appear smaller in the distance and larger up close. If you were to look at a set of parallel lines, such as a railroad track, they seem to meet at some point in the distance even though they are parallel. The point where they appear to meet is called the vanishing point.

In creating a garden-railroad scene, we can use this concept to create the illusion of greater space and depth. The easiest way to do this is to taper features that would normally have parallel lines; streets or roadways, for example. Instead of making their sides parallel, draw them toward one another as they recede into the distance. Curving the road will enhance the effect. This is most effective when you are working with an area that will usually be seen from a single spot.

This is called "forced perspective." You are creating the illusion of distance by changing the parallel lines into converging lines. The same principle can be used with dry washes and waterways. Tapering and curving them will give them greater apparent depth.

Another trick in forcing perspective is to make background things smaller. For example, use smaller rocks at the top of the mountain than at the base. if you are using flat rocks, place the smaller end toward the vanishing point.

Using smaller-scale buildings in the distance can also force perspective. For example, if you use 1:22.5-scale building in the foreground, try using a 1:24-scale or 1:32-scale building in the background. If the building is far away, you might even be able to use an O-scale (1:48) structure. This would work best if placed in an area where it cannot be closely observed.

Try experimenting with this concept. You'll be amazed and pleased with some of the effects you can create.

Developing this thought even further, I now look at every railroad project as picture or painting. In circumstances where the railway is visible from the house, I stand inside and use the window as a picture frame, then design the railroad to fit in the frame.

Bob and Rose Ann Bell had contacted me about helping them design a garden railroad for their backyard. Their backyard was pie shaped, with the apex of the triangle being farthest from the house. It turned out that this yard was perfectly shaped for the creation of a dramatic view, especially from the house through the window. Bob had designed and built his home himself and he built in several large windows so one could view the yard from the dining room, the living room, and other living spaces.

Keeping the above information in mind, I designed the railroad's landscape based on what the view would be from the house. The first problem was how to deal with the pie shape. This turned out to be relatively simple. The shape created a natural way to force perspective. Everything was designed to lead the eye toward the apex of the yard.

The first decision we made was to raise the railroad. A retaining wall was built up to a height of about 3 feet on two sides of the pie. This wall is not visible from the viewing side of the railroad. Next, a trackplan, a simple folded dogbone, was designed to fit into this space. The plan was enhanced with sidings and a secondary railroad line, but the basic design was quite simple.

Since there were two basic areas from which to view the miniature landscape, two dry washes were created; one on the left and one on the right, with a peninsula in the center. As these dry washes recede into the distance, they narrow to give the illusion of greater distance and to lead the eye into the scene. This is called forced perspective.

In the final plan, the floor of the dry wash turned into a concrete walkway. The concrete is contoured to follow the canyon wall and it narrows to meet the natural rock landscape. As you look further up the canyon, you see a high-level waterfall at the farthest depths of the canyon. Whether you are sitting on the patio or in the dining room, you are treated to a view of this distant waterfall and high mountains. It is pleasing even without the railroad running.

A few basic things were done to enhance the scene when the landscape was built. The waterways were curved so the water never flows in a straight line. In other words, the water is always coming from somewhere around the bend, so you never really see its source. This also provides a variety of viewing angles. The water flow starts at a high point, but not at the top of the mountain. Full-sized waterfalls generally appear to start somewhere in the middle of a mountainside, rather than at the very top. In making dry washes, the same rules apply. They will look longer if they are curved and tapered as they go off into the distance.

The railroad was kept at about the center of the scene (from top to bottom). This made the mountains seem larger and the trains smaller. Elevating both the railroad and its landscaping was a key factor in creating a spectacular scene. You must look up to see all the scenery. This would not have been nearly as dramatic if it were built at ground level.

Raise your railroad

Jim Hudson

A proper viewpoint is of prime importance for realism, and for practical purposes, that means moving the trains up from toe level to something approximating eye level. Yes, raising your garden railway can be quite a bit of work, and you'll have to do it at the beginning, when you're really inspired and itching to be laying track and running trains, instead of shoveling wheelbarrows of fill dirt.

How high is up?

Just how, and how much, to elevate your railroad is up to you and your resources. An existing retaining wall is a great base to start from, at a very handy 3 feet above the ground. Any mountains built up above this level already have a head start, from the viewer's perspective. Unless you're a pro basketball player, you'll be looking up at the peak of a 4-foot-tall mountain, just as you'd look up at a real mountain. Combine the mountains with some 2- or 3-foot-deep valleys and you have some pretty dramatic topography.

If you can't raise your whole railroad, maybe you can raise part of it. If your yard slopes away from the house to the back fence, your track can start at ground level by the back porch. Then, as the ground gently slopes down, the track can gradually rise.

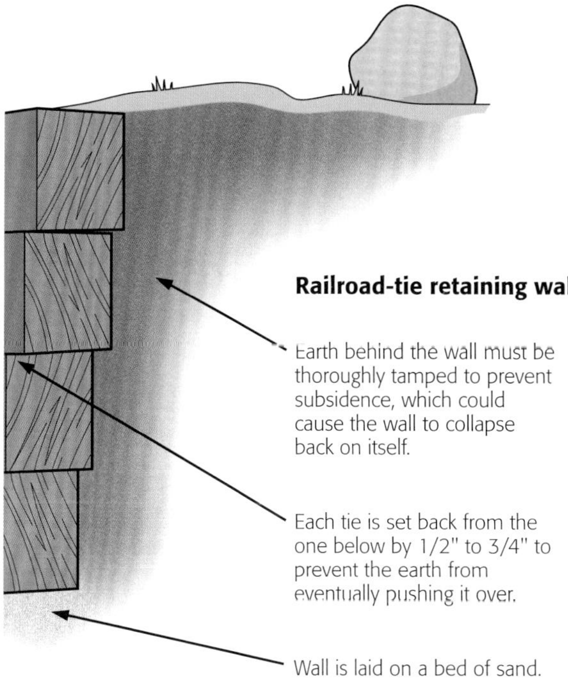

Railroad-tie retaining wall

SECTION 4

Laying the groundwork

Jim Hudson

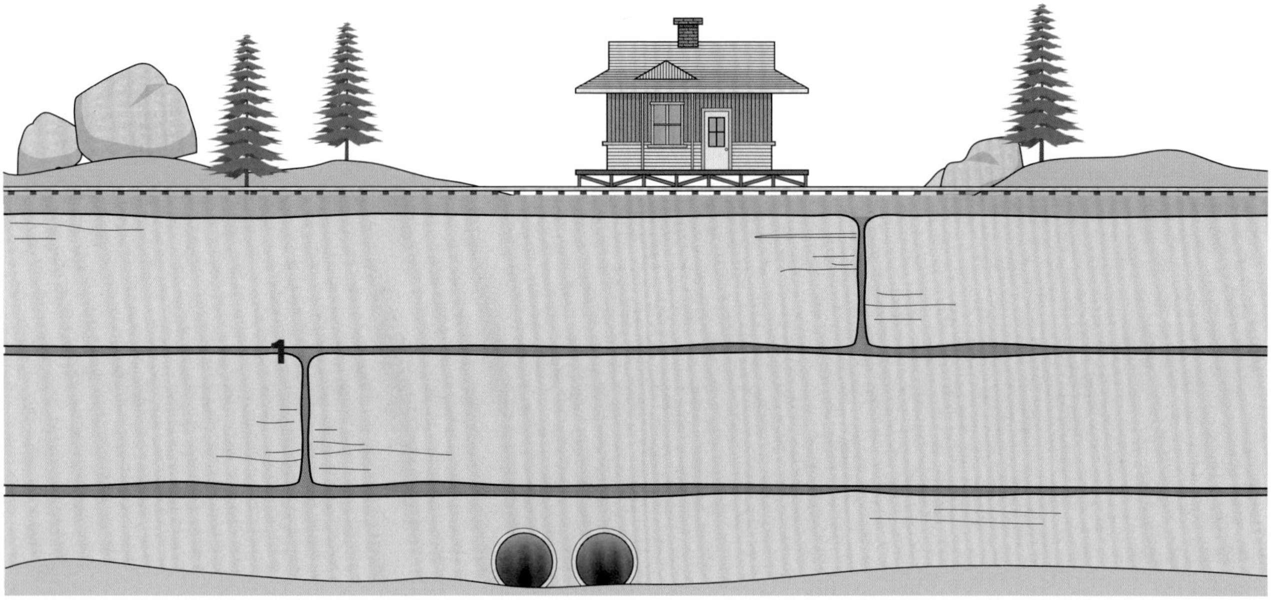

1a

Have you ever wondered why it seems that the construction crews can work for ages on a building site with little visible progress, and then suddenly the walls seem to go up almost overnight? There's a lot more to a building than meets the eye. Surveying, engineering, and grading the site may take months. Beyond the obvious things, such as shaping the earth to the desired contours, great amounts of time may be spent just scraping away the soil, then replacing it, only this time carefully compacting it so it doesn't settle and sink. Trenches must be dug for all kinds of utilities—plumbing, storm drains, electricity, and more. Then there is the foundation itself. Any mistakes or shortcuts here can lead to serious problems later.

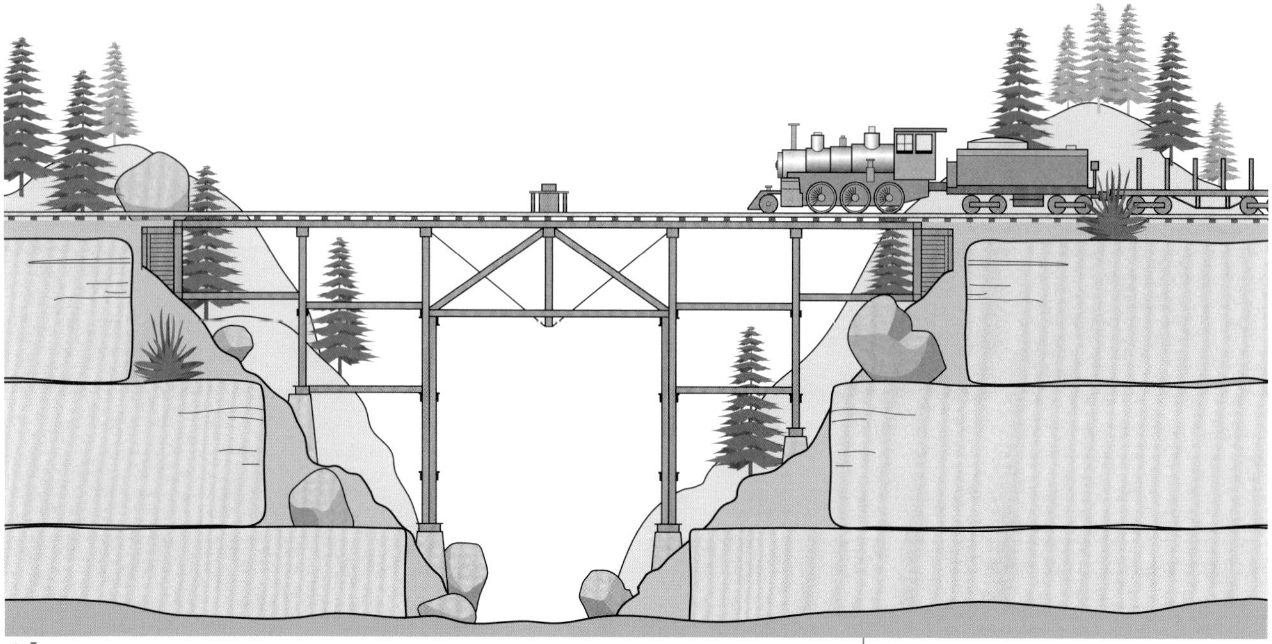

1b

There are some parallels between constructing a building and a garden railway. As you continue to refine the design of your railway and move into the construction phase, you'll find you have a lot more to consider and deal with than just laying track.

Proper drainage

You'll need to allow for proper runoff and drainage, especially if you decide to raise your railroad above the surrounding area. You may find that your raised garden-railway "platform" creates a fine dam for rainwater, resulting in a pond in the middle of the backyard. You can follow the practice of highway and railroad engineers and make simple culverts out of plastic pipe to carry the water under your railroad (fig. 1a) to the other side.

Culverts are certainly a functional approach, but you might want to take advantage of the situation and make a feature out of a necessary evil. Instead of a culvert, consider dropping the railway's terrain to make a sort of dry wash (fig. 1b). Tracks can run across on a dramatic bridge, and the wash will serve as a drainage channel when the need arises. Now you have a scenic element and a bit of added drama.

There is one other point regarding drainage that should be obvious, but it's an easy trap to fall into. Make sure the middle area of your garden railroad is not the lowest point unless you—actually intend to have a pond.

You can't get there from here

Consider how you will gain access to all parts of your railway for construction and maintenance. A simple approach would be to make your garden railroad no more than a few feet wide at any point, so you can just reach over to clean a track, trim a bush, or rerail a locomotive. But you may want wider sections for scenic purposes, or you may need that extra dimension for things like reversing loops. In these cases, you need to be creative in allowing yourself ways to gain access to those points.

You may find that a dry wash or roadway makes a convenient pathway for full-size foot traffic. On the slopes of a mountain, a well-placed rock of the proper shape can become a comfortable place to step, kneel, or sit while you work on the railroad.

Time for the heavy earthwork

Once you have some sort of wall built to raise the level of your railroad, it's time to backfill the area. Resist the temptation to grab a few wheelbarrows-full from the nearest dirt pile. You'll want to use the right materials as a base for your garden railway. You need soil that is stable and drains well.

Expansive soil (that with a high clay content) will swell up like a sponge every time it rains, then shrink as it dries. Soil with organic material, such as dead plants, trees, compost, or garbage, won't compact firmly and will continue to settle as whatever is in it decomposes. It's probably also wise to avoid the "fill dirt" you see advertised for sale around construction sites. This may contain, clay, compost, or worse.

The ideal fill material is what is called decomposed granite (DG). In most areas you should be able to get this inexpensively by the truckload from a local building-supply store or rock yard. If DG is tough to find, you can also use what is known as construction sand (not beach sand, which has a very high salt content), as long as it is constrained or held in place by something solid on all sides.

If you have a large volume to fill, say raising your railroad up 3 or 4 feet, it's fine to use solid materials such as rock or old concrete as a base. Just finish off the last foot or so with good material and be sure to allow for large pockets of planting soil wherever you want trees or large plants. One garden railroader near me recently used chunks of concrete from a driveway a neighbor was tearing up. The neighbor was glad to save the expense of hauling it away. By layering and carefully filling in all the voids around the concrete pieces with decomposed granite, the garden-railway builder also saved a bit of money.

Figs. 1a & 1b. A culvert in the form of a pipe can be used to drain certain areas of the railway. Alternatively, a dry wash can be created, giving the railway a natural gap to bridge.

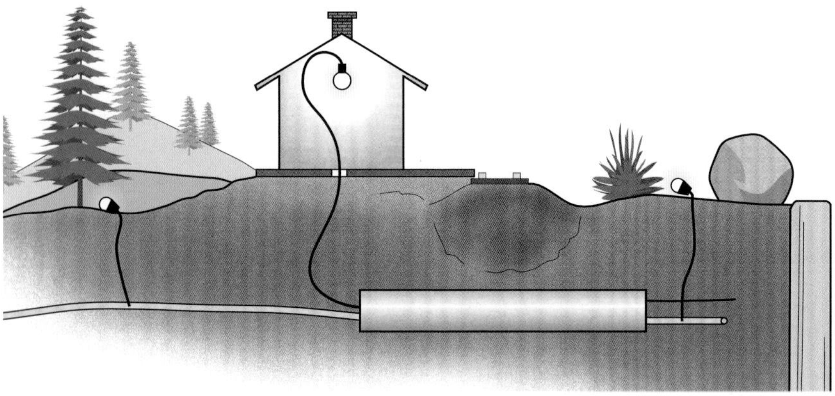

Trenches for irrigation pipes and electrical conduits will need to be dug before the track is laid.

2

Underground utilities for your miniature world

Even though we've not yet discussed how you are going to power your trains (track power? Radio control? live-steam?), now is the time to plan for some kind of access under the track at a few strategic points. In addition to any track wiring, you'll also likely want to run wires for electrical accessories such as building lights and switch machines, plus piping for sprinklers and pond pumps, hoses for drip irrigation, and a bunch of other things you can't always anticipate (fig. 2).

You can minimize the need to tear up tracks by placing a few lengths of plastic conduit across, under the roadbed, before you lay the track. You can get fancy if you want, with pull boxes and covers, or just bury a piece of heavy plastic pipe a few inches beneath the track. (I prefer what's called "schedule 80" pipe, about 2″ diameter.) Even the simplest efforts will save you headaches down the road.

Rocks by the ton

From observing a number of garden railways, I think one of the things that sets some apart from the others is the use of rocks, generally fairly big ones. I admit that I've seen some great-looking garden railways with artificial rocks, but for this discussion I'm presuming that you're going for the natural approach. The reason this whole subject comes up at this point in construction is that you may need to build the bigger rocks into your landscape before you start laying track in a particular area. A rock just a couple feet across can weigh several hundred pounds, and you don't want to drag or roll it over your beautifully laid tracks.

It's usually evident when garden-railway builders have spent some time choosing their rocks, then carefully placing and integrating them into the whole scene. If you're modeling something along the lines of the Grand Canyon Railway, your rocks might need to look like the dry, red sandstone of the western desert. If you are trying to capture feel of the Pennsylvania Railroad, you may want dark gray, moss-covered rocks with bursts of iron-ore stains. Obviously, it's going to be easier—and cheaper—to use what you have available locally, but importing rocks from across the country is possible if you have the desire and the budget.

If you are after realism, don't mix a number of types and colors of rocks. Pick one type of rock and use it in quantity. Also, pay careful attention to the orientation of your rocks. If the rocks you choose have a natural stratification (grain pattern) or some typical shape characteristics, be consistent in positioning them (figs. 3a and 3b). It helps to study the real thing. Follow the way nature lays out those rocks and you'll be miles ahead in the realism department.

Next in importance, if you want your rocks to have dramatic impact, is to use the biggest rocks you can manage. A couple of strong backs with pry bars can probably wrestle 150- to 200-pound rocks into place. Moving up into really big rocks, you may need to rent a small tractor or the services of a professional landscaper. It all depends on what level of effort and expense you decide is appropriate to dedicate to this portion of the whole process of building your garden railway.

3a

In good rock placement, the strata are aligned and altitude is gained by stacking the rocks in a natural manner.

3b

In this example, stratifications are not naturally aligned and height has been gained by unnaturally turning a rock on end.

Tools
of the trade

Jack Verducci

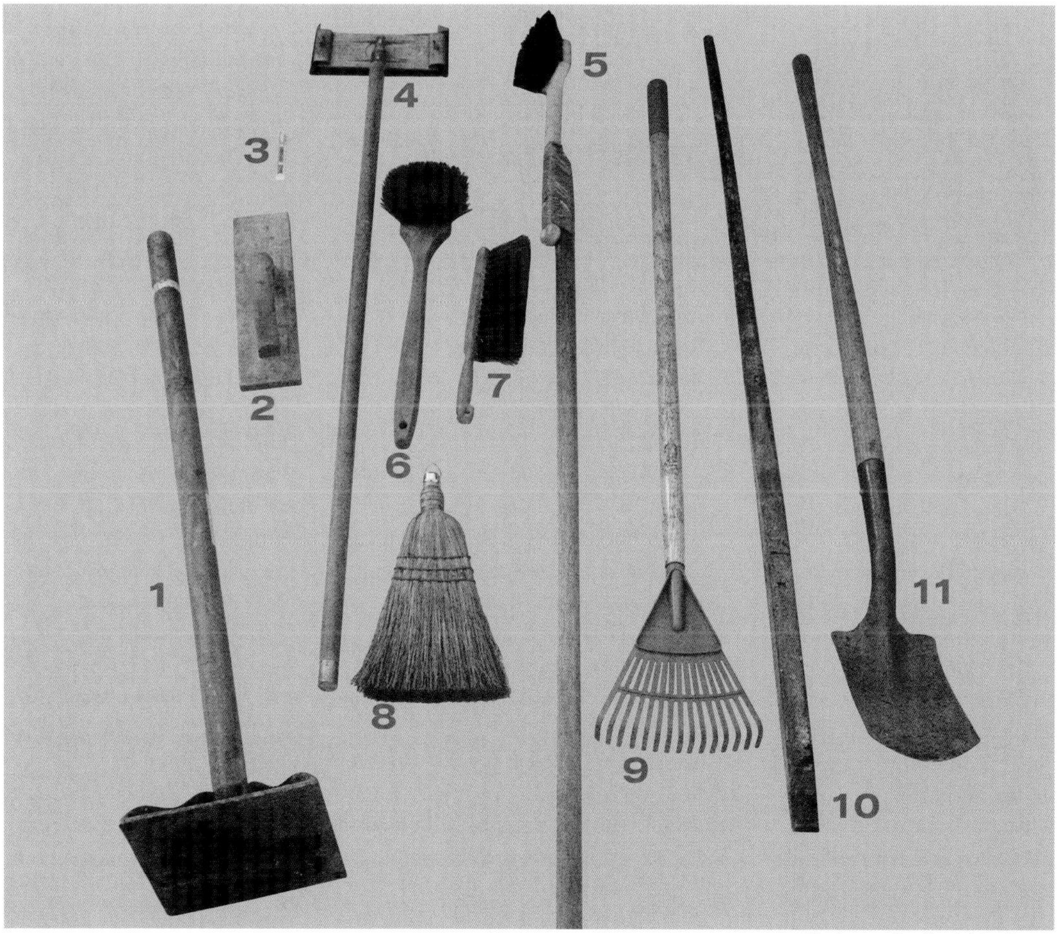

All photos by Jack Verducci

These tools, except for the long prybar, are the basic tools for building and maintaining roadbed. 1. Six-inch-square tamper. 2. Mason's wooden float. 3. Plastic torpedo level. 4. Drywall sander. 5. Gong brush mounted on a broom handle. 6. Gong brush. 7. Counterbrush (foxtail). 8. Whisk broom. 9. Shrubbery rake. 10. Prybar. 11. Trenching shovel.

Let's depart the realm of design, planning, and theory and enter the realm of actual construction methods and techniques. In this chapter, we'll begin with a discussion of tools and how they are used in garden-railroad construction.

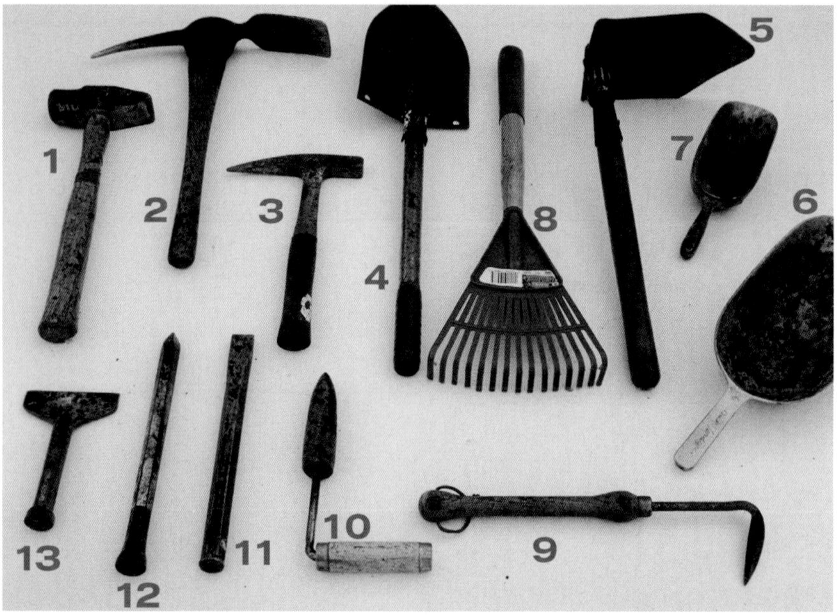

These tools are used for a variety of landscaping and roadworking jobs. Except for the chisels, they are short-handled tools that can be used while you are seated or lying down. 1. Short-handled sledgehammer. 2. Short-handled pick. 3. Rock hammer. 4. Folding shovel (in shovel position) 5. Folding shovel (in pick or hoe position). 6. Large material scoop. 7. Small material scoop. 8. Short-handled rake. 9. New England weeder. 10. Dibble. 11. One-inch cold chisel. 12. Bull-point chisel. 13. Brick-cutting chisel.

A **tamper** is for packing down the earth and is especially useful in compacting subroadbed. Tampers are usually offered in two sizes: 6″ x 6″ and 9″ x 9″. The small one can get into tighter areas and takes less energy to use and is well suited for tamping roadbeds. Tamp the earth while it is dry, then water it in.

A **mason's wooden float** is useful for making roadways and doing small tamping jobs. It is also helpful in making flat areas on which to place buildings. It can be used like a miniature road grader. Use it to smooth and level materials such as sand and crusher fines. If you like, you can glue a little level to the top of the blade to help you level small areas.

A small, **plastic torpedo level** is the ideal tool for side-to-side leveling of track. It fits easily in your pocket and, since it is plastic, it can be laid across the track even while the power is on.

The **pole sander or drywall sander** is a relatively painless way to manually clean track and is a tool that everyone who runs track-powered trains should have. It features an abrasive pad on a swivel and allows you to clean the rails while standing up. it is long enough to clean inside most tunnels. Use a medium grade, drywall-sanding mesh. This is an open-mesh sanding cloth that looks like a piece of window screen.

A **gong brush** can be used for spreading ballast and general cleanup.

The **long-handled gong brush** is a standard brush taped to a broom handle. This brush is useful for cleaning out tunnels and spreading ballast inside them.

A **foxtail broom or counter brush** can be used to clean and spread ballast, but it is especially good for brushing excess soil off rocks.

A **whisk broom** can be used to do the same jobs as a gong brush or foxtail.

A **shrubbery rake** is a must-have for any garden railroader. They are available in metal or plastic, with wooden handles. The advantage of the plastic rake is that you can use it while trains are running and it won't short the track. This rake is used to clear debris from the line.

The **prybar** is used to pry rocks loose or to break up large rocks by working it into cracks and crevices. A lifting and dropping action is used. This tool can be useful where you cannot swing a pick.

A **drain spade** is the tool to use for digging drainage ditches, pipeline ditches, or for placing ballast inside tunnels. It is long, narrow, and cupped, and is designed to dig a deep, narrow trench.

A **short-handled sledgehammer** is useful for breaking rocks and driving stakes and rebar.

The **short-handled pick** is a real prize. This is the hand tool that I use the most when landscaping. A short-handled pick can be used while you are seated or lying on the ground (which you will probably be doing a lot of when building a garden railroad).

A **rock hammer** is used to break up rocks. Unlike the sledge hammer, it can be very precise. You can chip away a rock a little at a time until it is just the shape and size you want.

Folding shovel (in shovel position). This tool can be used while you are seated or prone. It is excellent for rock placement and moving small amounts of dirt.

Folding shovel (in pick or hoe position). In this configuration, the tool can be used to move small amounts of dirt when you are seated or lying down.

Material scoops (large and small) are excellent all-round hand tools for a garden railroader. They are useful for ballast application and light material transfers, such as spreading mulch.

A **short-handled rake** is a good ground-maintenance tool, especially when you are trimming trees in the seated or prone position.

A **New England weeder** is a good tool for removing excess ballast from beneath the track. It's also useful for small trenching—laying low-voltage lighting wire, for example.

A **dibble** is a tool with a (usually) wooden handle and a metal point. It is used to make a hole in the soil by pushing it into the ground and is useful for planting, especially when planting in between rocks or in tight areas.

The **1-inch cold chisel** can be used for precision rock breaking.

A **bull-nose chisel** can be used to split rocks.

The **brick chisel** is used to cut brick or to make large cuts in masonry.

More tools of the trade

Jack Verducci

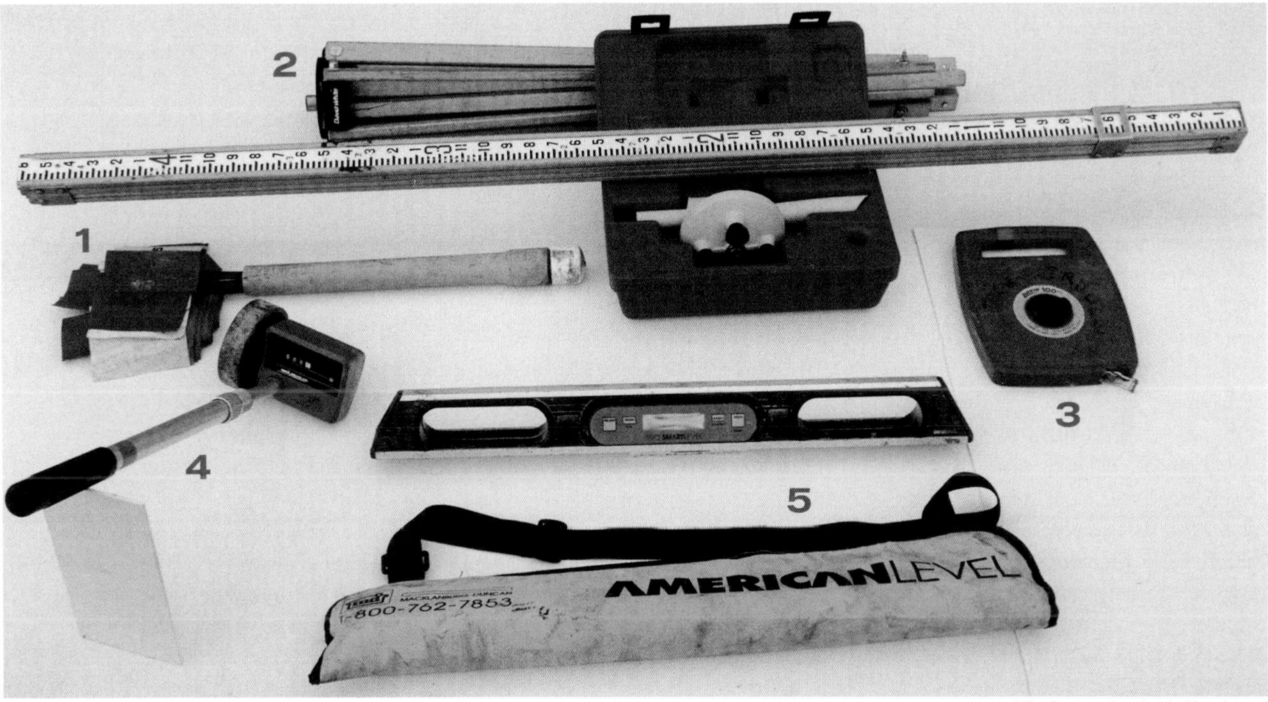

All photos by Jack Verducci

1. Marker flags. 2. Builder's level. 3. 100' tape measure. 4. Measuring wheel. 5. Smart level.

There are some highly specialized professional tools that most people will not own, but may have to rent or borrow.

Marker flags are used to mark the position of grade stakes, sprinkler heads, wire runs, and so forth.

A **builder's level or transit** is used to set grade.

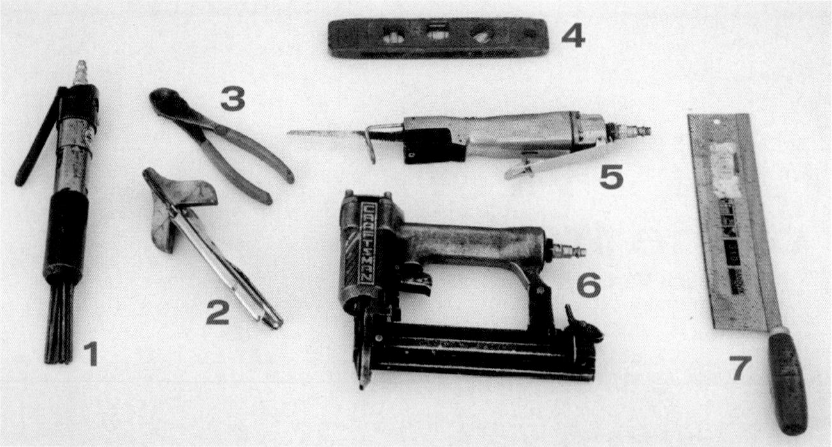

‹ 1. Needle gun or scaler. 2. Wood-cutting tool. 3. Side cutters. 4. Torpedo level. 5. Air saw. 6. Brad gun. 7. Dovetail saw.

› 1. 175-watt soldering iron. 2. Allen wrenches with screwdriver handle and T-handle. 3. Air ratchet. 4. Atlas Super Saw. 5. Rail bender. 6. Allen-wrench set. 7. Resistance soldering unit. 8. Pliers. 9. Stainless-steel wire brush. 10. Dic grinder with extra cutting wheel. 11. Microtorch. 12. Butane gas.

A **100′ cloth tape** measure is useful for measuring long distances and can also be laid around curves, since it is not rigid like a metal tape.

A **measuring wheel** can be used to measure distance. You walk the wheel along the area to be measured. This is a good tool to have when working alone.

A **"smart" level** is an electronic level with a simulated bubble that measures in several modes, including degrees of elevation, percent of elevation, and inches-per-foot drop or rise. This is useful for checking grade over a short distance, say between two grade stakes set 5′ apart.

Straightedge. Mine is a 1″ x 1″ x 72″ steel bar. I use it in conjunction with the smart level to cover distances longer than the level can reach by itself. You can also buy a longer frame for the level to accomplish the same end, but a steel bar is cheaper. I find the shorter version of the smart level easier to store. The metal bar can be thrown anywhere.

A **needle gun or scaler** is an air-powered tool that is used to scale excess cement from rocks. I also use it to clean caked-on dirt or cement from tools.

My **wood-cutting tool** is similar in function to a pair of scissors. Normally it would be used in the workshop for cutting small pieces of wood to size; model shingles, for example. In the garden it is handy for cutting trestle braces to size.

Side cutters can be used to remove brads when necessary. They are also useful in cutting plastic tie strips.

The **small torpedo level** reads in either a horizontal or vertical position. It is used to set up trestle bents so they are vertical. Its size makes it easier to use than a large carpenter's level. It can also be used as a ruler to set spacing.

An **air-powered body saw** is a metal-cutting saw fitted with a wood-cutting blade. It is used to cut small pieces of wood, such as those used in trestle construction. I find it very versatile and it has replaced the saber saw in my tool box. In real life it is used to cut sheet metal in auto-body shops.

A **brad gun** is extremely useful for building a variety of wooden items for your railroad, but it is an absolute must for trestle construction and installation. It allows you to nail a trestle together without banging or having to drill pilot holes. Brad guns are available powered by air or electricity.

Dovetail saw. Sometimes it is necessary to make a small precision cut. A dovetail saw gives you the control you need.

A **175-watt soldering iron** is the minimum-voltage soldering iron required to solder track.

Allen wrenches with T-handles are good for tightening easy-to-get-to Allen-head screws. Wrenches with screwdriver handles with ball ends are needed for tightening Allen screws at an angle. These are good for tightening rail joiners and servicing other tools fitted with Allen-head screws.

An **Atlas Super Saw** is the fastest manual tool for cutting track, and it can also be used for cutting wood. It is a throw-away item that can be used dozens of times before the blade becomes dull. Look for one at your hobby shop.

A **rail bender,** as the name suggests, is used to prebend rail to make curved track sections to fit your specific needs. It comes with a hand crank but I fitted mine with a drill chuck so an air ratchet can be used to powered it.

A **resistance-soldering unit** is another tool that can be used to solder rails.

Pliers. A large pair is used to align rails after solder has been applied, before it cools.

A **small stainless-steel brush** can be used to clean rails before they are soldered and to clean slag and soot from soldered joints.

An **air-powered die grinder** is the quickest and easiest way to cut track. It has just the right amount of speed and power. A spare cutting wheel is good to have around just in case.

A **small torch,** in my opinion, is the best way to solder rails.

Butane gas is the fuel for the torch.

A **demolition hammer** is a small electric jackhammer that can be fitted with various attachments. The tamping attachment is useful for compacting roadbed or soil. A spade or digging blade is good for breaking up hard ground and can sometimes be used in place of a pick. With a chisel attachment you can break up rocks or, with a bull point, concrete.

Here are some additional common tools (not pictured):

A **square-point shovel** is designed to move materials. For example, it is good for shoveling dirt from the pile in the driveway into a wheelbarrow or moving loose dirt from one spot to another. It is also useful for leveling roadbed. Since the nose is square, you can cut a flat path for the roadbed. While not so good for digging a hole, it is good for edging where you want a square cut, say in making the walls or sides of a railroad cut.

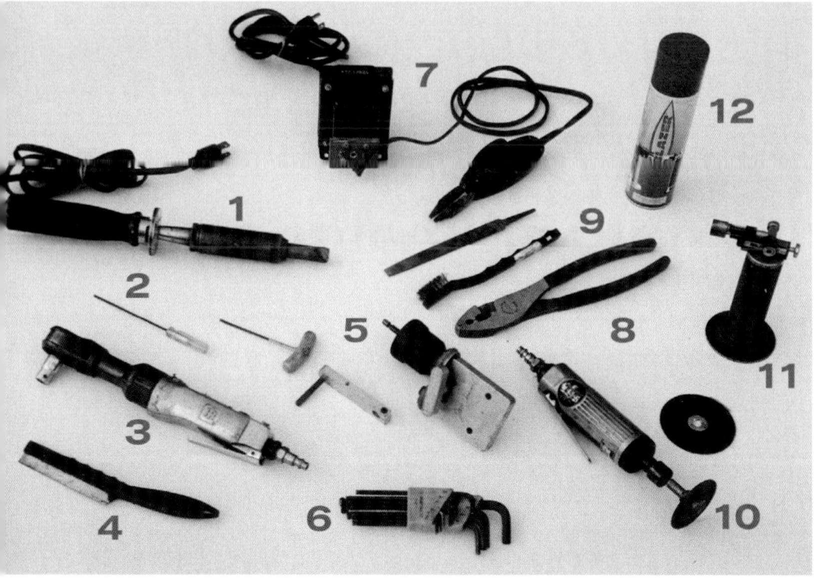

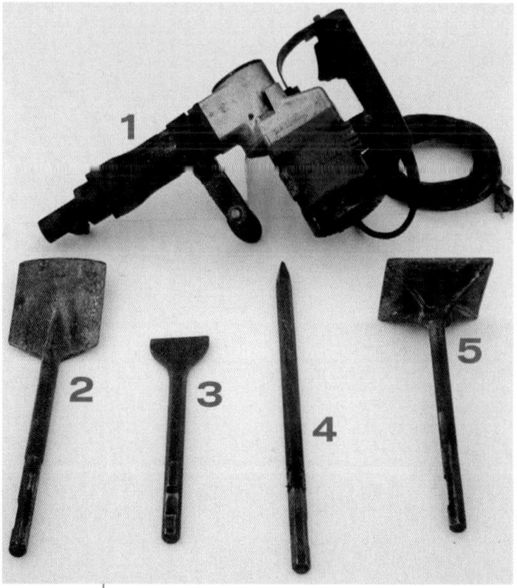

1. Demolition hammer. 2. Spade or digger. 3. Chisel tip. 4. Bullnose. 5. Tamper attachment.

An **old fashioned wood-handled shovel** works fine if you already have one on hand. If you are going to buy a new one, may I suggest one with a Fiberglas handle? This type is four times as expensive, but will last forever if not abused. The handle is very strong and it will not rot. Best of all it is lighter weight. After shoveling ten yards of dirt you will be grateful for that feature.

The **pointed shovel** is the digging tool. It is not good practice to use a pointed shovel for moving materials from a driveway or other hard surface. This win destroy the point. Again, a Fiberglas handle is recommended.

A **pick** is the main tool of the mountain-railroad builder. It is used to break the ground to make cuttings and dig tunnels. Use the pick first to break up the dirt, then use the pointed shovel to clear it out. These two tools work together. Be careful the pick can be a real back breaker. If you don't swing one for a living, take it easy or you will pay the price the next day. Watch your toes and make sure the surrounding area affords clear swinging space.

A **polaski** is a cross between a pick, an standard axe, and a broad axe. It is used to cut through buried roots. One side of this tool is like a conventional axe, the other is like a broad axe. In other words, one blade is horizontal and one is vertical. The blades need to be kept sharp. A polaski can cut through medium-size roots fairly quickly. Larger roots will take more work. This tool will work where a chain saw will not.

A good **wheelbarrow** can be a big asset in constructing a railroad. Choosing the right one is important. Here are some things to consider. Don't even think of buying a wheelbarrow that does not have a pneumatic tire. This is very important when moving heavy loads over rough terrain. I have found that a 6-cubic-foot capacity is about right. With a smaller one you have to make too many trips and a larger one becomes too hard to handle. Contractors' wheelbarrows are nice, but you may find them a little heavy to handle. I prefer the smaller version.

A **metal rake** is good for spreading topsoil and other materials. For larger jobs, an asphalt rake makes fast work of the project. This rake is 36″ wide and is made of aluminum.

A **5-gallon bucket** is a wonderful tool to have on hand. You can buy them or find them lying by the side of the road (they like to blow out of truck beds). A bucket is useful for moving small amounts of materials like ballast or soil to places where a wheelbarrow cannot go. You will find that as your railroad approaches completion, access for materials becomes trickier. A bucket can solve the problem.

Buckets are also useful for mixing and storing things. Be sure to cover any buckets used for storing materials outdoors. A bucket of topsoil can turn into ooze if it gets rained on—a bucket usually does not have a drain hole. A better way to store these types of materials is in 5- or 15-gallon planting pots that have drain holes in the bottom.

Marking paint can be used to mark roadbed and other locations. You can buy spray paint that is designed to be sprayed while the can is upside down.

A cement mixer is a handy tool for mixing large batches of mortar, concrete, or Gulapata (see the December 1997 *Garden Railways*). It can also be used for mixing special soils for planting.

A good pair of **scissors** is helpful for cutting pond liners and other materials. Also useful are garden or bonsai scissors to trim plants as you plant them.

This is by no means intended to be complete nor is it to be considered a must-have list. It is intended to be an overview of tools that garden railroaders might find useful. The size and complexity of your railway and landscaping will be a big determining factor in which tools you ultimately need. A good rule of thumb is to purchase what you need, when you need it. It isn't necessary to get everything all at once.

Miniature
landscaping with natural materials
Jack Verducci

Jack Verducci

When I discovered garden railroading, a whole new world opened up to me. It was the trains that lead me to the hobby at first, but later I actually became interested in gardening. The challenge of creating realistic settings for the trains using natural material eventually became a major interest.

◀ These rock outcroppings on the author's railway were constructed with head- and double-head-size stones. Groundcover has helped make these well-planted rocks look like they have been there for millions of years.

▶ Large rocks that must be moved with heavy equipment should be chosen for specific situations on the railway, like this one, where a huge stone is used as a mesa on Barb and Marc Horovitz's Ogden Botanical Railway.

Marc Horovitz

Over the years I have developed a real love of miniature landscaping. I believe that a well-designed garden railway will stand on its own as a beautiful landscape, even without the train. The majority of the time you see the landscape without the train running, even if you run your trains a lot. So it is worth the effort to make landscaping a high priority in your overall plan.

The basic concept in landscaping is to create a scene that you will enjoy, one that is pleasing to the eye. Garden-railroad landscaping shares many things with Japanese-style gardens. One of these things is to try to make a space look larger by using smaller features in it, such as miniature plants and rocks.

An introduction to landscaping materials

Some of the materials mentioned in this chapter and subsequent ones may be called by different names in your area. So, with that in mind, I will try to describe the characteristics of each material and show a photo of each one so you will know what to look for. My goal is to give you enough information for you to choose the right rock for the job.

Rock

Rock is one of the mainstays of garden-railroad construction. Not only is it part of the structure of the landscape, but stone contributes to the overall look and mood of the railroad.

There are an infinite variety of rocks that will work in a garden railroad. I will describe the types of rock that I believe work best in creating a believable miniature landscape.

Rocks for use in making mountains

My first consideration in choosing rock is its overall appearance. This includes two primary attributes. First, and most important, is shape and texture; second is color.

Size is another consideration. Generally speaking, larger rocks work better for making mountains. I usually use rocks that are head and double-head size. Head and double-head are terms used to indicate the size of a rock. As implied, head size is about the size of a human head. Double head is twice as big. These are sizes that can be manhandled.

If larger rocks are used, special machinery may be required to handle them. Anything larger than double-head size should be carefully selected with a specific application in mind. It is easier to make rock formations out of smaller rocks than out of huge rocks.

It is interesting how much weight difference there is between various types of stone of equal dimensions. When you're at the rockyard, pick up and carry a sample of your rock of choice to see how easy or difficult it will be to move around.

Marc Horovitz

Double-head-size rocks (and sometimes even larger) can be easily moved with a two-wheel hand truck.

Rock types and shapes

Jack Verducci

All photos by Jack Verducci

When examining rocks, visualize how they will look if viewed from a scale prospective. Individually, some rocks may look like mountains in miniature. Other rocks, working together, can make formations like those found on a cliff side or in an area that has been blown or cut away to make the roadbed of a railroad or highway.

1

4

5

2

3

6

‹ Feather rock is an amazing material. It can be carved, cut, and shaped and it will accept dye, so it can be colored if you don't like gray.

1 Flat lava rock is useful for service walkways. It comes in sizes ranging from less than 1 square foot to as large as 10 square feet. Its darker color makes it blend well with holey wall rock or other similar-colored rock. These rocks can be set on edge to form a steep canyon wall or the edge of a railroad cut.

2 Cold Water Canyon (CWC) is an interesting rock in that it is bi-colored. One side is reddish brown while the other is dark brown with some black. CWC can be used as stepping stones, but it can get slippery, since it's relatively smooth and is usually crowned. It is best used for dry washes or as part of a rock face when stacked horizontally. Since it is crowned and has some strata, it can be used on edge as a rock face.

3 Gnarly boulder is just one of many specialty rocks that can be found. This particular stone would make a mountain all by itself.

4 Holey wall rock is my favorite rock. It is very versatile and its irregular shape can be used to create interesting rock formations, either stand-alone or used together with others rocks to make up a larger formation.

5 Desert cloud is another specialty fieldstone. This material looks good sitting in the rock yard, but how will it look in your railway's landscape? Plan how you are going to use it. It can be stacked horizontally or placed vertically.

6 Water-washed flagstone looks good when stacked horizontally. This size is a little large to be used in a scale stream bed.

Irregular rocks

I prefer rocks with irregular shapes, ones that have natural crevices, small holes, and rough forms, such as "roping." Roping is twisted strata that look like a rope or eroded earth.

My favorite rock is a type called **holey wall rock.** It may also be called by other names, such as mossy wall rock. Holey wall rock contains many small holes and comes in all kinds of shapes, sizes, and textures. The particular variety that I use looks volcanic rock but is not as light as pumice. Because these rocks are not round, they will interlock with each other, making them structurally suitable for miniature mountain building.

Fieldstone comes in many types. Generally, it is not as rough as holey wall rock but can still be used to form mountains. Fieldstone is a good rock from which to make walls. It's heavy and somewhat uniform in shape. Napa fieldstone is more irregular in shape, making it a better choice for mountain building, while Sonoma is a little more uniform in shape, which makes it a better choice for walls.

Flat rocks

Flagstone is usually tan in color, although there are many other colors available. This flat rock can be as thin as ½″ and has an almost-smooth texture. Flagstone is normally used to make walkways and patios. In a garden railroad, it can be used to create mountains by flat-stacking it, which gives you horizontal strata.

Flat lava and Cold Water Canyon are local names for another class of flat rock

1 Napa fieldstone has some strata. It is smoother than holey wall rock and is my second choice for making mountains. Napa fieldstone is more irregular in shape than Sonoma, making it a better choice for mountain building.

2 Sonoma fieldstone, also know as Sonoma wall rock, is a typical, common fieldstone. It is basically round, with some strata, and is most useful as wall rock. The main advantage of Sonoma (and Napa) wall rock over others is its weight and uniform shape. These are a plus when it comes to building a wall but they are a disadvantage when used to make a mountain or other landscape feature.

3 Green basalt is a heavy rock that can be used for fill or as large rock formations in a miniature landscape.

4 New England wall rock is a flat, gray stone with rounded edges. Since it does not have a lot of strata it would probably look best stacked horizontally.

5 Peach, buckskin, buff, and oak flagstone are useful for stepping stones and in dry washes. They are relatively smooth and can also be stacked horizontally for a rock face.

1

2

3

4

5

that may be called by other names in your area. The stones have more texture than flagstone and so are not as suitable for walkway use. They can be used to make horizontal strata, as with flagstone, or they can be used to form mountainsides by setting them upright so that one edge is in the ground. The flat side then becomes the mountainside. This method makes for nice rock formations along the tracks, especially at tunnel openings or in simulated cuts.

Round rocks

Round rocks and smooth rocks, such as river rocks, are generally not suitable for miniature mountains. I call these goose eggs. They are usually off-white or gray in color, but can be found in other colors, too. In proportion to the garden-railway landscape, they are much too large to use for most landscape features. They can be used as fill, though.

Smaller sizes of round rock can be used in dry washes. You may have to bury one-half or more of each stone. Another thing you can do is to break these rocks up into smaller pieces to give you some rough edges to work with. I prefer not to use round rocks at all, since it takes a lot of effort to make them look natural.

Specialty rock

A variety of special rocks can be found in rock yards and in nature. This should be chosen carefully. Sometimes a rock looks interesting by itself, but it may not look so good integrated into the landscape.

Feather rock is a most interesting volcanic rock. In fact, it is actually glass. It is, as its name implies, very lightweight. Its other interesting feature is that it can be cut and split with relative ease and can also be carved.

Mexican Bowl rock is a volcanic stone that has many irregular edges and depressions. **Desert Rose** is a reddish-brown rock that is very rough and comes in long, skinny pieces that can be used for desert rock formations. These rocks can be used to enhance water features made using a bowl or watercourse.

Small rock and gravel

Jack Verducci

All photos by Jack Verducci

When planting a rock for use as an outcropping, its base should be buried so the rock looks like it is part of the landscape and not just lying on the ground. Here, groundcover helps these rocks look like they have been there for millions of years.

Small rock ranges in size from 1/4″ to 3/4″. These sizes are considered gravel or sand, but in our small world they can be used as small boulders, broken rocks, or, in dry washes and streambeds, as water-washed rock. Some can be used as decorative ballast. However, I would not recommend these materials for working ballast, since they do not interlock or pack down.

1

2

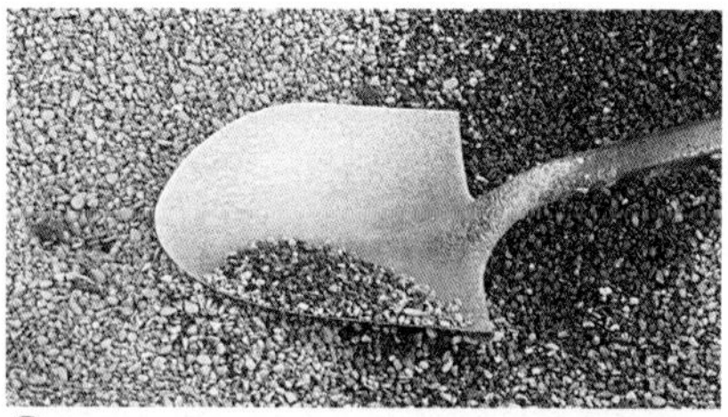

3

4

5

6

7

8

Pea gravel comes in 1/4″ to 3/8″ sizes. It can be used for walkways, riverbeds, and as chips that have fallen from larger rock. Pea gravel is also useful for drainage.

Aquarium sand, a clean, washed sand with a nice mixture of black, white, and gray tones. I use it as decorative ballast. It is perfect for river and pond bottoms.

Quartz, a light-colored rock, might make a good base for a water feature.

LaPaz rock, normally used for exposed aggregate in patios, has a lot of color.

Lin Creek. In its smaller size, this makes a good base for water features.

Red or brown lava rock (1/4″, 3/8″, 1/2″) is useful as a soil amendment. It helps keep the soil loose so water can penetrate. In some cases, you can use this smaller rock as mulch to cover bare soil.

Rock debris. Rock chips can be used to imitate broken rock that has fallen from a larger rock formation.

Crushed rock

This material is useful for many things, including subroadbeds, ballast, fill material, roadways, and bases under buildings.

Crushed granite is usually found in three sizes: 1/4″, 1/2″, and 3/4″. In some places you can buy no. 10 crushed granite, sometimes called chicken grit.

Drain rock is less expensive. Three-quarter inch is the best size for drainage.

Fines are similar to crushed rock except they have been reduced to pieces that are usually 1/4″ inch or smaller.

Blue and gray fines make excellent fill. They compact quickly and do not take as long to settle as common fill dirt does.

Gold fines or gold dust (decomposed granite) is a fines material with color.

1 La Paz mix is a colorful mix of gray tones that makes good dry-wash and stream-bed rock.

2 Half-inch Salmon Bay is a pebble that matches the color of gold fines.

3 Quarter-inch pea gravel is useful as either decorative ballast or drain rock. It is cheaper, smoother, and darker than crushed granite.

4 Quarter-inch Pami pebble can be used in a dry wash.

5 Quarter-inch quartz is a light-colored aggregate. It is often too bright for use in a garden railway.

6 Gold fines is a crushed-rock product sometimes called decomposed granite. The section below the shovel has been tamped. It can be made smooth for roadways or left rough.

7 Red lava is available in many sizes. It can be used as a soil amendment to help keep soil loose and allow water to penetrate.

8 Gray fines is best used for subroadbeds or working ballast. It packs hard, almost like cement. When packing, wet it down to help it set.

Working with rock

Jack Verducci

All photos by Jack Verducci

This rock face was made of holey wall rock, which was used because it looks like eroded soil or broken rock. The outcropping serves as both an erosion-control device and a decorative part of the landscape. Smaller stones at the base simulate broken rocks that have fallen over the years. Also note the moss and lichen on the rocks.

How do you lay out rocks so they will stay in place? In making mountains, rocks serve two purposes. One is visual. Rocks give the appearance of rugged outcroppings and stone faces. The second function is to hold the mountain up. So, when using rocks in making a mountain, you must keep two things in mind: one, make sure the good face of the rock is showing and, two, install the rock in such a way that it supports the structure.

Bad

Good

Better

Setting rock into the ground

A more natural look can be realized by burying the bottom of the rock, making it look like it has been in place for centuries. Adding smaller or crushed rocks around the base helps to achieve this look.

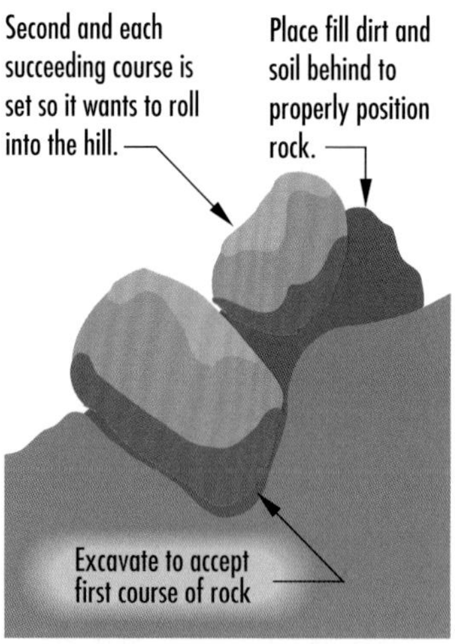

Mountain building with rocks

The first course set in the ground becomes the foundation. The second is laid so that it wants to roll back into the hill. Gravity will hold it in place. Miniature trees should be planted as the mountain is being built, which will help hold it together.

In choosing the side to show, use your own judgment. I look for interesting features like crevices and other texture. If the rocks have moss, you'll probably want that showing. However, do not let moss be the only determining factor. You can always get moss to grow if you choose the non-mossy side (see the sidebar on moss).

Using rock for support takes a little thought. You need to interlock the rocks to form a structure that will be held together by gravity. The sequence I use is called "dirt-rock-trees." You stack up dirt, place a rock, and plant a tree.

Here's how it works. If you simply piled up dirt to make a mountain, you'd need a large area at the base to support a tall mountain. By using rocks, you can make a taller mountain in less space because the rock will support the dirt and prevent it from spreading. In placing the rocks, I set them in place in such a way that the rock wants to roll back into the mountain, sort of pivoting on its bottom side. Balance the rock with one hand to keep it from rolling into the mountain, then back fill behind and under it with soil. This tendency of the rock to roll back into the mountain insures that gravity will hold it in place permanently. If this is not done, the rock may pop out later due the weight of the soil behind it or the flow of draining water.

I plant the trees at this time because I like to stack the rocks close. Planting later would be more difficult because the rocks will be too close to each other. I have always been impressed by trees in the mountains that grow right out of rock. By stacking rocks closely together and planting the tree in between, this can be replicated.

As you build up the rocks from side to side, interlock the ends of the individual stones. This helps hold them in place. As you go, step the next rock back a little so it wants to fall back into the mountain. When done this way, it should be difficult to pull a rock out of place with your bare hands. Even though we are building a mountain, we are using wall-building techniques. What makes the structure look like a mountain is the use of trees. When constructing a mountain, leave some space for soil to plant groundcover.

Color is another important consideration. I rank it second only because you can change a rock's color if desired. Natural rock can be found in just about any color you can imagine. However, you should be careful here. Sometimes something that looks striking in real life may look out of place in a miniature setting. For this reason, I tend to use rock with less vivid colors. I try for an overall "look." For example, I want viewers to see a mountainside, not a group of individual rocks. Therefore, I use rocks of similar color to form a larger formation that looks like it might be one piece.

Color also sets mood or feeling. More subdued colors look cooler and may give the feeling of a rain forest or coastal, wooded mountains. One the other hand, brighter colors, such as red, may lend a desert feel to the landscape or, when used with trees, you may get the feeling of being in the San Juan Mountains.

Color carries over to ballast. Gray ballast looks cooler, gold or red ballast looks warmer. All of these colors and more are to be found in the full-size world.

In nature you may find an odd-colored rock in the midst of a larger formation. You must determine if a similar rock in miniature will enhance your mountain's appearance or distract from it. Multicolor rocks work well for southwest-desert-looking landscapes. Here, color is what distinguishes the landscaping. In this case, brighter colors are appropriate.

A word of caution: sometimes multicolored rocks look great sitting at the rock yard, but when you get home and try to work them into your landscape, you may find that they just don't look right. Try picking up several samples first to see how they look in your setting.

Coloring rocks

It is always best to find rocks that are naturally the color you want. However,

Dry washes, canyons, and draws

One of the concepts in miniature landscaping is to create the illusion of space. The following techniques will help reinforce this effect.

When laying out a dry wash, box canyon, or draw, taper it so that it is smaller at the end farthest from the viewer. Another technique is to curve the feature so that its origin is hidden. This will make it look like it goes on beyond the bend. On the floor of the canyon or wash, use larger rocks in front and smaller ones in back. This adds to the illusion of distance.

San Pedro pebbles were used for the dry wash. The canyon walls are made of a combination of holey wall rock, Cold Water Canyon, and Napa fieldstone. Rocks in a waterway or dry washes are often much lighter in color than the surrounding rocks. Note the use of forced perspective. The dry wash tapers and turns, making it appear longer and larger than it really is.

this is not always possible. Sometimes you will find a rock with just the right texture and strata, but the wrong color.

There are several ways to color rock. One is with cans of spray paint. To make the rock look right, just dust on the paint. Shoot from a distance and use several colors. For example, along with brown, you might dust on a little black or some beige. Real rocks are not one, pure color—they are a subtle blend of colors. The secret is to spray lightly and mix the colors.

A natural-looking color can be achieve with dry, powdered concrete dye. Paint the rock with a clear coat of lacquer or acrylic sealer. This will give the dye something to stick to. Next, sprinkle on the dry powder (while the sealer is till wet) or mix it with water and spray it on when the rock is dry.

When the water evaporates, you will have a dry, powdery finish that looks natural. This finish can be sealed with a clear coating, if you like.

A variety of mosses and lichens can be found on rocks. This adds much to their overall appearance.

Moss for your rocks

Years ago I heard that if you put buttermilk on a rock, moss would grow. I could never get this to work. I kept painting my rocks with buttermilk, but the only result was stinky rocks.

Then I read in a garden catalog that you have to harvest moss, put it in a blender with buttermilk, then paint it on the rocks. This does work. However, I found another way.

I harvest some moss by carefully scraping it off rocks in the wild, then I use buttermilk to "glue" the harvested moss to rocks on my railway. After that, I make sure it stays wet. Now the rock has moss on it. Note, though, that this technique will not grow moss in areas when moss is not normally found. Moss will only grow in the right conditions of shade and water, and is often dormant in dry seasons.

Flat rocks
and dirt

Jack Verducci

Jack Verducci

To form this natural-looking cutting, flat rocks were set on edge. Stone cuttings like this are often found at the mouths of tunnels. Once the groundcover has taken hold, the stones look like they've been there for eons.

In some cases, you may want to take flat rock and set it up on edge so its flat side becomes a rock face. This works well with rocks like cold water canyon and flat lava rock, mainly because they have some strata. Rocks such as flagstone are smooth and may not be the best choice for this application.

A typical use of rock in this manner would be where you have cut into the natural hillside, leaving bare dirt. If left to nature, the dirt will eventually erode onto the track. You can anchor a flat rock to help stabilize the cut.

Flat rock can also be used to line pond edges. The edge of the pond liner can be held in place with flat rocks. Use mortar to blend flat rock into the pond's sides, creating a cliff-like appearance.

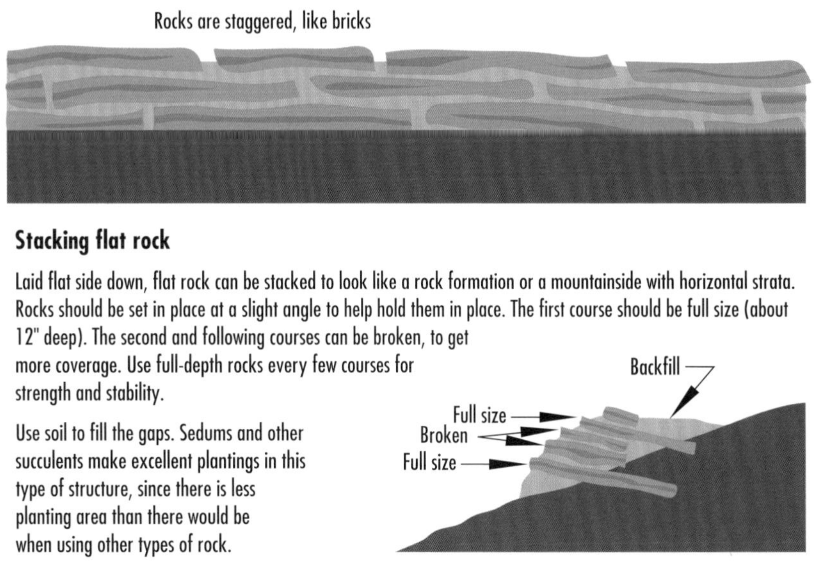

Stacking flat rock

Laid flat side down, flat rock can be stacked to look like a rock formation or a mountainside with horizontal strata. Rocks should be set in place at a slight angle to help hold them in place. The first course should be full size (about 12" deep). The second and following courses can be broken, to get more coverage. Use full-depth rocks every few courses for strength and stability.

Use soil to fill the gaps. Sedums and other succulents make excellent plantings in this type of structure, since there is less planting area than there would be when using other types of rock.

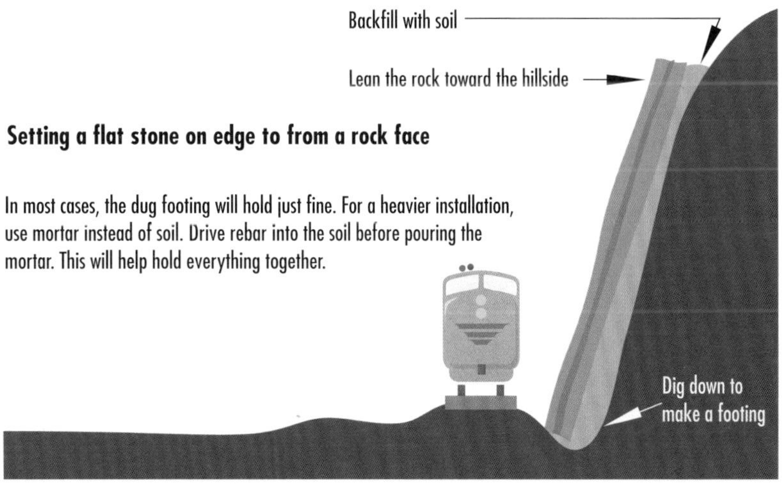

Setting a flat stone on edge to from a rock face

In most cases, the dug footing will hold just fine. For a heavier installation, use mortar instead of soil. Drive rebar into the soil before pouring the mortar. This will help hold everything together.

Planting or placing rocks on the ground

If you are placing rocks on the ground to represent mountains, or if you are setting stones up to look like a rock outcropping in a meadow, here are some hints. Don't just set a rock on the ground. To make it look like part of the landscape and give it age, bury part of it in the ground. Another trick to make a rock look natural is to add smaller pieces of stone around its base.

In some cases, you can use this smaller rock as mulch to cover bare soil, either temporarily until groundcover is planted or permanently in the place of living groundcover. If you decide to plant groundcover later on, just mix soil in with the crushed rock.

Dirt

You might think that dirt is dirt, but there are actually several kinds to consider when building a landscape.

Clean fill is dirt (or other material) that can be used as fill. This is the cheapest dirt. It should be free of organic waste, such as roots, leaves, pine needles, and scrap wood. Materials that can be used as clean fill include fill sand, excavated dirt from swimming pools or building foundations, and broken concrete, such as from an old driveway.

Top soil or sandy loam (sometimes called heavy soil) is a high-quality fill soil to be used over clean fill and as a sub-layer for nursery mix or planting soil.

Nursery mix or planting soil is topsoil that has had amendments added, such as compost, chicken manure, horticultural-grade lava, sand, and other things. Ideally you should have at least 12" of planting mix for miniature trees; less is required for low growing groundcovers. This should be over a sub-layer of topsoil.

To quickly review, your landscape should start with clean fill at the bottom. Form the basic features with this material. Next, cover the clean fill with a layer of topsoil and finish with planting mix and rocks. The rocks are your erosion control. Inbetween the rock, plant your trees as you set in your rocks. To finish, fill the voids with small crushed rock, such as 3/8" lava or crushed granite (choose a color that closely matches the large rocks) or plant groundcover.

Screening and road building

If you are using fines to make a road, a trick you can use is to screen down the material. This can be done using a piece of hardware cloth with about 1/4" spaces. Place the screen over a bucket, scoop the fines onto it, and sift them through the screen. You will get a smooth, uniform material that can be dry-troweled (I use a wooden float) right onto the ground or over a base coat to create a believable roadway.

These fines can be held in place by spraying on a mixture of concrete adhesive and water (25 percent adhesive, 75 percent water, and a few drops of dish soap). This will penetrate and lock the material in place. This works best if the sifted fines are installed over a firm base and the sifted fines are not too thick.

Roadbed construction

Jack Verducci

Jack Verducci

There is an old saying: If you want to keep friends, don't argue politics or religion. Or, to rephrase it for our hobby: If you want to keep friends, don't discuss roadbed or ballast. I have been in garden railroading for over 10 years and I have read a lot of articles on roadbed and ballast. I am also sure this will not be the last article that you will see on the subject, for it seems to be a rich and deep topic for discussion. In any case, here is my two-cents worth.

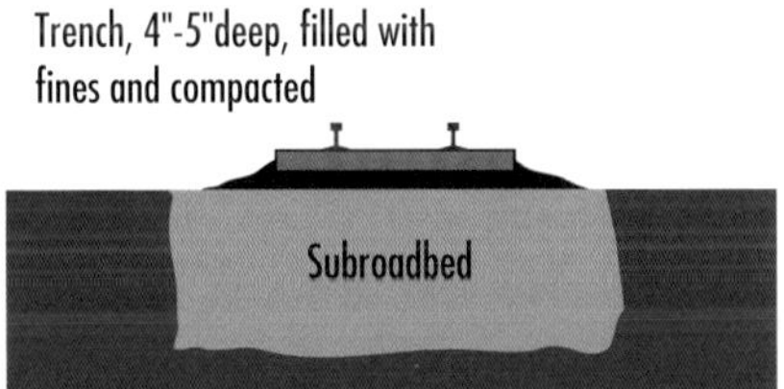

Figure 1
Ground-level roadbed

‹ Finish ballast is being applied over the working ballast on this bridge abutment. Rock retaining walls create a place for the roadbed.

If you want a railroad that will survive earthquakes, floods, and the next Ice Age, then you might want to build your roadbed out of steel encased in concrete, with pilings every 5 feet, sunk well below the frost line and tested by the Army Corps of Engineers. This seems to be the mindset of some. Too many people want to do it the hard way! A good rule to follow when building a garden railroad is to use prototype practice wherever possible. The same applies here. If your roadbed is done right, you do not need to use concrete or concrete block.

The most important thing about roadbed construction is to create a substructure to retain the ballast and support the track. If you are building the railroad right on the ground, the earth can serve as this structure.

For ground-level roadbed, dig a trench about 4″ or 5″ below grade level and about three times wider than the track. This will form a place to hold the subroadbed ballast. If you are creating mountains, you could use boulders to form a plateau, or bed, upon which the roadbed can be built. Use the boulders to form a retaining wall that looks like a natural cliff.

Ballast

I put ballast into two categories: working ballast and decorative, or finish, ballast. Working ballast does the real work of supporting the track, trains, and humans. It goes in first and is often covered later by decorative ballast. Decorative, or finish, ballast can be anything you like (more on this later).

I am very selective as to what I use for working ballast. My material of choice is "gray fines" or the equivalent. This is made up of 1/4″ and smaller crushed rock. It is sometimes called "quarter minus," "fines," "crusher fines," or "quarry waste." In any case, there is a lot of dust and fine material in it. This product, when packed and wetted, sets up almost like concrete, but remains porous and can be easily broken back down to its original state with a pick or other excavating tool. It can be piled up and will hold a 45° angle.

The thing that makes ballast work is its mass. Ballast holds the track in place by interlocking around and under the ties. The heavier and denser the ballast, the better it will hold.

The list of what not to use for subroadbed is much longer. Don't use crushed granite, pea gravel, lava rock, aquarium sand, chicken grit, sand, or kitty litter. These do not have the interlocking properties or the mass and density that fines have. However, if you like the look of these materials, they can be used as decorative ballast on the surface.

Decorative ballast is used to finish off the roadbed. This is the layer you will see. Decorative ballast is applied over the top of the working ballast and is for looks only. Since it is just a surface coating, you will not need much of it.

Decorative ballast

One problem with fines is they are dull and plain to look at. You can use decorative ballast to add color to the line. The color you choose will help set a tone or mood.

For example, aquarium sand that has a mixture of colors, such as black, gray, white, and some brown, will offer a cool appearance, while fines that are yellow/gold will give a warm feel, like the desert. In a different setting, gold fines could look like earthen ballast. Red lava rock gives a warm look. Chicken grit is uniformly gray in color but has a very nice texture. Kitty litter also has a nice texture.

In real life, a variety of materials are used for ballast. There is also a wide variety of colors used. Some railroads spread cinders out over ballast, giving it a black color, while other lines use snow-white rock. The important thing is to use a material that is the right size. Too large, and the ballast will not do its job, for it will have too many gaps or voids between the rocks. Too small, and the material will wash away. A good size for finish ballast is no. 10, which is a small rock about the size of a BB.

Working with ballast

The bulk of the working ballast should be installed before laying track. Application can be done with a shovel. A tamper is used to pack the material down.

Using the grade-stake system, fill the roadbed nearly to the top of the grade stakes with working ballast. Next, tamp the material down. Always tamp the material when it is dry. If you wet it before tamping, it will stick to the tamper. After the dry material is tamped, you can wet it to help pack it even more.

Next, lay the track. You will see that there will be high and low spots in the ballast. You can use the track as a guide for how much more or less ballast to use. The track should be lying on top of the grade stakes. (If you live in a climate where frost heave is a problem, remove the grade stakes before laying the track.) Next, using a material scoop and a whisk broom or fox-tail brush, start pouring ballast over the track and working it in with the brush. The grade stake will help you keep the track at the proper elevation. Use a torpedo level to level the track from side to side. At this point we are still using fines.

Next water the ballast. This should be done over a few days, "wetting in" the roadbed a little more each day. You will notice the ballast material will settle a little, creating small voids that should be filled.

Now you can use your choice of decorative ballast to finish the job. Be aware the ballast will settle over time. This is natural. As it settles, you can continue to add your choice of decorative ballast until that is all you see. If there are areas that have settled excessively, add more sub roadbed materials. A roadbed is like a fine wine. It needs to be aged, and it gets better with time.

The main advantage of this system is that the roadbed is flexible and is easily rebuilt. It can move with the ground. If the ground heaves, the roadbed will go

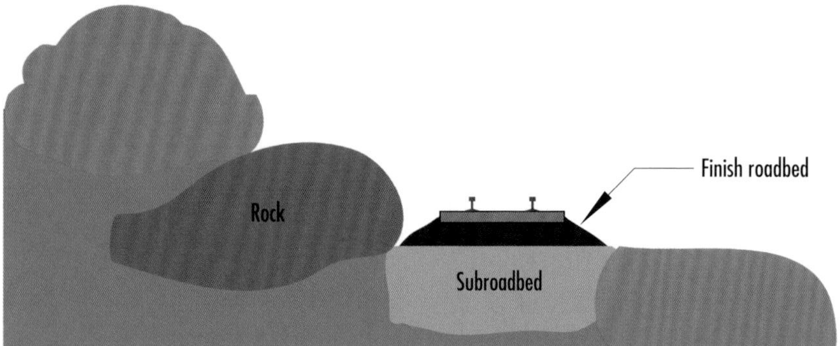

Figure 2
Natural-looking boulders can be used as a retaining wall, forming a plateau or ridge on which to lay track.

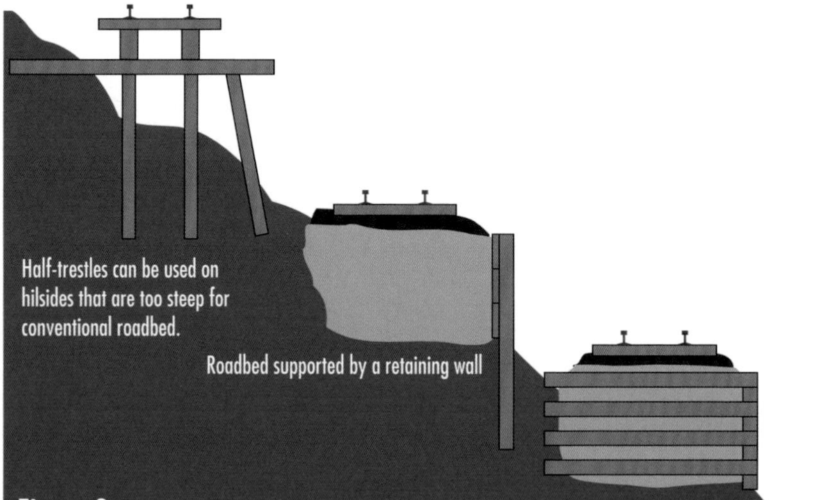

Figure 3

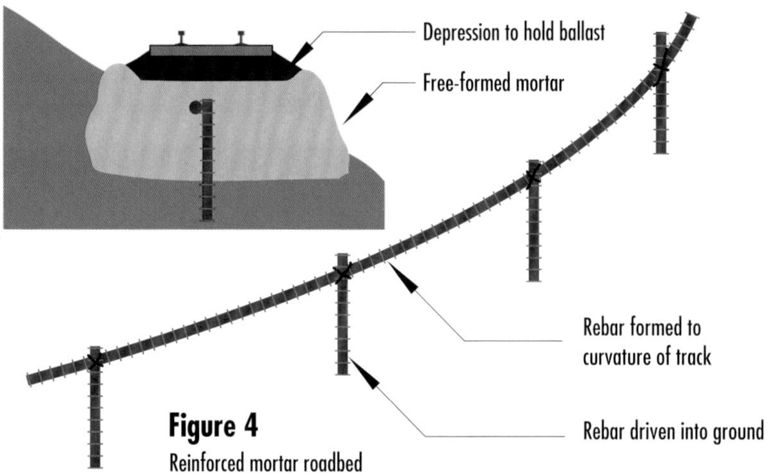

Figure 4
Reinforced mortar roadbed

with the flow. If the ground sinks, simply add more ballast. This is what prototype railroads do. The secret is using the right working ballast.

Weed block, such as landscape fabric, is a waste of time. Weeds will grow in your ballast with or without weed block. A problem with weed block is that it acts as a barrier between the ballast and the earth, which prevents the ballast from locking to the earth. This is the same problem with cement subroadbeds, and roadbeds such as pavers (special sidewalk bricks). The ballast does not lock to the surface of the cement and is allowed to slide around too much. Ballast is meant to hold the track in position from right to left as well as in the horizontal plane.

There are some cases where a concrete roadbed may be needed. In these instances, I like a free-form method using mortar and rebar (a metal bar used for reinforcing concrete). Drive the rebar into the ground in the same way you would install a grade stake. Next, form a piece of rebar to the track curvature. Wire the rebar together, forming a rebar spine under the track. Next, mix a batch of mortar and spread it over the rebar to form a roadbed. When the mortar has cured, the rebar will lock the roadbed together.

While the mortar is still workable, spread finish ballast over it and work it in to create an exposed-aggregate look. If you need to add additional finish ballast to the roadbed later, it can be applied using concrete adhesive. Do not anchor the track to the roadbed! In almost all cases, track should not be fastened in any way to the roadbed. The ballast will hold the track in position. This is how you allow for expansion and contraction. The track actually slides around a little in the ballast.

Finishing touches

Looking at prototype railroad roadbed, you will notice that it is really a very narrow band crossing the landscape. When building your roadbed, employ the working ballast liberally, using as much as you need to support the roadbed. But when you are done, dress the edges with soil or plant materials to create that narrow band, just like the full-size railroad.

Strong wooden cribbing is used to retain the earth, providing an abutment for the trestle.

Cribbing

When constructed like the prototype, cribbing is the best man-made method of retaining a hillside. A series of boxes is created by laying the timbers out in squares, then nailing them together. The drawing shows the basic system. Cribbing can be used between boulders, for bridge abutments, and for a variety of other duties.

When filled with ballast, you will only see the ends of one set of timbers and the sides of the other set. The buried parts become "deadmen," which do the work of holding the wall in place. You can drive the deadmen into the hillside if you are working with dirt.

The basic system is the same, whether you are going up one or two inches or several feet. To expand it, you just keep adding layers of timbers. If you have a brad gun, it's easier to build your cribbing on the site.

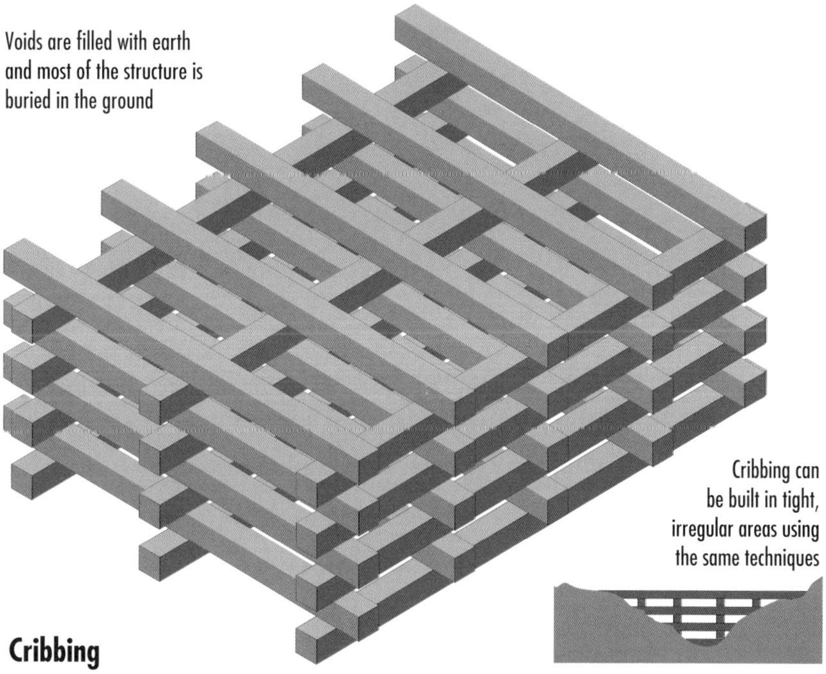

Cribbing

SECTION 5

The track game

Sorting it all out—a buyer's guide

Richard Schafer and Marc Horovitz

All photos Mark Horovitz

Twenty-plus years ago, when we happened into this marvelous world of large-scale trains, a buyer's guide to gauge 1 track of the day would have been quite a brief document. The major players at that time were LGB of Germany and Kalamazoo Toy Trains from Michigan. Both offered a line of heavy, solid brass, sectional track in support of their respective G-scale trains. GarGraves was around then as well. Their smaller gauge 1 rails on wooden ties proved to be popular on some of our modular, indoor railroads. It wasn't long, though, before flex track in brass and aluminum were on the market. Now, we've got at least a dozen options at hand when it comes time to build a gauge 1 railroad.

Aristo-Craft Trains offers an extensive line of solid brass or stainless-steel, code-332 rail mounted on wood-textured plastic tie strips in both European and American styles. Sectional track, flex track, and switches are available.

Bachmann Industries has a limited selection of tubular, tinplate track, primarily suited to indoor use. One-foot straights, rigid curves, and manual switches are listed as well.

GarGraves Trackage Corporation has a half-century or more in the track business, and continues to serve gauge 1 with tubular track in either tinplate or stainless-steel, code-215 rail. Tie strips are rigid or flexible, are untextured, and appear to be narrower and shorter than prototype practice.

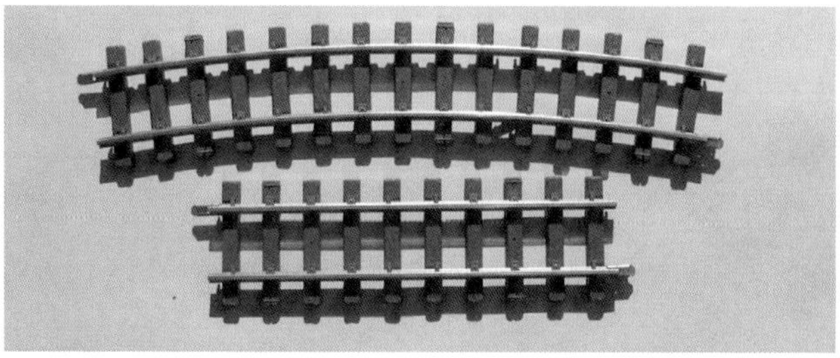

H&R Trains imports the A-2 Line of stainless-steel, code-332 track from France. Tie strips are light brown and wood-textured, with a derelict look about them. Concrete-style ties are also available. Sections have snap-together joiner assembly.

A look at the technicalities

All too often, we seem to mix up some of the basic language of the hobby. Two terms that are especially troublesome are "scale" and "gauge." Scale is a comparison of the model to the full-sized object in terms of proportions. It is expressed as a ratio, such as 1:32. This tells us that the model is one thirty-second of the size of the original (or prototype). We then know that parts, rolling stock, buildings, and all other parts of our railway operation need to maintain that same proportion to be "in scale," or to share a credible relationship size-wise.

Gauge, on the other hand, is not necessarily tied to scale. Gauge is simply the distance between the rails that guide our trains' wheels as measured from the inside edges of the rails. Gauge 1 is a historic model-railroading standard that uses rails separated by a distance of 45mm. When it first came about, it was the smallest of three standardized gauges developed by Märklin in the late 1800s.

A rich variety of scales can be used on the same gauge rails. On gauge 1 track, for instance, we could operate a 1:32-scale train (often referred to as "standard gauge" or "mainline," with the gauge representing rails that are 4'8½" apart) or a 1:20.3-scale consist (with gauge 1 now reflecting a 3-foot, narrow-gauge operation). All the track discussed in this feature is gauge 1 (45mm).

Just to confuse the issue, you'll note in this document that some track is described as being 1:32-scale or standard gauge. This is because a manufacturer has opted to represent the smaller ties, tie spacing, and rail proportioned to a scale (1:32) that is popular in many aspects of gauge 1 railroading, especially in live steam. Conversely, track described by manufacturers as being "narrow gauge" has fewer, larger ties, often represented in a well-worn state, intended to complement larger scale, narrow-gauge locomotives and rolling stock.

Another point of confusion centers around the often-used misnomer, "G gauge." G is a scale (1:22.5), not a gauge.

The term "code" is used to designate the height of our model rails. See the sidebar for a more complete discussion of code.

Each manufacturer makes a decision on the sizes and spacing of ties, based on their individual criteria. Most often, the hobbyist can consult the company's Web site or printed material to determine the rationale for these decisions. Sunset Valley Railroad, for instance, offers three different tie strips to be used with their code-250 brass, nickel-silver, or aluminum rail to produce "branchline," "mainline," or "dual gauge" (both gauge 0 and gauge 1) track. The branchline and dual-gauge ties are over a quarter of an inch longer than the mainline version and are spaced at 10 ties per foot versus the

‹ There is a huge selection of lengths and radii of sectional track, flex-track types, and rail materials out there today. This chapter will attempt to make some sense of it all.

J&W Model Trains offers the P.H.S. Rail line of track (from Canada), which includes codes 250 and 332 aluminum rail in weathered brown, natural aluminum, or anodized-black finishes. Rail comes in 6'1" lengths.

LGB of America offers a complete line of German-made, solid brass, code-332 track. There are some 30 track items in their catalog, ranging from very short makeup pieces to a 1.5-meter length of flex track. Look for a new large-radius curve coming soon to your LGB dealer.

Llagas Creek Railways has assembled flex track in 6' sections, offered in 12 combinations. Their rail is code 215 or 250, in aluminum or nickel silver. Turnouts and components are available, as well as semaphores and switchstands.

Märklin has German-built, code-197, solid stainless-steel rails mounted to dark brown, 1:32-scale tie strips. Straights, curves, and switches are available, suitable for use inside or out. Märklin offers a unique rail-joiner system.

mainline variety's 16 per foot. In scale, these specifications closely reflect prototype U.S. practice.

In this guide, there are references to "European" and "American" (or "U.S.") styles. Most of these notes are in regard to the plastic tie strips and their molded-in details. European practice is reflected when the attachment of the tie to the rail is represented as a clamp with bolt-head detail. American practice is suggested with tie-plate and spike details. The latter approach, with the smaller spike heads, can result in tie strips that lack a strong grip on the rail and may require more careful assembly and use.

Sectional or flex track?

Sectional track is often thought to be the norm for model railroads. It has a number of advantages, not the least of which is the fact that it is typically factory-assembled and permits the building of a railroad in just a few minutes. Most of the components are relatively small and can be assembled and taken apart by children. Since it's easily stored and transported, it works well for portable or temporary railways. The modular nature of sectional track encourages exploration of different trackplans and makes expansion easy.

For the modeler who has ambitions or plans beyond the limited radii of rigid curves and cataloged straight sections, this approach might prove to be a limiting factor. Trackplans based exclusively on sectional components often appear to be imposed onto the landscape rather than being integrated into the garden. Many manufacturers offer both sectional and flex track, which can be easily combined in a railway's design.

With flex track, there are fewer connections between the longer continuous sections, resulting in easier installation and simpler maintenance of electrical circuits. The builder decides where the track should go, rather than being limited to preset sectional patterns. Trackplans are only limited by one's imagination. Although a number of manufacturers are introducing large-radius curved sections, flex track can simplify construction of more prototypical curves.

There are some drawbacks to using flex track. In the smaller scales, flex track comes premade and one merely has to bend it into shape by hand as it is being installed on the framework on an indoor

Micro Engineering has an established line of code-332 and -250 aluminum rail and code-250, nickel-silver rail. Sectional track, flex track, and switches are offered. A large number of optional accessories are available.

Peco Railway Products has an excellent reputation in the smaller scales and gauges. For gauge 1, the company offers codes 215 and 250 nickel-silver rail on 1:32-scale (standard gauge) and G-scale (narrow gauge) wood-textured ties. Sectional track and some flex components are available; made in England.

Sunset Valley Railroad offers a choice of code-250, weathered-brass, weathered nickel-silver, or aluminum rail in 6' lengths, as well as branchline, mainline, and dual-gauge configurations for their tie strips. Wyes and turnouts are available in brass or nickel silver.

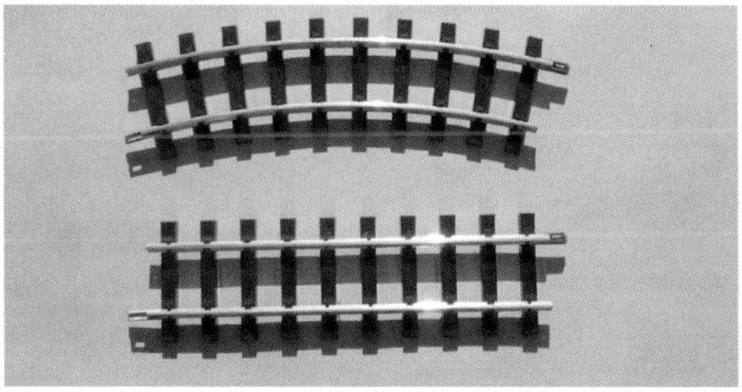

USA Trains has a limited offering of solid-brass, code-332, sectional straight and curved track. Illuminated switches are available. Track sections and rail joiners are nearly indistinguishable from Aristo-Craft's, except for wood-grain pattern on ties.

layout. With most gauge 1 track (GarGraves being the notable exception), you can't do this. The rails are considerably heavier and have a certain amount of spring and hardness to them. Rails must be prebent before the tie strips are slid on, which requires the purchase of a rail-bending tool. Flex track is sometimes sold preassembled, but many makers sell it as loose rail and a bundle of plastic tie strips, which the user must slide onto the rails after the rails have been appropriately bent.

Types of rail

Tubular-rail track is offered by two of our manufacturers, Bachmann and GarGraves. Tubular rail is hollow, made from strips of thin metal bent into the shape of a rail. Bachmann's track products are of tinplate construction and intended primarily for indoor use.

GarGraves offers both tinplate (tin-plated steel) and stainless-steel, folded-sheet-metal track. GarGraves recommends that its stainless-steel track be used outdoors. Brass pins are inserted into the rail ends to connect the track sections.

Solid rail that is extruded into a traditional T-shaped cross section is commonly used where a more realistic appearance and wear-and-tear are factors—such as in the majority of garden railways. A number of different approaches are taken by manufacturers in attaching rail ends to one another when the railroad is installed.

LGB uses a copper-and-zinc blend (different from the one used in their rail) to make a slide-on joiner designed to make a strong connection without screws or other fasteners. Aristo-Craft and USA Trains use small screws to secure joiners to rail sections. Märklin uses a slip-on metal joiner that is backed up by an interlocking, plastic-tab assembly molded into the tie strip.

Clamps can also be used to join rail ends. Sunset Valley Railroad offers a choice of clamps or slide-on joiners with their flex-track packages. Llagas Creek Railways offers slide-on joiners, and also has a product called Rail-blenders that can be used to make a transition from one code of rail to another. J&W Model Trains suggests that a third-party rail clamp be used with their P.H.S. Rail.

Gauge 1 track

Manufacturer/Importer	Description	Sectional straights	Sectional curves	Flex track	Switches	Comments
Aristo-Craft Trains 698 S. 21st Street Irvington NJ 07111 973-351-9800 www.aristocraft.com e-mail: aristo@mindspring.com	Solid brass, code 332 with plastic ties; European and American tie styles available; stainless steel, US style also offered; wood-textured ties; molded-in tie-plate detail	6", 1', 2', 3' & 5' lengths available in brass or stainless steel	Sectional curves available in 4', 5', 8', 10', and 20' diameters	Flex rail in brass, stainless steel; bender offered	Manual or remote, small radius and wide radius offered in brass or stainless steel	Screw-together rail joiners standard; ties treated for UV stability; 30° crossing, rerailer, reversing unit offered
Bachmann Industries, Inc. 1400 E. Erie Avenue Philadelphia PA 19124 215-533-1600 www.bachmanntrains.com	Tubular rail, shiny, tinplate finish; black plastic, wood-textured ties with some tie-plate detail;	1" length in package of 4	4' diameter in package of 4	No flex track	Manual left and right switches available	90° crossing available; primarily intended for indoor use
GarGraves Trackage Corp. 8967 Ridge Road North Rose NY 14516 315-483-6577 www.GarGraves.com	Tubular rail, shiny steel finish; smooth finish on ties; no tie-plate details; code 215 rails; pins used to align/join rails	37' straight track sections; available in rigid or flexible format	6 different radii, ranging from 72" to 138" in diameter	Straight track is available in a flexible variety	36"-radius switch to be introduced in near future	Stainless steel and tinplate versions available; s.s. is recommended for outdoor use
H&R Trains/A-2 Line 6901 US 19 North Pinellas Park FL 34665 727-526-4682 www.hrtrains.com e-mail: don@hrtrains.com	Code 332, solid stainless-steel rails; medium-brown plastic ties with "old wood" texture & detailing; bolt-head detail on tie plates; concrete-style ties also available; snap-together joiners	12" and 24" straight sections plus shorter make-up pieces available; also specialty track	10 different radii, with range from 24" to 100"	Flex track is available in lengths from 48" to 120"	48"- and 76"-radius switches are available	A-2 Line of track imported from France; line of accessories, 90° crossing, and other specialties also specialties also available
J&W Model Trains/P.H.S. Rail 6450 E. Becht Road Coloma MI 49038 800-443-0440 www.jwmodeltrains.com e-mail: jwtrains@cybersol.com	Code 250 and 332 aluminum rail, plastic tie strips; weathered, brown, natural aluminum and anodized-black finishes available	No sectional track	No sectional track	Flex track available in 6'1" lengths	No switches currently offered	Textured, brown-plastic ties with tie-plate and spike details; no rail joiners; rail clamps recommended
LGB of America 6444 Nancy Ridge Road San Diego CA 92121 858-535-9387 www.lgb.com	Solid brass, code 332 with textured, brown-plastic ties; European style, bolted tie plates molded in	Straight sections in 300mm (about 1"), 600mm, & 1200 mm lengths, plus 6 short make-up sections	Choice of 3 curved-track diameters; 50.8", 64.8" and 97.9"	Flex track, 1.5 meters in length, and tie sections available	Manual and electric switches in small & large radii, 3-way, & double slip; 30° crossing	UV resistant ties; rail joiners engineered for high conductivity without screws; larger radius curve (91.3") coming soon

Which track should I select?

There is no easy answer, simply because of the divergent interests of gauge 1 hobbyists and the fact that there are many excellent products available. However, here are some questions to ask yourself before making a final selection.

• What scale are you working in? If fidelity to the prototype is important, consider the scale sizes of the various rails available.

• How durable does the track have to be in your setting? Will it be permanently laid on a solid, strong sub-base or will it be loosely put down over uneven ground?

• What will be the minimum radius you'll be working with? (The bigger the better.) If you are constrained to small radii, sectional track may be a better choice than flex. If you have broad

Manufacturer/Importer	Description	Sectional straights	Sectional curves	Flex track	Switches	Comments
Llagas Creek Railways/ California & Oregon Coast Rwy. PO Box 57 Rogue River, OR 97537 800-866-8635 www.llagastrack.com e-mail: dmanley@cdsnet.net	Choice of code-215 or code-250 rail in either 6061-T6 aluminum or nickel silver; highly detailed tie strips in 3 scales (1:32, 1:22.5 & 1:20.3); US style	No sectional track	No sectional track	Assembled flex trak in 6' sections is offered in 12 different combinations	Variety of built-up turnouts available, as well as components	UV resistant ties; Tenmille ground throws & Del-Aire system supported; Lindsay railbender offered; semaphore & switchstand kits
Märklin, Inc. PO Box 510559 New Berlin, WI 53151 800-321-8811 www.marklin.com	Stainless-steel rails, code 197, mounted on dark brown, plastic tie strips with European-style tie plates; 1:32 scale	Sections of 1' and 3' are available, plus 3 shorter lengths	4 curve radii are offered, ranging from 24" to 46"	A "track kit" (3' long) allows construction of custom curves	Manual switches offered in small and larger radii; turnout mechanism is available separately	Designed for use with gauge-1 Maxi & Märklin trains; trackwork is weather resistant and useable outside or inside
Micro Engineering, Inc. 1120 Eagle Road Fenton MO 63026 636-349-1112	Codes 332 and 250 aluminum rail or code-250 nickel silver; US-style spike and tie plates on dark brown, textured-plastic tie strips	Sections range from 4" to 36" with 3 choices in each size	2', 4', 6', 8' & 10' radius curved sections are available	Flex rail components are offered in codes 250 & 332, both weathered or unweathered	Code 250 nickel-silver turnout kits are available; 10' radius	Useful accessories include 2 types of rail joiners, steel spikes, and white-metal tie plates
Peco Railway Products Pritchard Patent Product Co., Ltd. Beer Seaton Devon EX12 3NA England	Codes 215 and 250, nickel-silver rail on 1:32 scale and G scale, wood textured, brown-plastic ties	1' sections	2' radius	3' flex-track sections and component parts available	Pair of turnouts offered in 2' radius	Extensive program of track in virtually all scales; large number of optional accessories
Sunset Valley Railroad 13428 209th SE Issoquah WA 98027 425-255-2453 www.largescale.com/svrr e-mail: svrrted@sprynet.com	Choice of code 250, weathered brass, weathered nickel silver, or aluminum rail; 3 tie configurations in brown plastic (branch line, mainline, or dual gauge); US-style spikes & tie plates	No sectional track	No sectional track	Flex track in 6' lengths	12 varieties of turnouts & wyes in brass or nickel silver	2 crossings, switch-stands, spikes, tie plates, joiners, ground throws, rail clamps, and other accessories are available
USA Trains PO Box 100 Malden MA 02148 781-322-6084 www.usatrains.com	Solid brass, code 332, with black, plastic ties, wood texture, & European-style ties with bolt-head detail	Straight sections are available in 6", 12", 24" & 60" lengths	Curves are configured in 4', 5', 8' & 10' diameters	No flex track	4' diameter switches in manual & remote versions; lighted switch lantern	Screw-together rail joiners are identical to Aristo-Craft; rail also appears to be the same

expanses of real estate on which to build your empire, flex track will be better.

• Are you modeling standard or narrow gauge? This will influence your selection of tie strips and (possible) rail size.

• Are you willing and able to deal with bending and trimming your own rail to your desired curvatures and sliding on the tie strips, or does the simplicity and ease of sectional track make more sense to you?

• Will you be running your trains via track power, battery power, or live steam? This could affect your choice of rail material and rail joiners.

Talk with your local hobby shop or make connections through garden-railway societies in your area. There's a plethora of chat groups on the Internet, where you will find correspondents who are willing to share their experiences. Conventions and hobby shows also provide resources for those in need of information.

Rail materials

Rail types
There are three (sort of) rail types in use today. The most common is solid, extruded rail (left) in a variety of materials. Bachmann (center) uses its own system of "tubular" rail. It is actually a U-shaped, folded, sheet-metal rail that fits over a plastic inner rail underneath. GarGraves' system (right) is unique. It is a folded, sheet-metal rail with a "tang" built into the foot, which retains the rail in wedge-shaped slots in the ties.

Rail for garden railroads is currently available in aluminum, brass, nickel-silver, and stainless steel. Steel has been available in the past and you can sometimes still find it on the second-hand market. Each material has advantages and disadvantages. Here are some of them.

Aluminum rail is by far the cheapest, which is its primary advantage. There appear to be different alloys on the market with different properties. Some is relatively hard, which adds significantly to the structural integrity of the track. On the other hand, some is dead soft and easily bent. Generally speaking, aluminum is softer than other metals and can even be curved by hand if you wear a pair of leather gloves. However, aluminum rail is more prone to damage and kinking outdoors and it tends to expand more in hot weather.

Aluminum is light in color, which looks unprototypical (if that is important to you), and it does not darken with age. Also, aluminum track, while fine for live-steam and battery operation, presents conductivity problems at joints when used for track-powered trains. Although aluminum itself is an excellent conductor, its oxide is not. This problem can be mitigated somewhat with conductive grease inserted into the rail joints and tinned-copper jumpers held with stainless-steel screws.

Certain aluminum alloys seem to have a tendency to gum up wheels (especially plastic ones) more than other types of rail. Make sure you know what you are getting. Also, aluminum cannot be easily soldered, making switch building and wire attachment problematic.

Steel is the most prototypical material, since that is what full-size railroads use. It usually costs less than other metals, except aluminum, but may be difficult to find. Its biggest problem is that it is prone to corrosion. I have seen code-215 steel rail completely eaten away by acid rain. However, it was the garden railroader's rail of choice for decades in damp old Britain. A little kerosene was applied to the rail from time to time, often by a specially built tank car, which kept the rails like new for years on end.

Steel can be soldered, though not as easily as some other materials. It has been used successfully for track-powered trains. It's a hard metal and is more difficult to work and bend than many of the others, but it makes rugged track. Code-332 steel rail can even be welded to steel ties if you wish. Because of the need to preserve the rail, steel track may require more maintenance than others.

Brass is easy to work, it solders nicely, the cost is moderate, and most brass rail weathers to a prototypically near-black color. Code-332 brass rail may have variable weathering characteristics. LGB's rail weathers quickly while Aristo-Craft's rail will retain its bright-yellow appearance for months. Brass is excellent for live-steam and battery-powered lines, but may have to be cleaned regularly for track-powered trains.

Nickel-silver has many of the same qualities as brass. It's big advantage is that it oxidizes very little, minimizing track cleaning. Its bright-silver appearance can be removed with chemical blackeners. While more expensive on a per-pound basis, this rail is easy to work and it solders well.

Stainless-steel rail is available in certain sizes. It is the most expensive, but is impervious to just about everything. It's a hard metal and can be difficult to work. It does not conduct electricity as well as some of the other metals but, given the relatively large sizes of the rail we use, this should not be a problem. Some alloys can be easily soldered, while others cannot.

All of the above materials, with the exception of aluminum, can be intermixed with little problem. However, electrolytic problems can occur when mixing aluminum and other metals, particularly brass and steel. Stainless steel is more-or-less inert and can be used with any other metal.

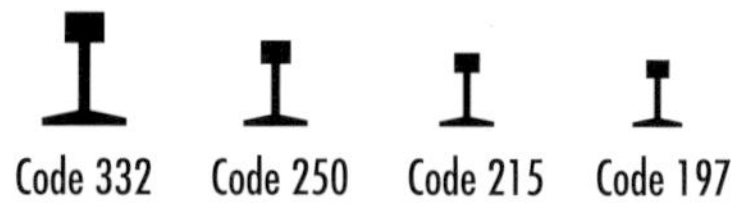

Rail sizes (actual size)

Rail codes

The size of model-train rail in any scale is referred to by "code." For instance, in large-scale railroading we commonly use code-332, code-250, or code-215 rail, although code-197 is also sometimes used. There's nothing secret about this "code"; it's just the height of the rail measured in thousandths of an inch. So, code-250 rail is .250″ tall, or $\frac{1}{4}$″. Code-332 is a little taller and code-215 is a little shorter.

Trackwork
for your garden railway

Jack Verducci

Marc Horovitz

Broad, sweeping curves, like those seen here on Betty and Jud Swedberg's railroad in Northern California, are easily attainable using the methods described in this chapter.

Now that we've designed our railway and built our roadbed, it's time to lay some track. A wide variety of track is available today, and which type is best for you depends on your circumstances. Basically, there are four choices of rail materials: brass, nickel-silver, aluminum, and stainless steel.

Jack Verducci

Jack Verducci

‹ Code-250 rail, with American-style ties and spikes, is closer to scale height and the spikes and tie plates are correct. Code-250 track with plastic ties is fragile, though. I recommend that it be used in areas where it is visible, but is not likely to be stepped on.

▲ Code-332 rail is much taller than scale and the bolts and brackets are European, but this track is very robust and will take a lot of abuse. On my own line, 90 percent of the track is code 332 and 10 percent is code 250.

Brass costs less than nickel-silver, but more than aluminum. It is not the best choice of materials, but it is, in my opinion, a reasonable choice. It is easy to work with and solders well. It does, though, require frequent cleaning if your trains are track-powered.

Nickel-silver is harder to work with. It is tougher than brass and more difficult to solder. It requires less frequent cleaning than brass, but still requires occasional cleaning.

Aluminum is the least expensive material. It is also the softest material of the four and can't be soldered. A sound mechanical/electrical connection is required for electric operation, which can be troublesome with aluminum rail. My advice is to avoid aluminum track.

Stainless steel is relatively new to the U.S. market and is very expensive. Manufacturers claim that no cleaning is required. The material is very hard and can't be soldered. H&RTrains, which markets a line of stainless track, offers rail joiners designed to clamp down on the rail by means of spring action to make a good electrical connection. If stainless-steel flex track is used, it is mandatory that a rail bender be employed and that the rails be bent to the exact curvature. Stainless steel may be a good choice for an electric railway running where track cleaning would be difficult.

Selecting your track

The next thing to know about rail is its "code," which refers to the height of the rail. Code is nothing more than the height of the rail, measured in thousandths of an inch. LGB is code 332, or .332″ high (the standard for most mass manufacturers of G-scale equipment). Also available are smaller rails in codes 250 and 215.

Why code 250 or 215? If you are a scale hound and you look at code-332 track from a low angle or scale eye level, you will notice that the rail is very tall, much taller than true scale. When codes 250 or 215 are viewed from the same angle, they appear more correctly proportioned. Personally, I like a scale look whenever possible.

LGB rails are supported by replicas of European sleepers (ties). In Europe, clamps and bolts are used to hold the rail in place. American rails are held down by smaller spike heads. This presents a problem in some garden railroads, especially those with limited or difficult access. Sometimes it's necessary to step on the track. Scale track does not handle foot traffic well. Due to the scale-size spike heads (represented by fragile plastic nubs), ties are easily stripped away from the rail when stepped on, creating a serious maintenance problem.

LGB track is more robust and more forgiving when abused. I personally recommend LGB flex track for general-purpose garden-railroad use. It is the easiest to work with, is strong, and has proven reliable.

If you prefer a more scale appearance, code-250 rail could be used in areas that are not subject to abuse. The two different rail sizes can be adapted to each other. Another trick with code-332 rail is to build the ballast up a little higher, over the tops of the ties, to make the rail look lower and to hide the European-style clamps and bolts.

In this chapter I will be discussing LGB flex track. I recommend it because it allows you to form your railroad exactly to the terrain. You are not limited by fixed curves or lengths. Once you understand a few basic things about flex track, you will see that it is easy and fun to work with.

Assembling and bending the track

There are three components to flex track: rail, ties, and rail joiners. Assembly is easy. If you are making a straight section, just slide on the ties and the rail joiners and connect it to the next piece. (If you are assembling several sections of flex track in advance, use a rubber-band wrapper around the rail ends to keep the ties from slipping off while you handle the track.) I cut the tabs off the LGB rail joiners, which allows me to slide the ties closer together at the joints.

As far as curved track, remember that any train will work best on wide-radius curves. There will be less drag on the train and it will have a more realistic appearance. As discussed in earlier installments of this series, all curves should be as wide as space permits. If you are making a curved section, you may have to use a rail bender to form the rail to the desired curve. Never bend flex track over your knee or around an object—this will only kink it.

The rail bender consists of three rollers, one of which is adjustable. By tightening the adjustable roller, you apply a force to the rail in such a way that it will bend between the other two rollers. As you rotate the crank, the rail passes through the rollers and is formed to shape. How much pressure you apply is a matter of trial and error. It seems that each rail bends a little differently than the next.

The best way to start is by increasing the pressure a little at a time until the rail assumes the proper shape. If you bend too far, you can put the rail through backwards and straighten it, then start over again.

A rail bender should always be used on rail that is going to be installed on a bridge or trestle or leading into a turnout. This eliminates the natural spring in the rail and ensures that the rail will not try to straighten out, knocking the trestle or switch out of alignment.

It may be necessary to cut some of the rail ends off when using a rail bender because most benders do not bend the last 1″ of rail. If the curve is sharp, the ends must be cut off; if the curve is very gradual, this may not be necessary.

Soldered track

I prefer not to use a rail bender where the track is laid on the ground (as opposed to being on a bridge or trestle). Instead, I solder the track.

First, assemble the flex-track sections. Each section is about 5′ long. Next, solder two sections together. You'll notice that the track will become more flexible as its length is increased. Solder as many pairs together as will be needed to cover the line. Next, take one of these double sections and lay it down where it will be installed, gently helping it conform to the roadbed. You will notice that the inside rail will be longer than the outside. Cut off the excess even with the outside rail. If your curve is on the tight side, you may have to hold the rail in place, then mark it where it is to be cut off. By following this procedure, you are letting the track lay down naturally. After trimming the first section of track, do the same for the next section.

The next step is to solder the two double sections together. What holds the track in shape is the fact that the inside rail has been cut to length and that each section is soldered to the next, creating a continuous, integrated length. The ballast, to be applied later, will also help hold the track in shape. The reason I like this method is that, when done correctly, you can actually form a smoother curve.

Adjustments to the line

Once the track is laid on your subroadbed and soldered, it's time to level and ballast it. Using a material scoop, pour ballast over the track and brush it in with a whisk broom or fox tail. Grade stakes are used here to ensure that the track is on grade. A torpedo level is used to level the track from side to side.

When using this method, you may occasionally run into a section of track that cannot be leveled from side to side with ballast. One side or the other seems to spring up. This is not a major problem—one rail or the other is simply too long.

To correct this, cut through the high rail, remove a small amount of it, then rejoin the ends with a rail joiner. It may take one or two cuts to remove just the right amount of rail. Once the rail is level, solder the track back together. This same method can be used to superelevate track.

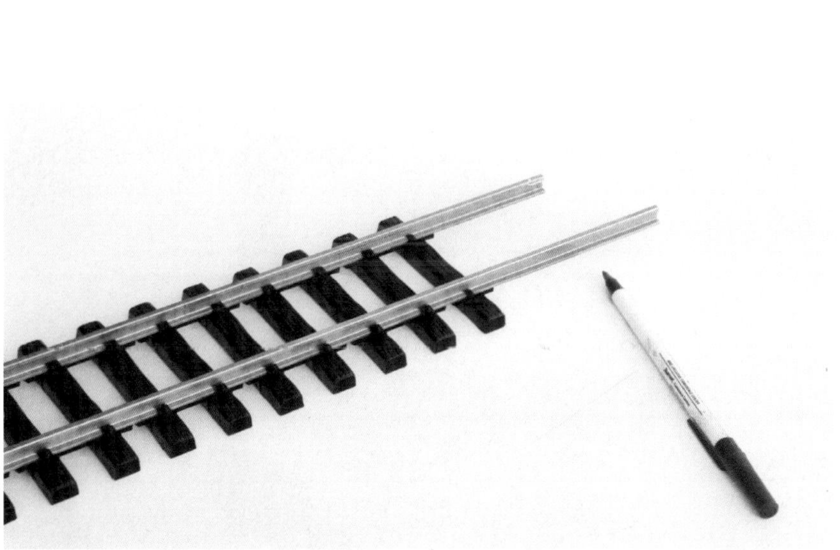

Jack Verducci

The rail on the inside radius of a curve is longer. Cut it off even with the outside rail.

Using clamps

Rail clamps are useful for joining rails to turnouts and they make removal easy. It is important for the lead-in rails to be lined up perfectly with the turnout rails. Clamps do not hold as securely as solder and a slight misalignment may cause a kink. This is why a rail bender should be used in these areas. Turnouts will be covered in more detail in another part of this series.

Conductive grease should be used where rail clamps are installed. A pipe cleaner or acid brush makes a good applicator.

Insulated rail clamps are used to make gaps for block control. Plastic screw-type joiners are far superior to the slip-on kind.

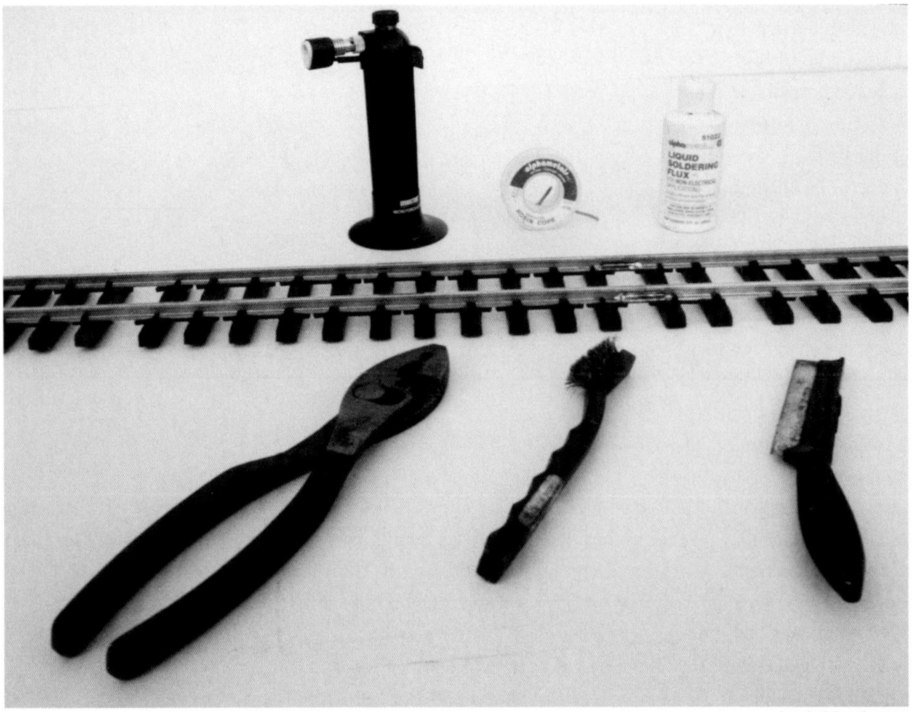

Jack Verducci

Soldering track

When I first became interested in garden railroading, I read all the articles I could find on trackwork. I discovered there was much controversy about soldering track. One of my biggest mistakes was not soldering my track when it was new. I strongly recommend soldering the track together (except at the turnouts—more on this later). Soldered rail joints eliminate electrical problems and also form a strong mechanical joint. I solder track even if the railroad is going to be battery- or steam-powered.

The arguments against soldering are weak at best. One is that you need expansion joints. This is bogus. Yes, if you have unsoldered joints you will see a gap open up when the temperature changes, but have you ever seen that gap close back up? Expansion and contraction of the track is handled by the roadbed. On a hot day the track will widen at the curves. On a cold day you may have a 10′ radius and on a hot it may be, say, 10′1″. This is why you should never anchor the track. It should be free to float in the ballast.

The other argument, which has some validity, concerns the desire to later change the trackplan. Still, this does not present a problem. You simply cut the track to remove it and resolder it where needed. The reliability of soldered joints is worth the extra effort this may take.

I do not solder rail joiners at turnouts. Instead, I clamp the ends with rail clamps, such as those manufactured by Richard Hillman. I have found that the majority of trackplan changes are made at turnouts.

Here is the method I use to solder flex track. I use 40/60, rosin-core, wire-type solder. With brand new flex track, the rosin in the solder will provide enough flux. If the track is tarnished, it will be necessary to use additional soldering flux. I use a liquid-acid type flux. (Paste flux is very messy when used in the garden—everything sticks to it—but it can be used if you are doing penance.) The function of flux is to clean the metal. You may see a warning that says acid flux should not be used on electrical connections. This does not apply to track. We are actually making a structural connection.

Soldering tools. Top row: mini torch; 40/60 rosin-core solder; liquid flux. Bottom row: heavy-duty pliers to align rails while the solder is hot; a wire brush for cleaning rail ends; and an Atlas Super Saw to cut the rails.

If you are trying to solder old track that has turned black, you will have to clean it first. I use copper-pot cleaner to start with and finish with flux. Once the rails have been prepared, slip on a rail joiner. If you are using acid flux, squirt a little into the joint. You are now ready to apply the heat.

There are several tools that can be used to solder track: a resistance-soldering unit; a large, electric soldering iron (175-200 watt chisel tip); or a micro torch. I have used all three and have found the micro torch is the best all-around tool. These sell in the range of $30 to $45.

The important thing about soldering is to get the work hot enough and to melt the solder into the work. Start by heating up the joint by passing the flame over it. This takes a little practice. Do not hold the flame too close to the work. The small blue tip of the flame should be about 1/8″ to 1/4″ from the work.

Securing track to trestles and bridges

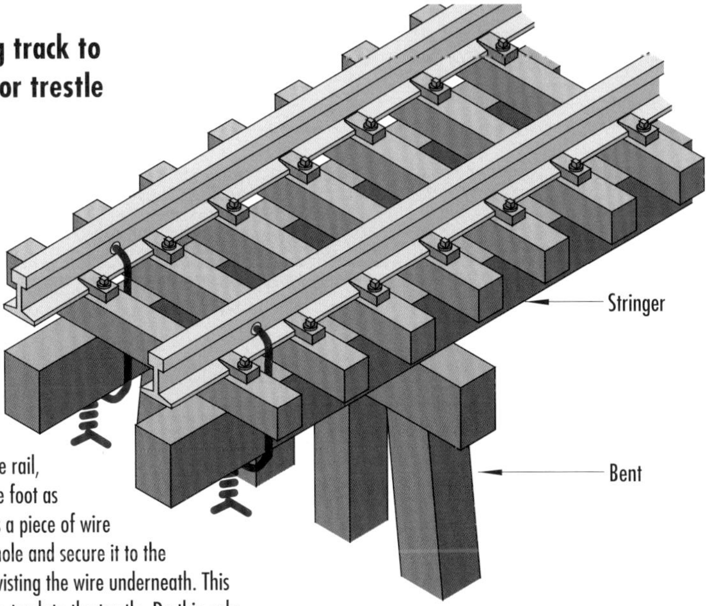

Bridges are the exception to my rule of not attaching the track to the ground. Securing the track in a few places can keep the track from sliding off.

Never screw the ties to the trestle. Over time that the ties will end up breaking and/or pulling away from the rail. If you must secure the track, drill a small hole in the web of the rail as close to the foot as possible. Then, using a piece of wire, tie the rail down to the trestle's stringer. Now the ties are actually held in place between the rail and the trestle and the track is anchored.

A little experimenting will teach you what the proper distance should be.

When the rail joiner starts to turn colors, this means it is coming up to temperature. Start applying solder at one end of the rail joiner on the opposite side of the rail from where the flame is being applied. Touch the solder to the end of the rail joiner and let the heat pull it into the joint. The flame should never actually touch the solder. The rail and joiner should be hot enough to melt the solder. Once solder is pulled into one end of the joiner, do the same at the other end. Then apply the heat to the other side of the rail and repeat the process. If done properly, the solder will be very shiny and will flow evenly.

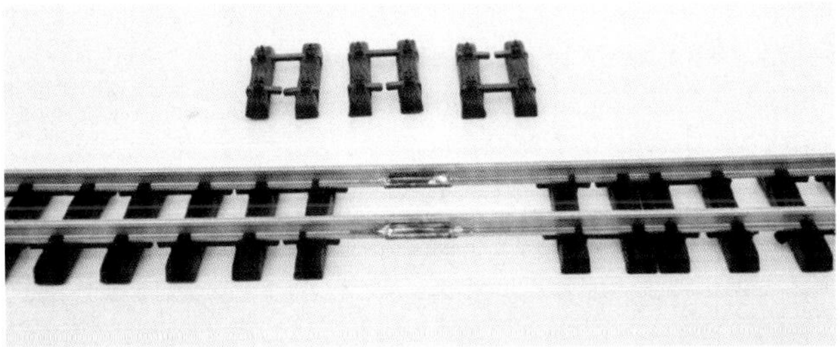

Jack Verducci

Here, two sections of flex track have been soldered. Notice that the solder has been drawn into the rail joiner at each end. To prevent melting ties, cut the tie strips into pairs and remove the web on the ends. Slide the ties out of the way (see right side). When the joint is cool, slide the ties back.

Next, take a large pair of pliers and grip the rails where they join. This will bring the rail heads into alignment and the pliers will act as a heat sink to help cool the joint. Let the joint cool until it is solid before releasing the pliers. Wash the joint off with water to remove the flux.

If done properly, there should be no beads or balls of solder on the joiners and the surface should be relatively smooth.

How to keep from melting ties

If you become proficient at soldering, you will be able to bond a joint without melting the plastic ties. The trick is to get in, get the metal hot enough to melt the solder, then get out.

Here is a trick that can help you until this skill is learned. Before installing the rail joiner, cut the webbing that connects the ties, so that you have three loose pairs of ties on either side of the joint. Remove the web completely from the ends of each pair. This will allow you to slide the ties safely away from the flame. When cool, slide them back into place.

Grading on the curve

Jim Hudson

All photos by Jim Hudson

Earlier in this book we discussed curves and the basic concept that wider radii are better for smooth operation and realistic appearance. But curves are not the only concern. Unless your railroad is going to be dead-flat and arrow-straight, your design will need to incorporate reasonable grades for your locomotives to climb and adequate clearances for your cars to pass safely.

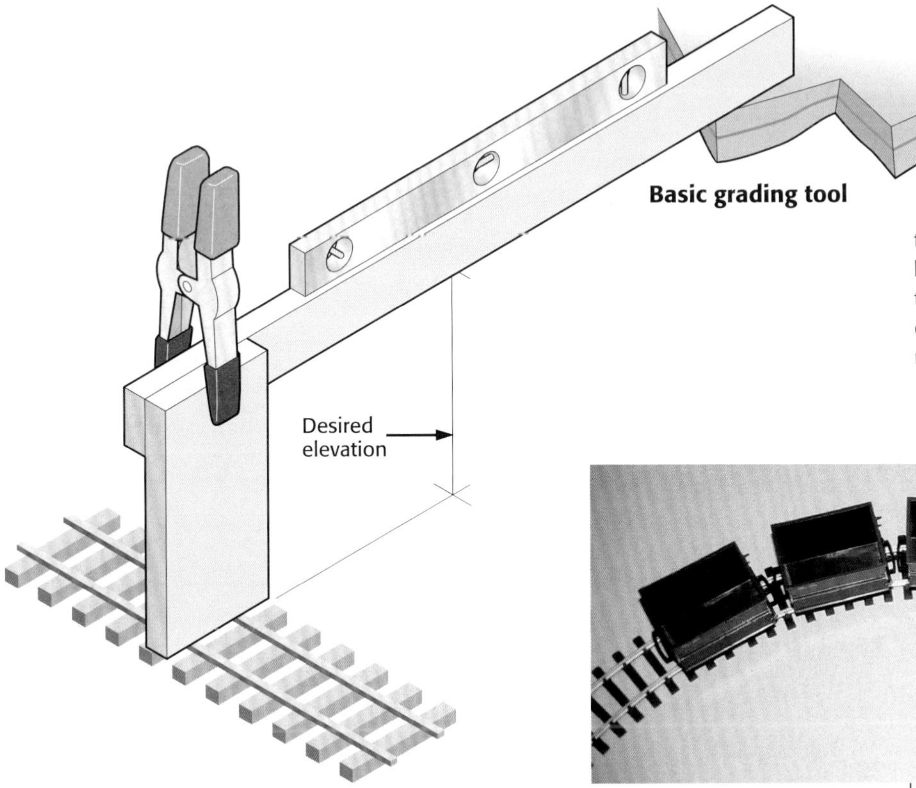

Select an object of known elevation, somewhat higher than the track, as a benchmark. Then measure and clamp the boards together at right angles to produce the desired difference. Set one end of the horizontal board on the fixed elevation, level it, then adjust the track to meet the vertical board. If the benchmark is below track level, just turn the tool around and set the vertical board on the benchmark and make the track meet the horizontal board.

< Track and roadbed under construction in what will be the inside of a tunnel. The planned clearance dimension of 4" (measured from the block wall to the centerline of the track) included a little room for error, since things often don't work out precisely according to plan. Happily, in this case, the track crews managed to keep the desired radius and even ended up with a bit of extra room.

^ Tiny rolling stock has little overhang at corners or sides, even on tight-radius track.

Let's start with some definitions. There are several recognized ways of indicating the steepness of a grade. In America, grades on a railroad are commonly expressed in percentages. For example, a 4 percent grade means the train will climb 4″ in 100″ of travel along the track. In Europe, that would be expressed as a 1:25 grade, in other words, 1″ of climb for 25″ of travel. Another common way of indicating grades in non-metric-system countries is to state the fraction of an inch of climb that occurs in a foot of travel. A ½″-per-foot grade climbs half an inch in a foot of travel. This grade figures out as a little bit steeper still, translating to 1:24, or approximately 4.17 percent.

Whatever method you use to quantify a grade in hard mathematical terms, it's more critical to know how steep the grade is in relative terms. For example, a ½″-per-foot or 4 percent grade is considered extremely severe in full-size railroading. If you study real railroads, you'll find that even the most notorious stretches of mainline track, whether in the Blue Ridge Mountains of Tennessee or the Tehachapis of California, seldom have grades over 1 to 2 percent. Lesser-used branch lines and many narrow-gauge railroads may have grades up to six percent or more, but such tortuous climbs are a definite source of headaches for railroaders.

On a model railroad, the consequences are less serious, but the same laws of physics still apply. There are no hard-and-fast rules, but you might expect a modern locomotive to pull only half as many cars on a 4 percent grade as on level track. Since locomotive wheels slipping on the rails can cause serious damage to an engine's gear train, the grades on your garden railway need to be gentle enough to safely allow you to run the lengths of trains you want. For most garden-railway applications, you'll be doing yourself a favor if you resist the temptation to create grades greater than 2 or 3 percent. If you plan to run live-steam locomotives, even 1 percent can be quite a bit unless your locomotive is radio-controlled so that you can give it more power when climbing a grade.

Since the friction of car and locomotive wheels against the rails increases greatly on curves, grades that occur on curves will also need to be reduced, perhaps by as much as half, depending on the sharpness of the curve. A 2-percent grade on a curve could produce the same effect as a 3- or 4-percent grade on straight track.

So what does that 2 or 3 percent limit mean? For one thing, it means that you'll need a lot of distance in order for your track to climb up and over itself. A vertical clearance of 10″ (measured from the top of the rail to any overhead obstruction) is a common minimum that will accommodate most G-scale rolling stock. You should always check each car or locomotive in advance! There is no such thing as too much clearance, but there can definitely be too little. A bit of math tells us that a track laid on a 2 percent grade requires almost 42 feet to climb 10″. Even

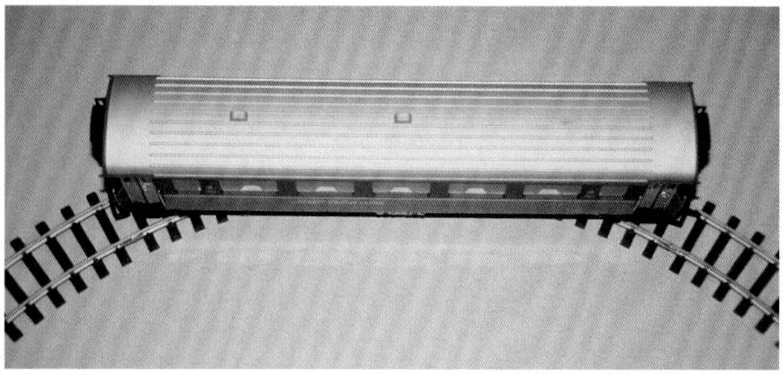

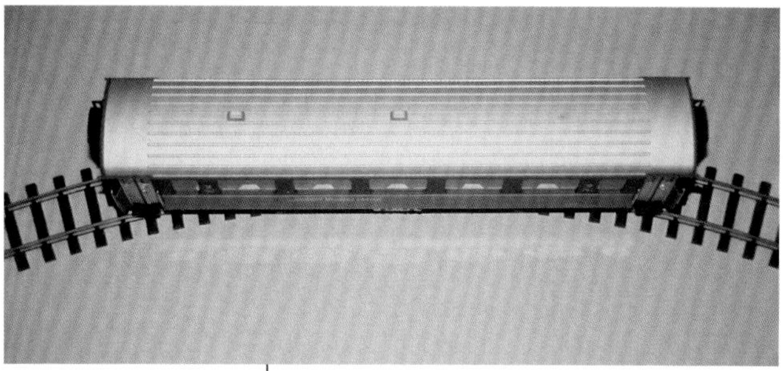

A very long car will have excessive overhang on outside corners and inside sides on tighter curves; not as much on more prototypical, wider-radius curves. Plan accordingly.

a 3 percent grade takes almost 28 feet.

Again, you may have to make some difficult choices and compromises to merge your garden-railroad dreams with the realities of the space available to you. You can quickly push some dirt around and temporarily lay some track in order to experiment with various grades. Try putting just a few drops of water on the rails and you'll get a feeling for what could happen when you run your railroad on a foggy morning.

Vertical curves

While you're busy figuring out how much distance, your track will require to climb a given height, don't forget to allow some extra for "vertical transition." While the term may sound technical, the concept is simple. Just as your automobile might bottom out when entering a steep driveway, your locomotives and cars will do much the same thing if you lay your track with an abrupt change from dead-level to a steep grade. On a real railroad, the transition would be algebraically calculated and built as a vertical hyperbolic curve, with the rails actually bending ever-so-slightly upwards at a continuously increasing slope.

For garden-railway purposes, you can bypass the tricky engineering. Just start your slope gently and then gradually work up to the full grade over several feet. Using that 4 percent grade as an example, you might start from level with a foot of track laid at 1 percent, then a foot at 2 percent, then another foot at 3 percent, before finally reaching your desired 4 percent. Even the crudest attempt at easing into the grade will offer a dramatic improvement in operation and visual appearance.

When planning grades on a garden railway, I like to roughly lay out a trackplan, then mark spot elevations at 1-foot increments along the track. If you know that a particular spot on a track is, say, 36″ above whatever benchmark you started from, then a ¼″-per-foot grade would mean that a spot a foot farther up the track would be at 36¼″ elevation. Another foot of travel would bring you to 36½″, and so on. This method allows you to quickly determine if your track can climb comfortably from one location to another in a given distance. As you proceed into track construction, you'll find that a tape measure, a level, and a couple of boards clamped together make a crude but effective grade tool for transferring your spot elevations from paper to the real thing. With an accurate indication of where your track should be, you can simply add or subtract fill material to place your track at the correct height.

Leave enough clearance

Unless you can be sure you'll never buy a big new car or locomotive, or that you'll never invite a friend to run some large equipment on your railroad, I'd recommend designing your garden railway with some extra clearance. Keep this in mind when you are planning the locations of parallel tracks, tunnels, bridges, station platforms, plants, and especially rocks!

Curve clearances for various sizes of cars and locos

Based on LGB track and equipment

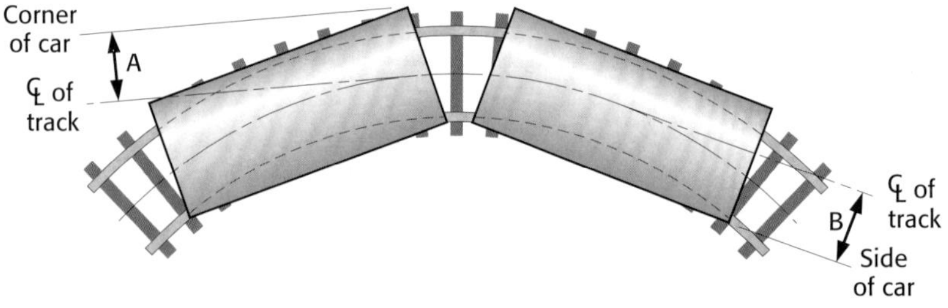

Curve Clearances

LGB 11000* curved track

	1	2	3	4
A	2"	3"	3½"	3½"
B	2"	2½"	3¾"	3½"

LGB 16000** curved track

	1	2	3	4
A	2"	2½"	2¾"	2¾"
B	2"	2¼"	3¼"	2¾"

1. Industrial mini-diesel and side-dump cars
2. "Standard" two-axle European cars
3. F7A diesel locomotive
4. RhB long passenger cars

*600mm/23¾" radius
**1175mm/46¼" radius

Turnout considerations

Jack Verducci

Jack Verducci

If you like to watch your trains run and do not get involved in routing, switching, or other operations, you should probably keep the number of turnouts, or switches, on your railroad to a minimum. There is good reason for this: Turnouts can be a source of irritation. Most derailments occur at turnouts; they can be the most frustrating part of running a railroad.

Fog Harbor Turnouts

Fog Harbor is a busy seaport that handles in- and outbound freight from ships and boats and also serves as a railhead for the Crystal Springs Lumber Company. The empty track in the center is the main line. At the left is a pair of dual-track sidings, a pair at each end of a switchback. (See the trackplan.) One pair services the piers (far end of the yard) and the other services the growers' exchange at the other end. The turnout that connects the main line to the switchback is just visible at the right of the station. To the right is the passing siding, with a turnout leading to the Crystal Spring Lumber Company's mill. This trackage belongs to the lumber company. Lumber is brought from the mill to be picked up by the CSRR. As you can see, there are endless switching and operational possibilities in this area, utilizing just a few switches.

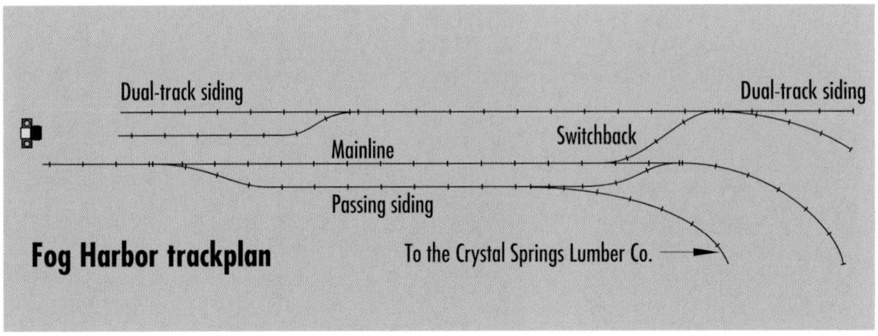

Fog Harbor trackplan

Despite this, turnouts are what a real railroad is all about. They enable trains to pass each other on a single-track main line, allow freight to be delivered to industries, permit routes to be changed, and so forth. A single turnout will transform a circle of track into an operating transportation system.

Types of turnouts

The basic turnouts are right-hand, left-hand, "Y," three-way, single-slip, double-slip, and a variety of combinations thereof (fig. 1). For reliable operation, avoid fancy stuff like three-way turnouts, double-slip switches, and so forth. These are problems looking for places to happen.

Turnout identification

Turnouts are identified by a number (such a no. 3 or a no. 4). These numbers refer to a ratio having to do with the amount of divergence over a given length from the point of the frog (fig. 2). The higher the number, the shallower the frog angle. This is important for smooth operation of trains. The larger the switch, the smoother the train will pass through it. The only problem with longer switches is space. A no. 8, for example, is 35″ long while a no. 3 is only 17″ long.

1

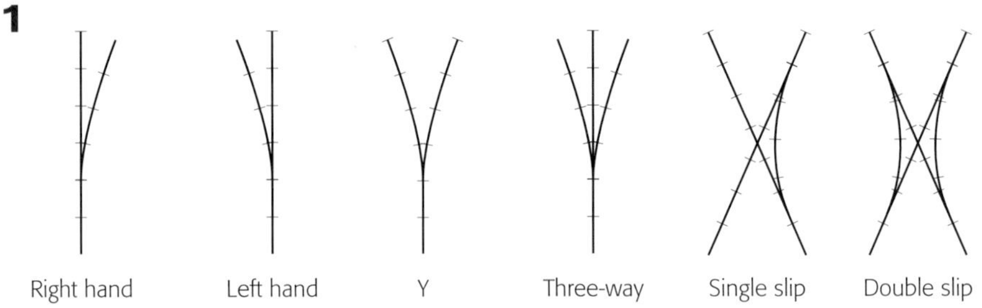

Types of switches

To find the frog number, select an arbitrary distance **x** from the point of the frog, then divide by the distance **y** at that point.

2

For instance, if **x** = 2.5" and **y** = .5",
2.5 ÷ .5 = 5
This would be a #5 switch.

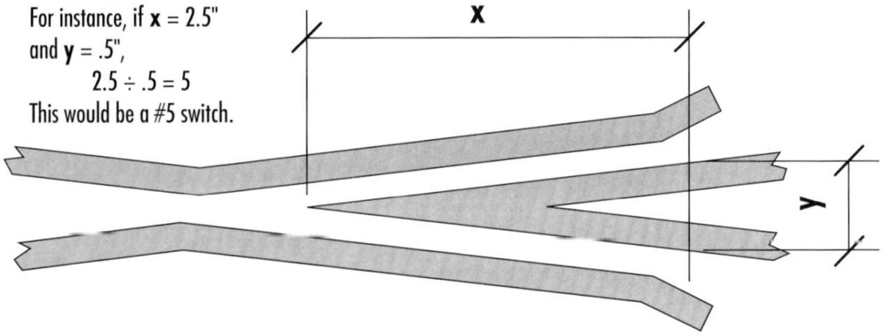

Finding the frog number

Tips on turnout placement
to help avoid problems

• Don't install a turnout in an inaccessible location, such as in a tunnel.

• Keep the number of turnouts on the main line to a minimum. If you want to have a large switching yard or industrial switching area, route the trains off the main line through a single switch, then spread the track out with as many turnouts as you like. This will reduce the likelihood of derailments on the main line. Trains in the yard run at a slower speed (called "yard speed"), which reduces the chance of derailments. You need to be able to run on the main line at higher speeds.

• Try to install turnouts so that the main line is routed through the straight side of the turnout. It is prototypically correct to run a main line through a curved section, but in model railroads it is not good practice because of the potential for derailments.

• Try to have a straight section of track leading into and out of a turnout. The purpose of this is to ensure that a speeding train is in balance and that its wheels are properly aligned as it enters the turnout. If a train is speeding around a corner, then suddenly comes into a switch, its momentum and centrifugal force may cause it to ride up the rail and off the turnout. A straight lead-in track gives the train time to align itself with the turnout.

• If you have a choice, set the turnouts up so that a train, in its normal direction of travel, enters the turnout at the opposite end from the points (frog-to-point direction). If the points are hard against the stock rail, the train will push them over as it goes through. When set up like this, the turnout is said to have "trailing" points (figure A). The train would have to back up to go into the siding.

• The opposite situation is said to have "facing" points. In facing-point installations, a partially thrown point would derail a train or cause it to split the switch—one truck goes west while the other goes east (figure B).

• If at all possible, avoid using "short turnouts" (such as LGB no. 12000 or no. 12050). These are intended for use in tight areas and with smaller rolling stock. They work fine with two-axle car, but larger four-axle cars usually have problems backing into short switches. The minimum turnout should be at least a 22° turnout, such as an LGB no.16050 or LGB no. 16150. Larger turnouts than these are better where space permits.

• Avoid goofy track configuration at the turnouts. For instance, stay away from S-curves between turnouts or turnouts aligned in a way that makes the train jog unnaturally. The train should be as stable as possible upon entering and leaving a turnout—smoother is better.

• Keep the turnouts level from side to side.

• If you run track-powered trains, it is a good idea to use a block system to prevent trains from entering the turnout while the points are set in the wrong position.

• Since turnouts require occasional maintenance, do not solder them in place. Use screw-on, clamp-type rail joiners to secure them to the adjoining rails.

• Be sure the roadbed under a turnout is firm. Excellent support is required under a turnout because of a weak point at the frog. Firmly compacted crusher fines will serve well. You may want to place a concrete paving block under the switches for support. Do not screw the switches down.

A

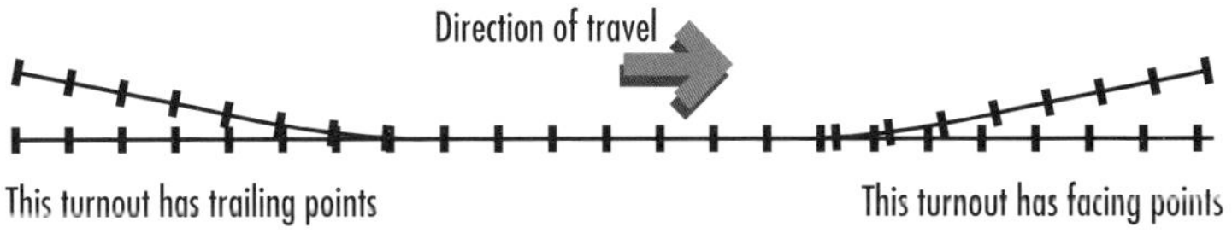

Trailing and facing points

B

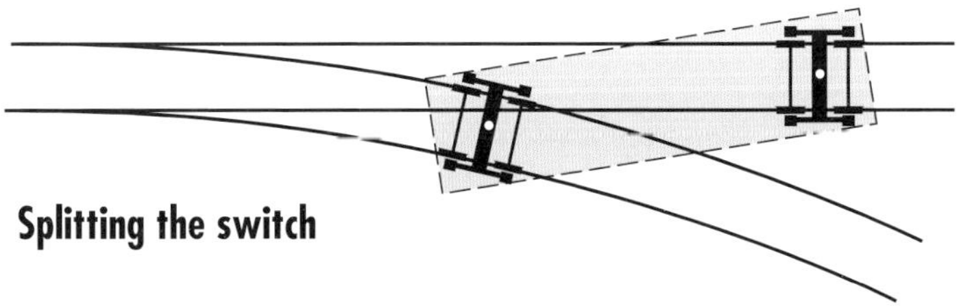

Splitting the switch

SECTION 6

Power for your trains

Jim Hudson

Jim Forbes

If you are itching to be outside putting down track, there are many ways to do it, some better than others. Before you get much track down, you may want to give some thought to how you will power your trains. You have more choices available today than any garden railroader has ever had. The matter involves far more than just choosing one power pack versus another. In addition to the staggering array of conventional power packs on the market, there is a wide variety of alternatives, including live steam, battery power, radio control (R/C), and digital command control (DCC). Now all you have to do is pick the one that's just right for you!

If you don't even know what some of those terms mean, let alone understand all the technical differences, how can you choose wisely? It may help to break the various systems down by categories or groups. To give you some basis for comparison, we'll also look at a few examples of the many components and systems available. Let me state now, for anyone who may feel I've overlooked their preferred method of powering trains, that this is certainly not my intent. For the sake of brevity, I've simply chosen what I feel are a few, fairly popular systems, each one representing a notably different approach from the others.

The most elementary difference in power is whether the energy source is carried aboard the train or is provided from something outside. In this chapter, we'll look at power provided from the outside, which generally means that the train receives its power through the rails. Most large-scale starter sets come with a small "power pack." You just hook up a couple of wires to the track, plug the cord into a wall outlet, and you're running trains. This approach is simple enough that almost anyone can use it without really understanding how it works. The train runs, so what more is there to know? Actually, quite a bit.

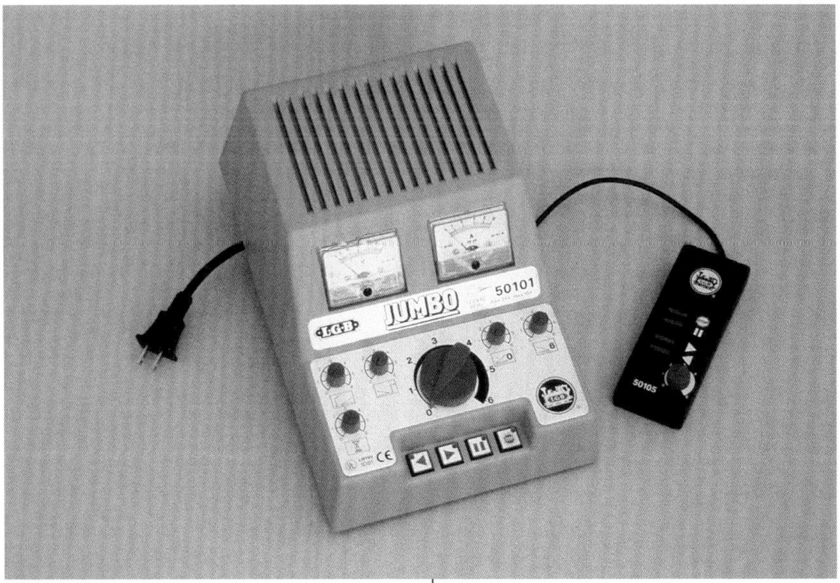

Jim Hudson

◂ A variety of control devices. From left: Märklin's simple power pack for its AC trains, Aristo-Craft's Train Engineer, and LGB's fully featured Jumbo pack.

▴ LGB's no. 50101 Jumbo Power Pack is a large conventional pack. It can be combined with the no. 50105 Tethered Remote Control. Similar power packs with tethered remotes are offered by MRC and Chicago Model International, although with lower power output and fewer options.

Terminology

First, let's get the terminology straight. The words transformer, throttle, and power pack are often confused and misused. A transformer changes, or transforms, the high voltage from the household mains to a safe, lower voltage (generally rectifying the alternating current into direct current in the process). A speed control, or throttle, regulates the amount of voltage and the polarity sent to the train through the rails. A power pack combines a transformer and a throttle in one unit.

Turning the power pack's control knob varies the amount of voltage sent to the rails and, eventually, to the electric motor in the locomotive, which moves the train down the track. Most large-scale trains are powered by direct current (DC) voltage, meaning that one rail is nominally positive and the other negative. The current flows in a loop from the power pack, through one wire to one rail, up through the electrical pickups on the locomotive, through the motor, back down through more pickups to the other rail, through the other wire and back to the power pack.

Reversing the train's direction is accomplished via a switch, either separate or integrated with the speed-control knob, which basically "flips" the polarity of the power on the rails. The rail that carried positive current becomes negative and vice versa. This causes the motor to turn in the opposite direction, thus reversing the train.

Options

Now that you understand the principles of how a conventional power pack works, you can look at options beyond the train set. The first thing most people experience is a need for more power. More and larger locomotives, lights in passenger cars, and electric switches and other accessories will likely soon tax the capacity of that small power pack from your starter set. This is fairly simply solved, at least in concept. Just look for a bigger power pack.

Do be cautious, though, of judging power packs solely by amperage ratings. You need to know the voltage that a pack can maintain while putting out a certain amperage. A wattage rating, abbreviated either as "W" or "VA" (for volt-amps) is a product of multiplying volts times amps. So, calling a pack a "3-amp" supply is rather vague, while "36VA" or "3 amps at 12 volts" is specific. If your train is drawing 2 amps of current, that pack may be able to provide 18 volts to move your train along at a good clip (36VA ÷ 2A = 18V). But that same pack may drop its output to only 10 or 12 volts if the train's current draw increases to 3 amps, such as when climbing a grade. That may leave your train barely crawling along. Three amps at 18 volts would require a 54VA rating.

Also, note that most power packs made for smaller trains (N or HO scales), are designed to provide 12 or perhaps 14 volts maximum. Large-scale trains use up to 24 volts and a single, large locomotive may need over 2 amps. Voltage losses through rails and wires over long distances on a garden railway only make the problem worse, so it's important to start with a high enough voltage and amperage from the power pack.

Jim Hudson

LGB's no. 50061 Transformer (right) is designed to stay indoors while the no. 51120 Outdoor Throttle, disguised as a signalman's shed, stays outside and controls the trains.

Ranking right up there with "more power" on the wish list is the ability to run two or more trains. You can just put two locomotives on the same track and watch them chase around until one overtakes the other. This isn't terribly realistic and, no matter if one train runs a bit faster than the other for a given voltage, both will still start and stop more or less at once and run in the same direction when you open the throttle. With DC power, it does no good to turn one locomotive around. Both will still travel the same direction, regardless of which way they are pointing.

With conventional track power, controlling multiple trains independently essentially implies dividing the track up into separate electrical sections or "blocks." Each locomotive or train must occupy its own block. Each block is then controlled separately by some means, ranging from a simple on-off switch that allows one train to stop while another runs, to separate throttles or power packs for each block, allowing actual independent speed and direction control.

Wiring for this kind of operation can become quite complex, but people do build large and elaborate systems this way. If you're heading in this direction for power, you'll need to incorporate conduits under the tracks and other obstacles to allow for all the wires you'll be installing and burying underground.

Safety first

Before you decide to buy a bigger power pack, let me suggest that a power pack may not be the best thing for your garden railway. There are two reasons—safety and convenience. First and foremost, remember that a power pack plugs into house current. House current has the power to give you a severe shock or even kill you. Of course, you should always look for the approval of a recognized safety testing agency, such as UL, on anything that plugs into house current. Beyond that, though, I have yet to see any model-train power pack or transformer that is recommended or approved for permanent outdoor use. All transformers have metal parts in them that can corrode. Many have ventilation openings. Even plastic housings that look like they are sealed are not actually watertight. Trains should be fun, not a worry, so please, put your power pack or transformer inside.

So, if your transformer is inside, how do you control your trains? You can't be running back to the house every time you want to start or stop a train. Fortunately, options exist that give you not only safety, but convenience. The simplest viable approach is to use a transformer that is separate from the speed control or throttle. The transformer stays indoors and low-voltage wires lead outdoors to the throttle. The track-power wires then go from the throttle to the track, perhaps through some sort of control panel or switches. Some throttles are not made for exposure to the weather, so even though you avoid the safety concern, you might

A caution about power supplies

If you'd just bought a new Ferrari and the manual said to use only high-octane gasoline, you wouldn't fill the tank with regular gas or diesel fuel. But many people do much the same thing with the power for their large-scale trains. Electrical power is not all the same. Different power supplies and controls put out different "wave forms" of electrical power. Some may cause harm to motors or electronics in your locomotives. Most will make your trains run, so you might not realize you are damaging your equipment until it's too late. You'd need electronics training and a test device like an oscilloscope to really tell the difference. Your retailer may mean well in recommending a particular power supply, but he is probably not an electrical engineer. Always check with the manufacturers of your locomotives for their recommendations on power supplies.

end up replacing a piece of expensive electronic hardware before too long unless you provide some protection from extremes of moisture, cold, and heat. Other throttles are actually designed to be permanently mounted outdoors.

You may find this method a bit constraining, since the controls are still in one fixed location. Several popular power packs in recent years have offered what is known as walk-around control. Small wires carry electrical signals—not track power—back and forth between a hand-held throttle and the actual power pack. Based on the throttle settings, the power pack then regulates the power and sends it directly to the control panel or track. The power pack still stays indoors. The important difference here is that the hand-held throttle, while it probably can't be left outdoors, most likely offers the option of a long enough cable or tether that you can take the throttle out to the railroad and follow your trains around. In practice, it really doesn't matter whether the power pack is right there with you or in the garage 50 feet away, as long as the train runs the way it should according to your commands.

From tethered walk-arounds, it's just a short leap of technology to radio-controlled (R/C), track-power devices. The train's speed and direction is still determined strictly by the voltage applied to the rails. The systems I'm familiar with require a separate transformer to provide power for a receiver or "base unit," which actually runs the trains. Here, the wires between the base unit and the hand-held controller are replaced by radio waves. As with tethered systems, there is no direct connection between the hand-held R/C transmitter and the track. The transmitter just sends signals to a receiver in the base unit, which then controls the power to the track.

The obvious advantage to R/C track power is the freedom to walk around without any cords getting underfoot. The transformer and base unit can be mounted in a weather-protected location, reasonably close to the railroad and situated for good radio contact. Some testing may be in order to make sure everything is operating properly before things are placed too permanently. For example, unless you can run an antenna outside, you might not want to put the base unit inside a concrete-block basement or a metal shed, since both of these do a pretty good job of blocking radio waves.

When shopping for an R/C system, ask what happens when radio interference occurs, because it absolutely will, no matter how good the components are. I'd look for a system that has safeguards to shut down power if a signal is garbled or if no signal is received for a certain amount of time. Without safeguards, trains may receive full power by mistake, or you may discover you've walked out of radio range and lost control just as your favorite locomotive is charging toward an open drawbridge. Don't be scared away by that scenario—just ask questions before you buy. For people who want track power, the option of controlling that power by radio offers great operating flexibility.

So far, we've just touched the tip of the iceberg on the subject of conventional track power and its variations. For some, this may be all you want to know about powering your trains. Others may be looking at recent technological developments, such as digital command control (DCC) or battery-powered radio control. Whatever way you choose to run your railroad, more power to you!

Jim Hudson

Aristo-Craft's Train Engineer R/C walk-around control with a base unit. This system still requires an indoor transformer to supply power to the base unit. The Instant R/C system from Reed's Hobby Shop and a model from Remote Control Systems can also be used for R/C track power.

More Power
for your trains
Jim Hudson

All photos by Jim Hudson

In the last chapter, we covered conventional track-power supplies. In this chapter we'll look at one more variation on track power, then move on to power sources carried aboard the train.

Digital command control

Digital Command Control, or DCC, was virtually unknown 10 or 15 years ago. Most DCC systems operate on the same basic principles: A transformer brings house current down to a safe voltage, usually between 12V and 24V. This is used to power a central command station, which acts somewhat like the central processing unit on a computer. The command station sends a constant "full" voltage to the tracks. For large-scale trains this might be something like 18V AC. AC?! Yes, a high-frequency current oscillating thousands of times per second. But most large-scale trains don't run on AC, and even if they do, at 18V, anything on the tracks would be moving right along, wouldn't it?

Here's the difference: Along with the constant voltage to the track, the command station sends digitally encoded signals over the rails. Each one of these electronic messages is addressed to a specific recipient. In each locomotive on the tracks, there is a special circuit board called a decoder. Each decoder has its own "address," so it only receives the messages sent to it. Here's one way to understand what the decoder does: Suppose the mail carrier in your neighborhood didn't put the mail in mailboxes, but instead, every resident came out to meet the carrier on the sidewalk, looked at all the addresses on all the envelopes, then took away only the ones addressed to them. This is sort of what decoders do, only they sort through all the mail in micro-seconds.

The decoder acts as a locomotive's own personal throttle. It takes the electricity from the tracks, then uses it to power the motors, making the locomotive go faster or slower, in forward or reverse, blow the whistle, or turn the headlight on or off, all based on the messages sent to it by the command station. The truly wonderful thing about all this is that a number of locomotives can be on the same track at the same time and each one can be doing something completely different from the others.

Besides operating flexibility and realism, DCC offers other benefits: Track wiring can be pretty simple—really nothing more than two wires to the track in most cases. You don't need complex electrical block wiring or control panels. And, with all that power on the rails, things like car lights and smoke generators can tap directly into it, so they work great even when a train is standing still.

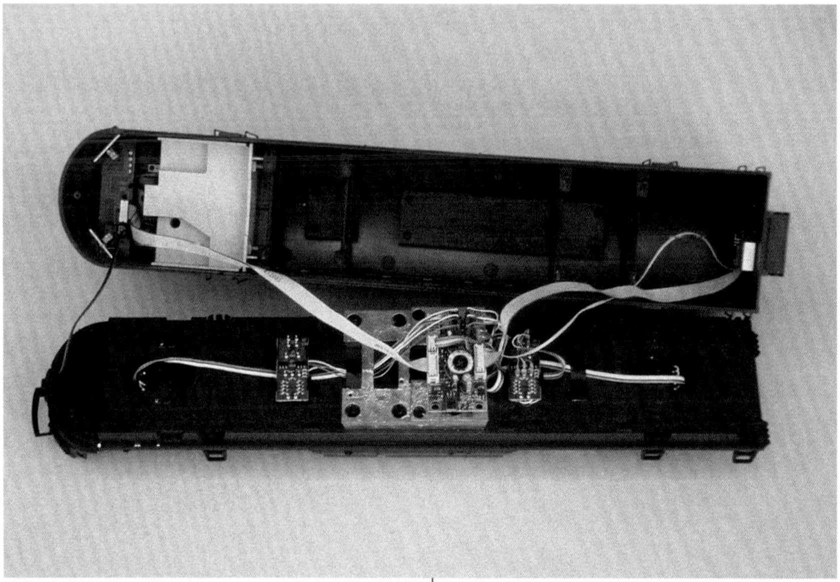

‹ Here's a digital command control (DCC) system. LGB no. 50111 AC transformer with no. 55000 Multi-Train System for DCC, consisting of a Central Station (command station), Train Mouse (tethered walk-around control) and a Decoder for installation in a locomotive. Märklin's Delta System is similar in function to LGB's. Both are designed for easy operation. A number of companies offer more complex DCC systems with additional features.

^ An LGB F-7A diesel with DCC decoders installed. This locomotive uses one decoder for each motor. The decoders can be seen fore and aft of the main locomotive circuit board, which is mounted to the large weight.

One of the drawbacks to DCC is that most locomotives require extensive electrical modifications to have the decoder circuit boards installed, especially if you want to control extra features like lights and sounds. In the smaller model-railroad scales, DCC has been growing steadily for a few years, so manufacturers and hobbyists have been working together to develop standards to minimize the amount of surgery that has to be done to a locomotive's electrical system.

In large-scale, so far LGB and Märklin are the only major manufacturers that I know of offering locomotives factory prepared for easy installation of decoders. In fact, many of their recent releases allow plug-in installation. Fortunately, a number of specialists, including some train manufacturers install decoders for those who don't want to tackle the job.

Most current DCC systems offer some form of hand-held, walk-around control, either tethered or via radio control. Most also offer the ability for several operators to each run a train or two, all on the same track. I've previously mentioned my preference for keeping things simple ,and this certainly applies to DCC. There are systems where you almost need to be a rocket scientist to operate them. If you can imagine it, these systems can control it—from multiple-diesel lashups to track switches to the bulb in the conductor's lantern. But beware: If your VCR is still blinking "12:00," these systems may not be for you. Other systems are more limited in function, but offer easier operation. You just move a lever to select the locomotive you want to run, then turn the throttle knob.

DCC can be a great way for non-technically oriented people, including children, to avoid the complexities of track wiring and just enjoy running trains. DCC systems might seem costly at first, but you may save in other areas

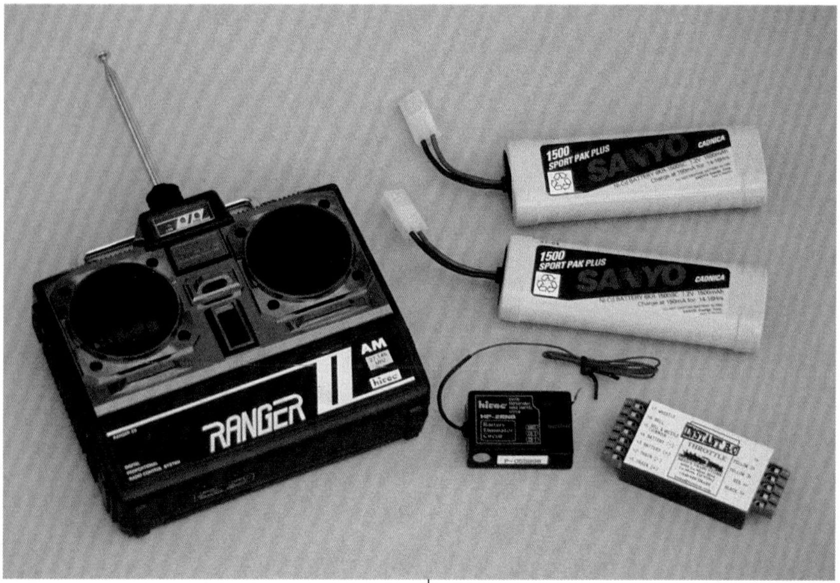

A typical battery-powered R/C system consists of a hand-held two-channel radio transmitter, a pair of nicad battery packs, a receiver, and a throttle or speed controller. Not shown is a charger for the batteries. This system is the Instant R/C System offered by Reed's Hobby Shop. Other similar systems are offered by Aristo-Craft and Remote Control Systems.

down the road—and it's hard to place a dollar value on the operating enjoyment.

Onboard systems

Finally, we come to power systems that are carried aboard the train. That could include live steam, clockwork (wind-up) mechanisms, or even miniature diesel engines driving tiny electrical generators to power traction motors, just as on a full-size diesel. Those last two are rather obscure. Live steam certainly isn't obscure, but it has developed as a sort of separate sub-group within the hobby of garden railroading.

One option that has gained considerable popularity in recent years is battery power. At its most basic, a battery-powered locomotive's mechanism can be as simple as a battery wired to a motor, with an on-off switch added for convenience. Part of the appeal seems to lie in an utter lack of sophistication. Though you may not choose to power most of your trains this way, it could be a way to get something moving on the track if you have a limited space or modest budget. You might try your own hand at building something along these lines, whether out of necessity or just for the fun of it.

Radio control

At the other end of the spectrum is battery power combined with radio control (R/C). The recent growth in the popularity of R/C systems has come hand-in-hand with technological developments. Radio controls from just a few years ago were often finicky and troublesome, but they did offer a few hardy, pioneer hobbyists enough of a glimpse of the possibilities to spur further progress. This eventually led to today's systems, some of which are quite reliable and suitable for the average garden railroader.

There are systems that allow one operator to control several locomotives, plus bells, whistles, turnouts, and just about everything else short of the kitchen sink. Here again, not unlike the DCC or live-steam aspects of the hobby, there seems to be a sort of special-interest group—people who are fascinated by all the neat technological things that can be done with radio control.

Rechargeable batteries are the most common power source. These provide power to a radio receiver and throttle that actually "runs" the train, based on signals sent from a radio transmitter held by the operator. Unlike radio-controlled track power, all of this equipment is carried either in the locomotive itself or in a car trailing behind the locomotive. Interestingly, it wasn't until the relatively recent huge growth in the popularity of large-scale trains—where there is room to carry the batteries and control gear aboard the train—that this technology found a popular model-railroad application.

As with DCC, the big advantage claimed by proponents of battery-powered R/C operation is freedom. A train can run anywhere, in any direction, with little regard for other trains except to avoid collisions, without the need for track wiring or even track itself, for that matter.

As with most good things, there are some drawbacks. Even with recent improvements, batteries to power a large-scale train for any length of time are still rather large and heavy. Radio receivers and throttles also take up a surprising amount of space. In larger locomotives, there may be room for batteries and controls inside the body shell. But with smaller engines, or when sound systems and other components occupy much of the interior of the locomotive, the R/C equipment may have to be carried in a car behind the engine. This means that the locomotive never goes anywhere alone; the R/C car always trails along, with cables strung between it and the loco.

This may, at first, sound bad, but there are benefits. If you have a number of locomotives, you probably won't run all of them at once, so you only need as many R/C cars as the number of trains you want to run at any one time.

Batteries

There are also choices in batteries. Using battery chargers designed specifically for the purpose, nickel-cadmium (nicad) batteries can be "fast charged" in a few minutes, but offer relatively limited running time. Nicads also tend to loose their capacity over a number of use/charge cycles.

Sealed lead-acid batteries, or so-called gel cells, pack more electrical punch and don't lose capacity with use, but have to be charged slowly over several hours. Each type of battery has its positives and negatives, so to speak. The need for charging means that you'll either have to leave the batteries in the car or locomotive and take it out of use while the batteries charge, or take the batteries out and replace them with charged ones to continue running.

There are also systems that advertise the ability to charge batteries from power in the rails while the train is running. Because these are somewhat hybrid in nature, they offer some of the benefits of R/C, such as freedom of operation, without the need for frequent battery changing, but with some of the drawbacks of track power, such as the need to wire and clean track.

Many of the same cautions apply to battery-powered R/C as were mentioned in the previous chapter in regard to track power. Before you buy a system, ask about things like proper electrical-wave forms for your motors and/or sound systems and safeguards to prevent runaway trains.

Like DCC, radio control can also require considerable modifications to locomotives. An absolute requirement when you are giving power to the motor from a source aboard the train is to remove the connection between the motor and the track power pickups. This avoids feeding power back through the locomotive to the rails. Again, the more features you want, the more wiring there is to be done. But there are people to help you with this, as well.

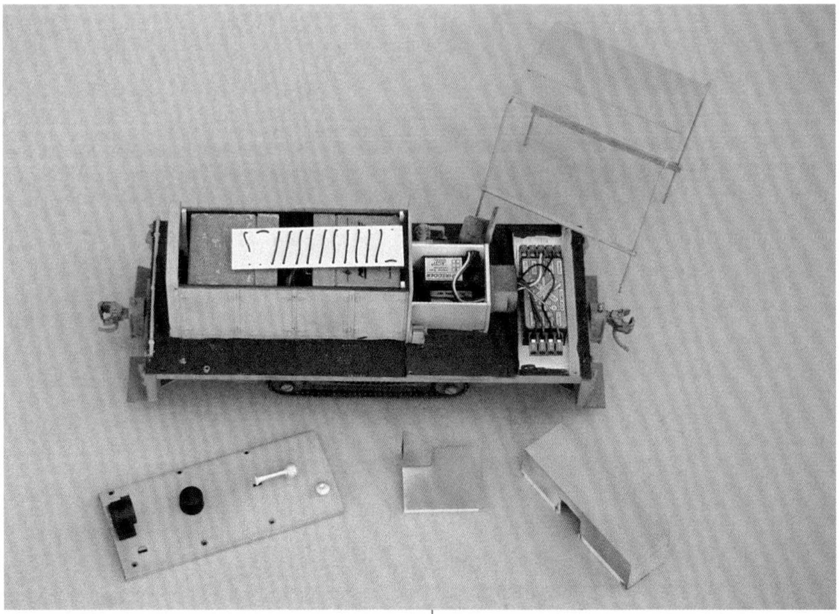

This battery-powered R/C system is carried entirely in the locomotive, in this case a modified LGB no. 20630 Rio Grande no. 50 diesel switcher. This setup uses gel-cell batteries concealed in the hood. Small boxes made from plastic sheet conceal the micro radio receiver and the throttle.

If you do decide to go with a DCC or R/C system, the choices may seem staggering at first, so do your homework. Find some people who are using a variety of systems and try them out for yourself. Talk to retailers and manufacturers about product and technical support. The more you understand about how each system compares to the others, the better equipped you'll be to decide which is best for you.

Suppliers, manufacturers, and installers

Suppliers, manufacturers, and installers of DCC and/or onboard R/C units

Aristo-Craft Trains
698 S. 21st St..
Irvington, NJ 07111-4109
Phone: 973-351-9800
Website:
http://www.aristocraft.com/aristo

Battery Backshop
18030 SW Lower Boones Ferry Road, #2
Tigard OR 97224
Phone: 503-624-7491

Digitrax, Inc.
Phone: 770-441-7992
Website: www.digitrax.com

Keithco, Inc.
POBox 1806
Lake Oswego OR 97035
Phone: 503-635-7604
Website: www.locolinc.com

LGB of America
6444 Nancy Ridge Drive
San Diego CA 92121
Phone:800-669-0607

Märklin
POBox 510559
New Berlin WI 53151
Phone: 800-825-0888
Website: www.marklin.com

Northwest Remote Control Systems
8026 NE 124th St.
Kirkland WA 98034
Phone: 425-823-3507

Power Systems Inc.
56 Bellis Circle
Cambridge MA 02140
Phone: 617-661-0660

Reed's Train Store
8039 La Mesa Boulevard
La Mesa CA 91941
Phone: 800-560-8724

Remote Control Systems
POBox 1118
Bayswater, Vic. 3153
Australia
US Phone: 800-490-6945
Website: www.alphalink.com.au/~rcs/

Getting power
to the railroad

Jim Hudson

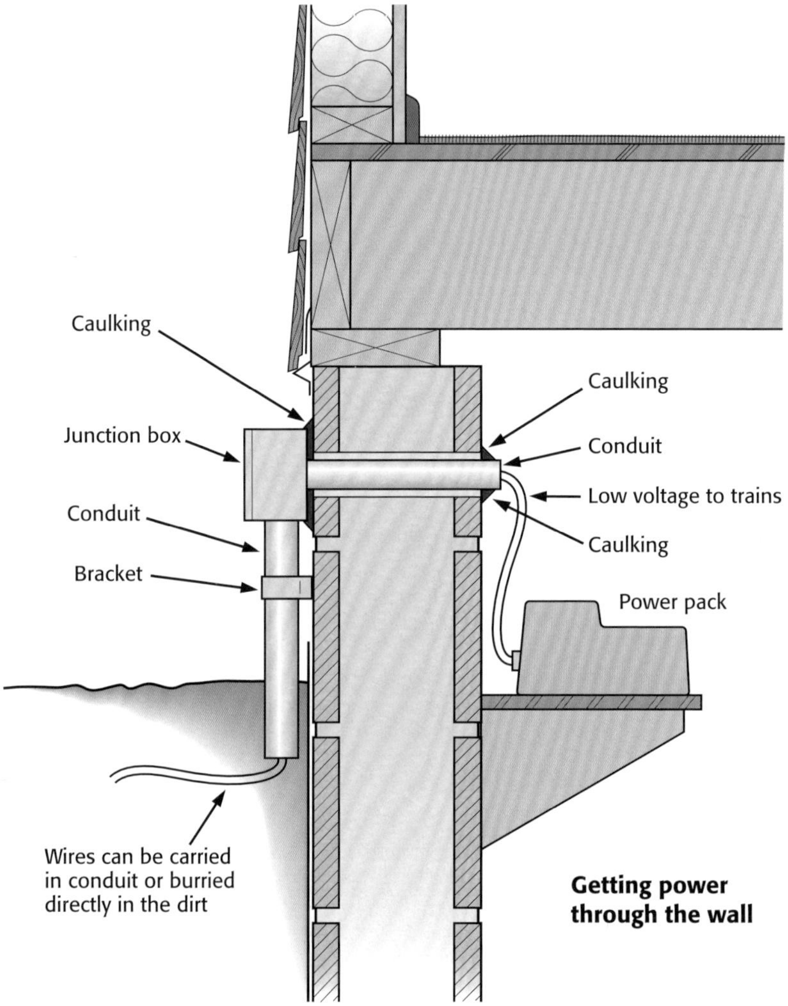

Getting power through the wall

Let's begin at the power source. The first challenge is to get stepped-down low-voltage power out of the house and into the garden. Chances are this will mean making a small hole (above ground level) through a wall to run a few wires out.

Run a short length of electrical conduit through the hole, caulk around it, and install a water-resistant electrical junction box on the outside of the wall (see drawing). Now you can pull a new wire through the conduit whenever you need to. From the junction box, extend a conduit straight down into the ground and terminate it a few inches below the surface, or extend it to or through the railway as needed.

If you need to get your wires across the backyard from the house to your garden railway, underground plastic conduit is probably the best way to go. This way, you can avoid tearing up the lawn just to run a new wire. Be sure to size the conduit larger than you think you'll ever need.

Once you reach the railroad, you have more choices. Telephone wire, bell wire, and ordinary household electrical wire are not well suited for outdoor use and should be avoided. You need something that is specifically made for direct burial in the ground, as well as exposure to the sun and temperature extremes.

I have some color-coded LGB wire on my garden railway that's been outside continuously for almost ten years with no ill effects. For longer distances or very large current requirements, check into the wire made for low-voltage landscape lighting. You can also buy Romex wire, but be sure to get the kind made for direct burial. All the landscape-lighting wire I've seen only comes in black, so you'll need to locate some decay resistant, color-code tags.

The longer the run your wire must make, the heavier the wire that you should use. A 12-gauge wire should be the heaviest required for most low-voltage applications. Try to make your runs with as few pieces of wire as possible.

I'm of the opinion that there is no substitute for a soldered connection. For heavy-gauge wire, you may need a 50 or 75-watt soldering iron or a small torch. Be sure to use only "electrical" type solder with a resin (not acid) flux.

Insulate all your connections with heat-shrink tubing, since even plastic tape tends to unravel over time. With a little care and practice, you can make a splice that you won't have to worry about, which will leave you more time to enjoy the rest of your garden railway.

Attaching the wire to the rail

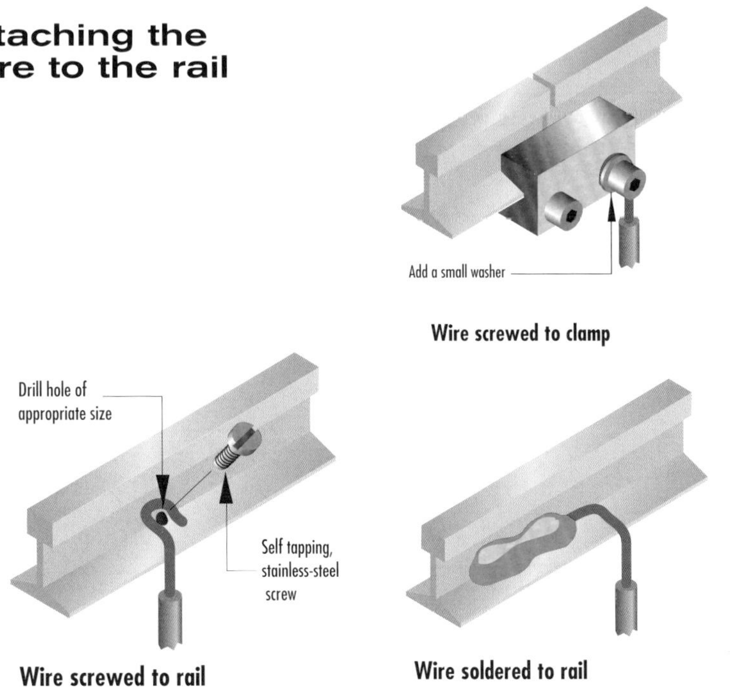

Steps in soldering a wire joint

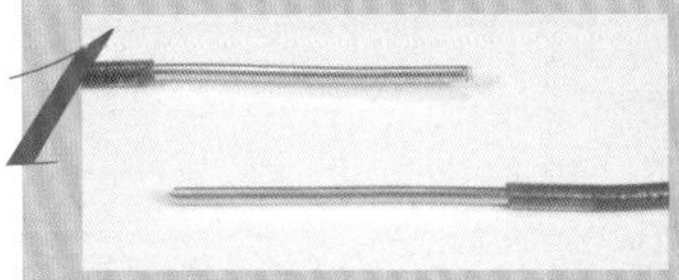

All photos by Marc Horovitz

1. Strip back the wire ends 1" or so.

2. Slip a 2" to 3" piece of heat-shrink tubing (available at Radio Shack or electronics-supply houses) over one wire and wrap the ends together.

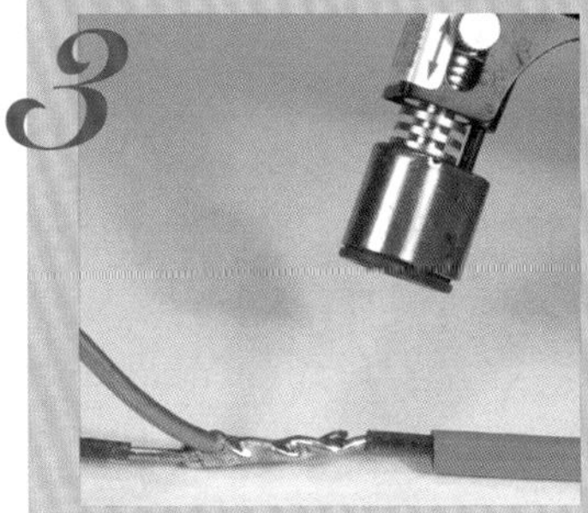

3. Apply flux to the joint, then heat the joint with either the iron or the torch. Apply the solder to the joint. The wires themselves must be hot enough to melt the solder. Don't direct the heat toward the solder. Heat one end of the joint and apply the solder to the other, letting it flow toward the heat. The finished joint should be bright and shiny. A "frosty" looking joint indicates a cold-soldered joint. Reheat the joint until the solder flows again–no need to add more.

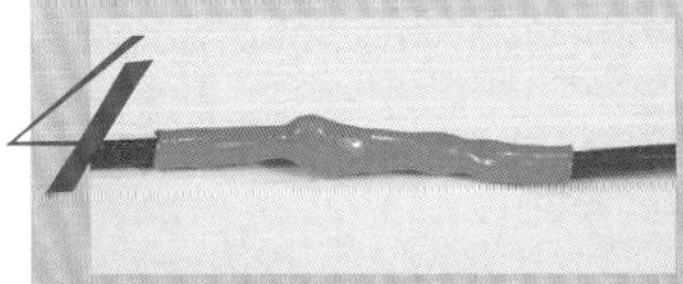

4. Slip the heat-shrink tubing over the new joint and shrink it in place with a hot-air gun, a torch, or heat from your soldering iron.

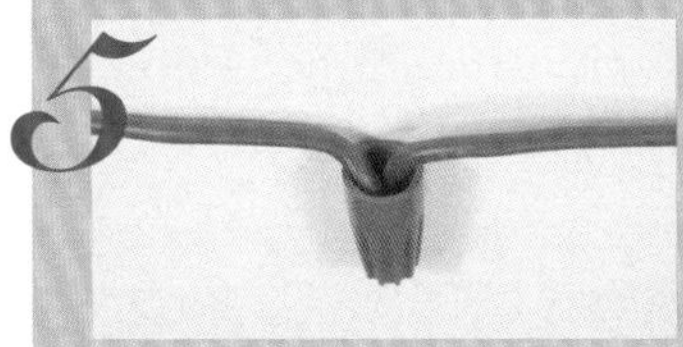

5. If you aren't up to soldering, wires can be joined with screw-on wire nuts, available at hardware stores. For burial in the ground, the nut can be filled with silicone sealer to keep out moisture.

Harnessing electrons to power your railroad

Jim Hudson

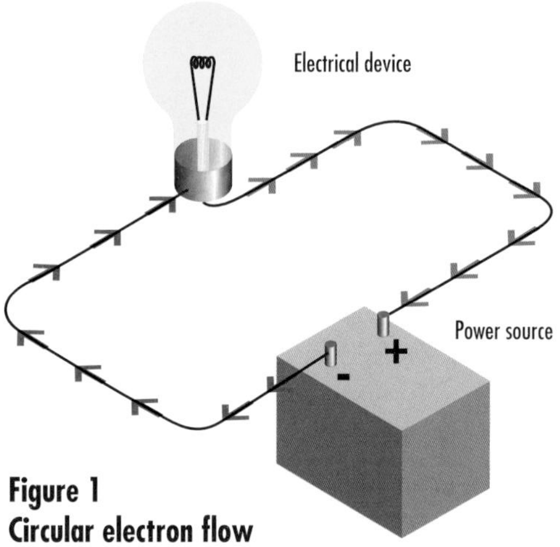

Figure 1
Circular electron flow

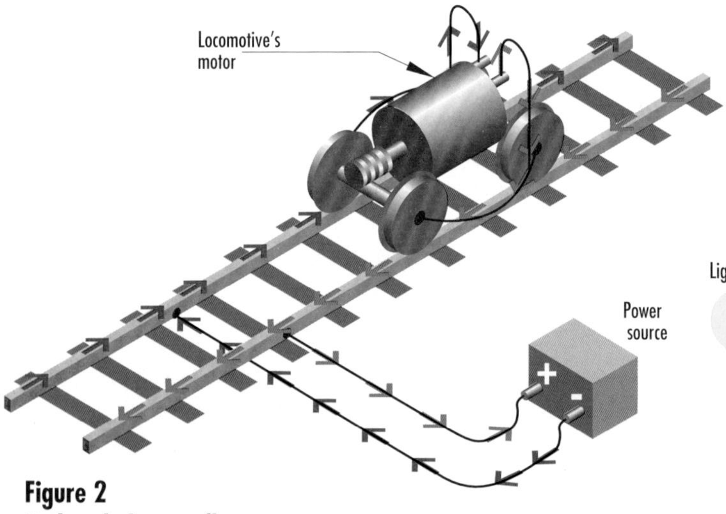

Figure 2
Railroad electron flow

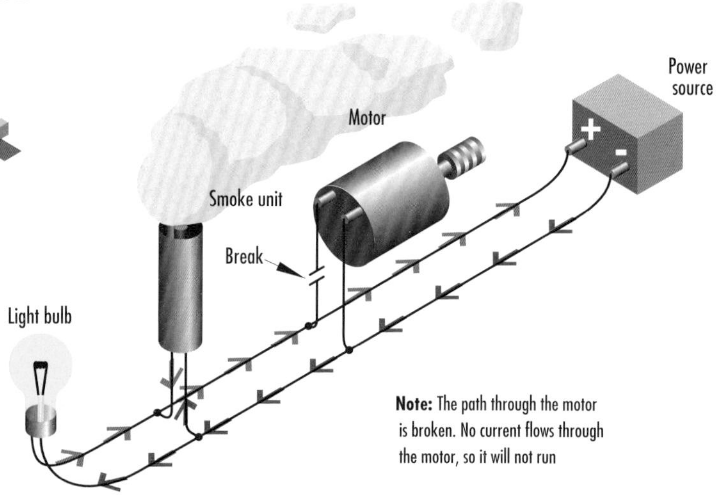

Figure 3
Electrical devices and alternate paths

Think of electricity as flowing in a circle (fig. 1), with the starting point being the power supply for your railroad. Visualize electrons flowing through one wire, to one rail, up the locomotive's electrical pickups (usually wheels or skates), and through the motor.

The path continues down through the pickups on the other side, through the opposite rail, then through the second wire back to the power supply (fig. 2).

All this happens in micro-seconds. While I've drastically oversimplified things here, when the circle is complete, the current flows. If you break the circle at any point, the current stops flowing.

The circle can also have an unlimited number of branch circles or alternate paths (fig. 3). These alternate routes can be good things, such as the several little branch circles formed by wiring for street lights in your miniature towns, or they can be bad, such as a short circuit that completes the circle when you thought you had the flow interrupted.

Rest assured, electricity works on cold, hard universal laws. If your locomotive is not running, the circular current path that should allow the electrons to flow through the motor is either interrupted somewhere, or the current is taking a shortcut (short circuit) somewhere else. Conversely, if you aren't able to stop your locomotive by flipping a switch that was supposed to do just that, there is only one conclusion—somewhere, the circle is being completed.

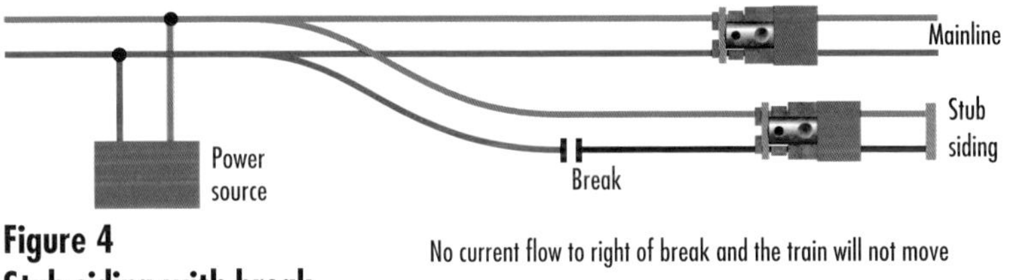

Figure 4
Stub siding with break

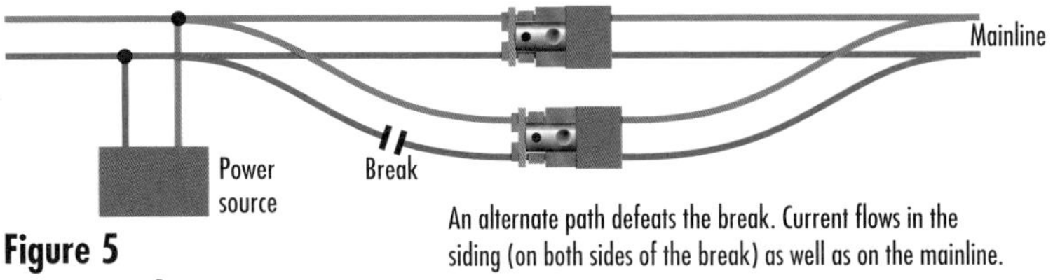

Figure 5
Passing siding

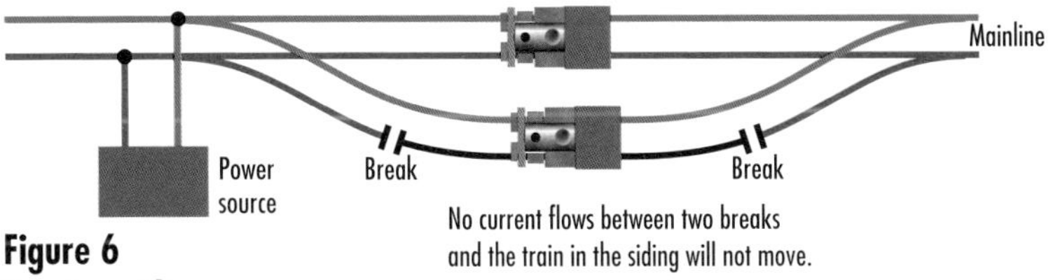

Figure 6
Passing siding

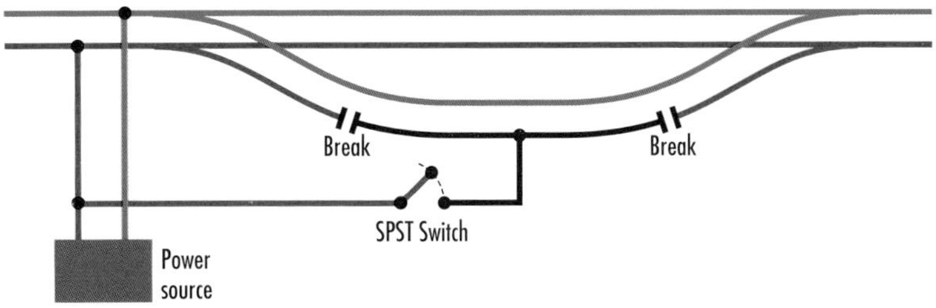

Figure 7—Wiring for a passing siding

Two-train operation

Let's take this knowledge and work towards a practical application on your railway. First, start with a **stub-ended siding.** If you make a break in one rail at the entrance to the siding, the circular current flow is interrupted to any point beyond the break (fig. 4).

A break in the rail can be made in several ways. You can simply take your hacksaw and cut through the rail, but you might want to insulate the cut rail's ends with a piece of plastic so they won't expand in the sun and touch each other.

A passing siding (a siding with a switch or turnout at both ends) adds an alternate path for the current to flow through (fig. 5), so you need to break the rail at both ends of the siding if you want to interrupt the circular current flow (fig. 6). Now you have a section of track between the two breaks where a locomotive will not run.

Of course, you need to be able to recomplete the electrical circle through the siding when you want to run a train. A couple of wires and a toggle switch will do the trick. A switch is really nothing more than a neat, formal substitute for touching two bare wire ends together. A good type of switch for this is what's called an "SPST" or "single-pole, single-throw" switch. The single-pole part means it controls just one wire. The single-throw part means it only gives you one set of choices: either "on" or "off."

Finally, it's time to put all this into practice by wiring up that siding. From the pair of wires that bring power to your main track, locate the wire that connects to the rail that has the same polarity (+ or -) as the one on the siding with the breaks. Run a branch wire off this wire to one terminal of your SPST switch. From the other switch terminal, run a wire to the isolated rail on the siding, somewhere between the breaks (fig. 7).

Done properly, this should provide one, and only one, complete current path for the siding. Turn the switch on and your train should run through the siding. Turn the switch off and the train in the siding should come to a halt.

SECTION 7

Plant hardiness

How does your garden grow?

Pat Hayward

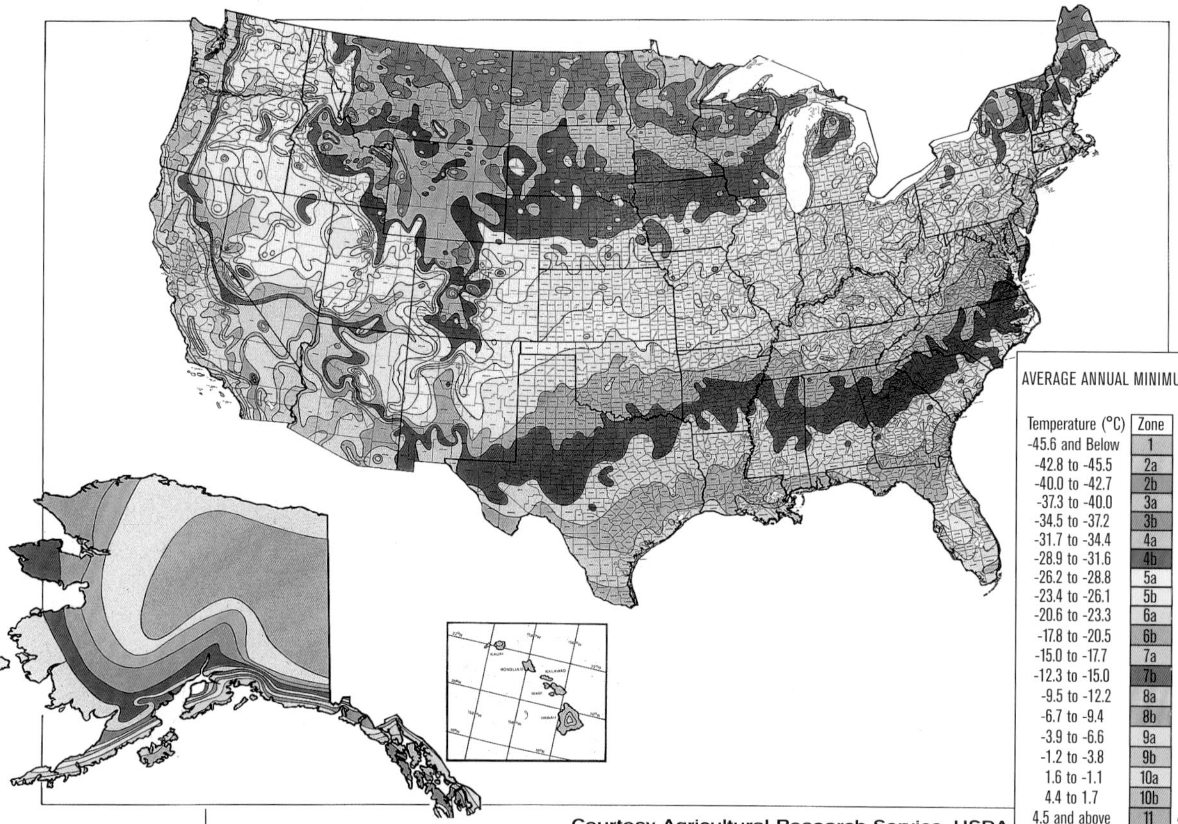

AVERAGE ANNUAL MINIMUM TEMPERATURE

Temperature (°C)	Zone	Temperature (°F)
-45.6 and Below	1	Below -50
-42.8 to -45.5	2a	-45 to -50
-40.0 to -42.7	2b	-40 to -45
-37.3 to -40.0	3a	-35 to -40
-34.5 to -37.2	3b	-30 to -35
-31.7 to -34.4	4a	-25 to -30
-28.9 to -31.6	4b	-20 to -25
-26.2 to -28.8	5a	-15 to -20
-23.4 to -26.1	5b	-10 to -15
-20.6 to -23.3	6a	-5 to -10
-17.8 to -20.5	6b	0 to -5
-15.0 to -17.7	7a	5 to 0
-12.3 to -15.0	7b	10 to 5
-9.5 to -12.2	8a	15 to 10
-6.7 to -9.4	8b	20 to 15
-3.9 to -6.6	9a	25 to 20
-1.2 to -3.8	9b	30 to 25
1.6 to -1.1	10a	35 to 30
4.4 to 1.7	10b	40 to 35
4.5 and above	11	40 and above

Courtesy Agricultural Research Service, USDA

USDA Plant Hardiness Zone Map for the United States. The lower the zone rating, the more cold hardy the plant is likely to be. Zone 11 is the only totally frost-free zone. The USDA has also developed plant hardiness zones for Canada and Mexico (these zones can be seen through the resources listed in the sidebar).

The last couple of winters have been very misleading, at least in my part of the country. Relatively warm temperatures have made many of us think our local climate is actually milder than it really is. We've begun to experiment with less hardy plants and take chances we wouldn't normally take. It's amazing how short (or selective) our memories can be. Some winter (maybe this one) we're going to get clobbered again and lose a few plants we've grown attached to.

Pat Hayward

Xeric and native plants are in abundance in my own garden because they're so well adapted to the hot, dry, windy conditions. Specialty growers are constantly offering new colors and improved varieties, such as this yellow form of Pineleaf penstemon (*P. pinifolius* 'Mersea Yellow').

In reality, we should probably always keep our eye on the big picture, the long-term climate instead of the short term. And that's where the United States Department of Agriculture's hardiness-zone map can help us make informed choices. Winter temperatures are the single most important factor in determining landscape plant survival, so when the map was first developed in 1960, the department collected minimum temperatures from 14,500 weather stations across North America. The map was then divided into 10 zones (1-10), each based on a 10°F difference in annual minimum temperature, zone 1 being the coldest and zone 10 the warmest. In 1990 it was further refined, separating each zone into two, 5° categories (a and b). They also added a zone 11 for tropical areas that never receive frost.

The zone ratings were intended to indicate excellent adaptability of the plants. Many plants may survive in warmer or colder zones, but mere survival doesn't count. They wanted these ratings to be a reliable indicator of plant hardiness for gardeners, not just technical data with little practical application. Most sources that describe garden plants (gardening books, plant catalogs, Garden Railways magazine's "Plant Portraits" column, Web sites, and so forth) use these USDA hardiness zones when offering hardiness information. (Many of the Sunset publications employ a completely different zone classification system. Check the introductions in your plant resources to verify that they are using the USDA Plant Hardiness Zone Map for their point of reference.) Hardiness zones are listed as general indicators to help you make informed decisions, especially when selecting plants that may be unfamiliar to you.

Low winter temperatures aren't the only factors that affects hardiness of your plants, however, and the map takes some of these into account. These other factors include environmental and cultural influences that can vary greatly from site to site, even within the same zone. When you really examine the question of plant hardiness, you'll find that plants are most likely to survive in garden conditions that most closely resemble their native habitats. And while some plants will only grow in a narrow range of conditions, fortunately for us there are hundreds of garden-railroad plants that are delightfully adaptable.

Some of the environmental factors that will affect plant hardiness in your own garden railroad include your soil type, drainage, soil and air temperatures, humidity, light, precipitation, fertility, and wind. To further complicate the issue, there are often different environmental climates (called microclimates) within the same garden. The most successful gardeners choose plants suited for the specific conditions their garden, rather than trying to make the garden satisfy the plants.

Every garden railroad has its own gardening challenges. In extreme climates, sometimes the easiest alternative is to find native plants or selections of native plants that offer miniature and dwarf features. These plants can often be manipulated to fit into railroad situations.

No matter where you live and garden, it's likely that the plants you're enjoying are native to many parts of the world and these same plants are hardy to more than one zone. The zone ratings are simply tools to help determine if a plant might work in your own garden. They're especially helpful when you're talking to gardeners from other parts of the country, when buying plants from out-of-state sources, or when reading plant descriptions in *Garden Railways.* They aren't absolutes; simply guidelines.

Winter temperatures may be the most critical when determining plant hardiness, but all the other environmental and cultural factors combine to create your own special microclimate. Use the zone ratings as a guide, but don't be afraid to try something new if you think it might work. As they say, sometimes it's a good thing plants don't read, because the books have been known to be wrong!

The Plant Heat Zone Map

Just as cold can be a limiting factor to plant health, so can extreme heat affect plant hardiness. The new Plant Heat Zone Map, developed by the American Horticultural Society, addresses the long-term effects that heat has on garden plants. It consists of 12 zones based on the number of "heat days" (days of over 86°F) in the region. Zone 1 has less than one heat day, while zone 12 has more than 210. Much newer than the USDA map, it will be several years before the majority of plants currently in cultivation have their designations determined. For those of you in warmer climates, this map and classification should prove to be invaluable. For more information, contact the American Horticultural Society at 800-777-7931 or visit their Plant Heat-Zone Web site at http://www.ahs.org/publications/heat_zone_map.htm

Resources

Online resource

http://www.usna.usda.gov/Hardzone/

This Web site goes into great detail on each of the environmental and cultural factors affecting plant hardiness and lists sample cities for each zone as well as sample plant lists for each zone. It contains the map for all of North America.

Print resource

The American Horticultural Society A-Z Encyclopedia of Garden Plants, DK Publishing, Inc. New York, 1996.

A healthy start

planning and planting

Pat Hayward

All photos by Joel Hayward

To understand how planning and planting affect the long-term health of your plants, first consider the future of a poorly planted tree or shrub in your railroad. It may die immediately, leading you to believe that maybe it wasn't a "good" plant to begin with. It might look sickly for weeks or even months, eventually perking up with lots of TLC, or it may die a lingering death. On the other hand, if that same healthy tree was properly planted, it might adapt to its new situation immediately, growing as if it never traveled between the nursery and into your backyard. What steps can you take to make sure all your plants turn out alive and well?

Planning and planting for a healthy start

1. Select the right plant for the right place in the garden
2. Make sure your plants are healthy from the beginning
3. Place the pots around the garden
4. Check the roots and planting mix
5. Dig the hole at the right depth
6. Set the plant in the hole and check the soil levels
7. Mix the backfill and refill the hole
8. Water the backfill when the hole is half filled
9. Fill hole to top with soil
10. Build a reservoir and water in
11. Water in again
12. Check for water needs regularly

1 A gentle tap releases the plant from its pot. These roots are healthy and vigorous.

2 Gently massage the roots away from the root ball. This allows them to grow into their new surrounding more quickly.

‹ Successful plantings begin with proper placement. Here, a staggered row of Jean's Dilly spruce trees are set in place before planting.

Good planning and planting techniques aren't complicated, they're just a result of understanding what living plants require to stay healthy. Selecting the right plant for the right place is always the first step to consider. Knowing the cultural needs (sun, water, soil type, and so forth) of your plants is usually a matter of reading the plant label, consulting a local gardening expert, or reading about their needs in books and catalogs.

Once you have a list of the plants you're interested in, go shopping. Picking plants out in person allows you the opportunity to select exactly the ones you want. If you purchase plants through mail-order or online sources, be sure to understand the company's guarantee (if any) beforehand.

Look your plants over carefully before planting them, inspecting the stems and leaves for signs of insects, diseases or stress. If roots are circling the top or bottom of the pot, the plant may be overgrown and already stressed. Stressed plants can grow into healthy specimens, but may need extra attention and care along the way.

Once you've determined your plants are healthy, set them around the garden (still in their pots) in the places where they'll eventually be planted. This step helps you visualize the new plants in place before you go through the work of planting them. Make sure all the pots are moderately moist before proceeding. If the soil is too wet, it may be too heavy to work with or may fall out in muddy clumps. If the soil's too dry, the plant will be difficult to work with and may suffer afterwards. Take this opportunity to change your mind and move the plants around until you're happy with the overall design.

Next, knock the plant out of its pot by turning it upside down and tapping the edge of the pot with your other hand. If the plant is loose in the pot, you'll want to do this gently to prevent large amounts of soil from falling out and possibly injuring the plant or its roots. If the plant is tight in the pot, tap the pot edge on a rock or other hard surface to dislodge the root ball.

At this point you'll be able to take a close look at the roots and the soil they're growing in. Are the roots loose in the soil, or are they tightly knitted and circling the root ball? Are the roots white and healthy, or are they brown and dead looking? If the roots are white and healthy, proceed to the next step. If the outer roots look unhealthy, gently shake off some of the soil until you find actively growing root tips. If still no healthy roots can be seen, it might be best to keep the plant in its container in a spot where you can care for it until new roots begin growing again.

If the roots are crowded and potbound, gently massage the root ball until you can tease the roots out and away from the tangle. Once the roots are slightly separated, they'll grow more quickly into the new surroundings.

Look carefully now at the potting mix the plant's been growing in to see how similar (or dissimilar) it is to your own garden soil. If the two are very different from each other, you may want to dig your planting hole a bit wider than if the two mixes are relatively similar. This larger hole allows you to "mediate" the situation by backfilling the planting hole with a mix that's a blend of the two soil types. My general recipe for backfill is a mixture of roughly one part excavated soil mixed with one part of the plant's potting mix.

Now that you've determined the health of the plant's root system and the soil mixes you're working with, it's time to start the actual planting process. Dig each hole only as you proceed through the garden. Even though you've already gone through the visualization process, you're

3 Build a small water reservoir around the base of the plant with your index finger.

4 Gently mound the dirt up and around the reservoir for support.

5 Fill the reservoir with water, let it drain, then fill it again.

still entitled to change your mind. The holes should be dug slightly wider (one-and-one-half to two times as wide) but no deeper than the root ball. Be sure to remove any large rocks or other objects exposed in the planting hole that may inhibit healthy root growth.

Set the root ball into the hole and determine that the soil levels of the plant and the existing garden soil are equal. Plants need to be set in the hole at (or slightly above) existing grade to ensure good air movement through the soil and down to the roots. If the hole is too deep, many of the surface roots will be covered and die from lack of oxygen. Gently refill the hole halfway with the backfill mixture and tamp in. Be sure to get rid of any large air pockets and make sure there's good contact between the root ball and the new backfill.

The plant should be watered when the backfill area is about half filled. This helps settle the soil and makes sure that the bottom half of the root ball is well-watered. Continue adding backfill until the hole is filled. Next, make a shallow reservoir by drawing a circle around the base of the plant using your index finger. Gently mound the dirt up and around this reservoir. Fill the reservoir with water and let the water soak down. After filling the reservoir a second time your plant is likely to be fully watered in. Some people believe adding root stimulators and vitamins specially formulated for planting helps plants establish more quickly. Add these at this time, if you wish.

Caring for your new plants after they're settled into your garden now is a matter of careful attention and weather watching. If it's hot and windy, they'll need more water, but if it's cool and shady, they'll need less. The best way to know when to water is to stick your finger into the base of the plant; when it's dry about 1″ down (more or less), it's time to water again. Be sure to water thoroughly, adding enough water to soak the entire root ball and the surrounding backfill. The reservoirs usually wear down naturally during that first season. If your plants seem to need extra water, keep the reservoir built up for as long as necessary. More new plants die from under-watering than from over-watering.

The rest is up to you, your plants, the weather, and whatever outside forces may enter into your garden railroad's environment. In the same way that eating a good breakfast each morning keeps you healthy and strong, starting your plants off properly will help them live a long, healthy life in your garden.

Plant portraits

Pat Hayward

Annuals

FLOSS FLOWER

Latin name: *Ageratum houstonianum*
Common name: Floss flower
Category: Annual
Plant size: 6"-8" tall, 8"-10" wide
USDA hardiness zone: Annual
Cultural needs: Sun, moderate water

A lovely, old-fashioned bedding plant, floss flower has many attributes that appeal to garden railroaders. Blooming all summer long, this easy-to-grow annual comes in many shades of blue, lavender, pink, and cream or white. In full sun and under dry conditions the plants stay shorter and more compact, but they also provide color in semi-shaded spots. The tiny, feathery blossoms are borne in clusters, new flowers covering up and replacing old ones all season long. Try planting floss flowers amidst small-leaved groundcovers where the slightly out-of-scale foliage can be hidden from view. Grow from seed or purchase in the spring as a bedding plant.

Joel Hayward

DWARF CONIFERS
DWARF ALBERTA SPRUCE

Latin name: *Picea glauca* 'Conica'
Common name: Dwarf Alberta spruce
Category: Dwarf conifer
Needle color: Bright green
Growth rate: 3"-4"/yr
USDA hardiness zone: 3-8
Cultural needs: Sun to part shade, moderate water

This dwarf spruce, originally found in a native stand of white spruce in Alberta, Canada, is today possibly the most popular garden-railroad "forest tree" in use. Evergreen, its tiny needles are less than ½" long. Dense, slow growth makes naturalistic pruning easy, even for the beginner, and the lower trunks can often be exposed to create a more natural, "treelike" appearance. Its name comes from its tight conical shape. Very cold-hardy, but gardeners in southern climes should protect these tiny trees from hot, drying conditions in the heat of summer. Western gardeners may need to protect them from winter sun when young.

Pat Hayward

Pat Hayward

DWARF CANADIAN HEMLOCK

Latin name: *Tsuga canadensis* 'Jervis'
Common name: Dwarf Canadian hemlock
Category: Dwarf conifer
Leaf color: Dark green
Growth rate: 1"-2" per year
USDA hardiness zone: 4-8
Cultural needs: Shade, moderate water, rich soil

Hemlocks are normally thought of as towering forest trees, but 'Jervis' is a variety that has been selected for its extremely slow growth and compact habit. Growing at about an inch or two a year, it will take years to outgrow the scale of a garden railroad. Regular moisture, rich soil, and a shaded spot will keep 'Jervis' healthy. The tiny, evergreen needles provide rich color all year long and the congested, upright growth habit can add a nice accent to a winter or summer railroad. This picture shows the fresh, light green of new spring growth on a young plant. Older examples of 'Jervis' can be selectively pruned to create a weathered, natural look.

DWARF IRISH JUNIPER

Pat Hayward

Latin name: *Juniperus communis* 'Compressa'
Common name: Dwarf Irish juniper
Category: Dwarf conifer
Needle color: Blue green
Growth rate: 1"-3"/yr.
USDA hardiness zone: 5-9
Cultural needs: Sun and well-drained soil

This upright and very narrow form of common juniper is a perfect complement to garden-railroad designs because of its distinctive form and small-scale features. Narrow, sharply pointed, blue-green needles are less than ½" long. Often referred to as a garden "exclamation point," this unique dwarf conifer adds a striking vertical accent when placed in small groups or in contrast to mounding or spreading railroad plants. 'Compressa' grows very slowly in most areas, and will stay tight and narrow when growing in full sun. Shaded sites may lead to faster growth and a more open habit. 'Sentinel' and 'Pencil Point' are two more similar cultivars that can also add verticality to a garden railroad.

Groundcovers

Pat Hayward

LIVING ASTROTURF

Latin name: *Bolax gummifera* 'Nana'
Common name: "Living Astro-turf"
Category: Groundcover
Flower color: Light yellow
Height: about 2"
USDA hardiness zone: 5-8
Cultural needs: Sun with well-drained soil

One touch of this low-growing groundcover and you may find it hard to believe it's real! The waxy, bright-green leaves form extremely tight rosettes as the plant spreads outward. Its common name, "living Astro-turf," describes it perfectly. It is a slow growing, rock-garden-type plant that needs well-drained soil to be at its best. Small-scale leaves and tiny flowers make it perfect for small garden-railroad "lawns" or other areas where a non-invasive groundcover is needed. This Bolax can survive in colder climates but may need snow cover or other protection to make it through harsh winters. It is somewhat rare at garden centers, but can usually be found through rock-garden or other specialty nurseries.

BLUE RUG JUNIPER

Pat Hayward

Latin name: *Juniperus horizontalis* 'Wiltoni'
Common name: Blue rug juniper
Category: Groundcover
Leaf color: Blue
Plant size: 4" tall x 6" wide
USDA hardiness zone: 3-9
Cultural needs: Full sun, moderate to dry soil

From the hundreds of juniper varieties to choose from, 'Wiltoni' is among the very best for garden railroads. Appropriately named for its tendency to stay tight and low to the ground, blue rug will form a carpet of silvery blue that's attractive all year long. Even the tiny needles are in scale with a railroad setting. As with most junipers, this is an easy-care plant that will continue to grow and spread for many years. As it becomes larger, it is easily kept in check with a pair of pruners—simply cut back the oldest, longest branches first and let the new, fresh growth take its place.

BLUE STAR CREEPER

Pat Hayward

Latin name: *Laurentia fluviatilis*
Common name: Blue Star Creeper
Category: Groundcover
Flower color: Light blue
Height: about 1"
USDA hardiness zone: 5-7
Cultural needs: Sun to part shade, moderate water

Native to Australia and New Zealand, this fast-spreading groundcover is perfect for the garden railroad, with its small (½"), round leaves and tiny, star-shaped flowers. In semi-shady areas with good moisture it will spread rapidly and grow up to 1" tall. Hotter, sunnier conditions cause it to form a slower-growing, tight mat with fewer flowers. Light blue, star-shaped blossoms appear in late spring. This perennial groundcover can take light foot traffic but may need winter protection (such as a light mulch) in colder climates. Easily divided by sections; simply dig up a piece that includes some healthy roots and transplant, being sure to keep both the original and new plants well-watered until established.

CREEPING PHLOX

Latin name: *Phlox subulata*
Common name: Creeping phlox
Category: Groundcover
Flower color: Pastels (blue, pink, white)
Plant size: 2"-6" tall x 12"-20" wide
USDA hardiness zone: 3-8
Cultural needs: Sun, moderate water

Joel Hayward

Many spring gardens would seem incomplete without the cheerful blossoms of creeping phlox. This low-growing, evergreen, perennial groundcover is easy to grow and fits well into the scale of a garden railroad. Try interplanting creeping phlox with spring bulbs, such as dwarf daffodils, to create a colorful spring display. The ¾"-long leaves are narrow and needle-like, and stay tidy-looking even when the plant is out of bloom. Though an adaptable plant, it prefers at least six hours of sun, moderate water, and normal garden-soil conditions. Creeping phlox can also be quite vigorous, so give it room to grow. For a smaller plant, try pruning it back after blooming or choose a more compact variety.

DRAGON'S BLOOD SEDUM

Pat Hayward

Latin name: *Sedum spurium* 'Dragon's Blood'
Common name: Dragon's blood sedum
Category: Groundcover
Flower color: Rose red
Plant size: 2"-4" tall x 18"-24"
USDA hardiness zone: 3-10
Cultural needs: Full sun, moderate to low water

Sometimes you really need a vigorous groundcover to cover a lot of space quickly. Dragon's blood sedum is one of the best for quick cover and easy care. Extremely adaptable, it tolerates most kinds of soil and can take fairly harsh, dry conditions because of its succulent leaves and stems. Rosy red flowers are produced in early summer, but should be removed as soon as they begin to fade in order to keep the plant tight and compact. It is also easy to propagate from divisions and stem cuttings. (This green-leaved form gets its name from dragons, which supposedly have green blood.) It is often confused with the red-leaved form called 'Red Carpet'.

GOLDEN CREEPING JENNY

Pat Hayward

Latin name: *Lysimachia nummularia* 'Aurea'
Common name: Golden creeping Jenny
Category: Groundcover
Flower color: Yellow
Plant size: 2" tall and spreading
USDA hardiness zone: 4-8
Cultural needs: Full to part shade

It's amazing how golden plants can brighten up dark corners and shady spots in a garden railroad. Also known as golden moneywort, this groundcover may be too vigorous if placed in the railroad itself, but it makes a wonderful transition plant between the railroad and the rest of the yard or garden. A few plants will cover a large area in a short time, given good soil and regular waterings. Golden creeping Jenny should be shaded from the hot afternoon sun, preferring morning sun or filtered shade. As it spreads, the stems will set roots so it can be easily divided. Yellow buttercup-like flowers will appear in summer. It can also be used as a submerged water plant.

HENS AND CHICKS

Pat Hayward

Latin name: *Sempervivum* sp.
Common name: Hens-and-chicks
Category: Groundcover
Flower color: Pink, yellow, or white
Leaf color: Varies
Plant size: 1"-3" tall x 2"-12" wide
USDA hardiness zone: 4-10
Cultural needs: Full sun, dry conditions once established

Perfect for rock walls and steep inclines, these succulent spreaders grow best in the toughest conditions. They're called hens-and-chicks because tiny offsets, or "chicks," surround the mother plant, or "hen." Historically known as houseleeks, these fast growers often rooted in thatched roofs of old England. There are many forms of "semps," ranging from bright green to silvery grey to blood red. Though grown for their attractive foliage and hardiness, spikes of flowers are produced in summer. After flowering, the original rosette will die, but is quickly replaced as the younger plants mature. They're easy to divide—just pull off a "chick" and replant. Keep new plants well-watered until established.

IRISH MOSS

Pat Hayward

Latin name: *Sagina subulata*
Common name: Irish moss
Category: Groundcover
Flower color: White
Plant size: 1½" tall x 8" wide
USDA hardiness zone: 4-7
Cultural needs: Sun to part shade, moderate water, well-drained soil

Garden-railroad meadows and hillsides are often covered in a carpet of green with extensive plantings of Irish moss. A dense groundcover that often stays under 1" tall, this relative of the carnation family is also known as pearlwort. It can grow in full sun with lots of water, but prefers partial shade, and must have good drainage in any situation. In summer the tiny, white, star-shaped flowers appear, less than ⅛" across, arising from the dense growth of the foliage. The miniature, needle-like leaves are almost spiky to the touch. Irish moss can also be used to depict lush lawns around residential areas in the railroad, but won't take real-life human foot traffic.

MT. ATLAS DAISY

Latin name: *Anacyclus pyrethrum* var. depressus
Common name: Mt. Atlas daisy
Category: Groundcover
Plant size: 3" tall x 10" wide
USDA hardiness zone: 4-8
Cultural needs: Adaptable

The rich green, finely cut leaves of Mt. Atlas daisy can form an almost-ferny groundcover for the middle areas of a garden railroad. This very-low-growing groundcover prefers a sunny site and can tolerate low-water conditions if necessary. It can even withstand a bit of foot traffic now and then. In early summer, 1" wide x 3" tall white daisies will appear for several months—you can leave these on to enjoy, or cut them off for a more scale-appropriate look. The flowers fold up at dusk, revealing beautiful red stripes on the undersides of the petals. Mt. Atlas spreads fairly rapidly, but can be divided or kept in check by gently pulling up rooted sections.

Pat Hayward

PARTRIDGE FEATHER

Latin name: *Tanacetum densum* var. amani
Common name: Partridge feather
Category: Groundcover
Flower color: Yellow
Plant size: 4" tall x 15" wide
USDA hardiness zone: 4-8
Cultural needs: Dry soil, full sun

Feathery gray leaves give this plant its common name of "partridge feather." Native to the mountains of Turkey, this hardy plant endures some of the harshest conditions. It thrives in very hot, sunny spots and prefers little water once established. The finely cut, silvery leaves hold their color most of the year. Yellow, button-like blossoms will appear in mid-summer, but should be cut back to keep the plant in scale with the rest of the railroad garden. It's best used as a groundcover in less scale-sensitive areas. Propagate from stem or root pieces or buy young plants in spring.

Pat Hayward

Pat Hayward

WIRE PLANT

Latin name: *Muehlenbeckia axillaris*
Common name: Wire plant
Category: Groundcover
Leaf color: Glossy green
Plant size: 2"-4" tall x 12"-15"+ wide
USDA hardiness zone: 6-10
Cultural needs: Well-drained soil, moderate moisture, full sun

This diminutive member of the bistort family, with its tiny leaves, minuscule flowers, and slender stems, can be a perfect groundcover for garden railroads. Wire plant is similar to baby tears, but on a slightly larger scale. When planted in sandy, well drained, and slightly acidic soil, this miniature groundcover can be quite vigorous, while heavier soils will slow its growth rate. Good drainage is a must. Rounded, glossy, green leaves, barely ¼" long, are attached to reddish, wiry stems. In warmer climates, wire plant will be somewhat evergreen, but in colder areas it will die back when frosts begin. It's also easy to propagate by division or stem cuttings.

WOOLLY VERONICA

Pat Hayward

Latin name: *Veronica pectinata*
Common name: Woolly veronica
Category: Groundcover
Flower color: Blue
Plant size: 1" tall x 14" wide
USDA hardiness zone: 3-8
Cultural needs: Sun, adaptable

Among the groundcover veronicas, the woolly variety is one of the very best. The bright blue flowers in early summer last for several weeks, and the gray-green, fuzzy foliage is nearly evergreen. Perfect for rock walls and slopes, woolly veronica will root along as it grows. This wonderful plant stays tight and compact in situations with full sun and can tolerate fairly dry conditions once established. Shear the flowers off after blooming for a neater appearance. Woolly veronica is easily propagated from cuttings stuck in sand or by division. A pink woolly veronica (*V. pectinata* 'Rosea') is also available.

Perennials

ALPINE STORKSBILL

Pat Hayward

Latin name: *Erodium reichardii*
Common name: Alpine storksbill
Category: Perennial
Flower color: Pink
Height: 2"-3" tall x 6" wide
USDA hardiness zone: 6-9
Cultural needs: Sun, moderate water, well-drained soil

Realistic flowering plants for garden railroads that stay small are often difficult to find. This Mediterranean alpine plant forms a perfect, slightly spreading mound, easily representing a wonderfully proportioned, scale-sized shrub in a miniature landscape. The tiny pink flowers are less than ½" wide and resemble miniature geraniums. It blooms practically all summer, but even when not in bloom the gently scalloped leaves are a rich green and are attractive nearly year round. Also known as alpine geranium, this perennial needs at least part-day sun and a well-drained soil for long life. The name "storksbill" comes from the shape of the seed capsule when ripening. It may survive in colder climates with extra mulch for winter protection.

CYPRESS SPURGE

Latin name: *Euphorbia cyparrisias*
Common name: Cypress spurge, poor-man's pine
Category: Perennial
Flower color: Greenish-yellow
Plant size: 8"-12" x 12"-18"
USDA hardiness zone: 5-10
Cultural needs: Adaptable

Even garden railroaders with brown thumbs can grow this easy, fast-spreading perennial. Though adaptable to most gardens, it prefers sunny, dry conditions. Cypress spurge spreads by underground runners and can be left to grow naturally, providing a taller groundcover. It can also be pruned up several inches to simulate soft, garden-railroad-scale evergreen trees (hence the other name, "poor-man's pine"). Semi-evergreen, this plant provides year-round interest and texture in milder climates. Producing insignificant greenish-yellow flowers in late spring, this North American native is related to poinsettias. Those with sensitive skin should wear gloves when working with spurge relatives, as the leaves contain a milky sap that can sometimes be irritating.

Pat Hayward

DWARF LAVENDER COTTON

Latin name: *Santolina chamaecyparissus* 'Nana'
Common name: Dwarf lavender cotton
Category: Perennial
Leaf color: Silvery gray
Plant size: 8-10" tall x 18" wide
USDA hardiness zone: 4-9
Cultural needs: Full sun, well-drained soil

Silver is a soothing color in any garden and dwarf lavender cotton is one of the best silver-gray plants for garden railroaders. This shrubby perennial has stiff, upright stems and feathery, gray leaves. It usually forms a dense mound, but can be pruned out for a more open effect. The yellow button-like flowers that begin to emerge in early summer should be removed before opening to keep the plant more compact. Full sun and drier conditions will keep this plant at its best. Propagation is done by stem cuttings in sand and can take 6-8 weeks to root. There is also a larger, green-leaved form of this perennial, *Santolina rosmarinifolia.*

Pat Hayward

SEA PINKS

Latin name: *Armeria* spp
Common name: Sea pinks
Category: Perennial
Flower color: Pink, white
Plant size: 3"-8" tall x 5"-10" wide
USDA hardiness zone: 4-9
Cultural needs: Sun, adaptable

Sea pinks are one of the easiest perennial plants for garden railroaders to grow. They require little care and seem to tolerate a wide range of conditions. The tufts of tiny grass-like leaves are practically evergreen, and little pom-pon-like flowers appear in early summer for several weeks. The more common species, *A. maritima,* grows to about 8" tall in bloom and to about 10" wide at maturity. *A. rubrifolia* is a red-leaved version with pink flowers. Another species *(A. caespitosa)* is much tinier and even more in scale, barely 3" tall in bloom! 'Victor Reiter' is a miniature version with pink blossoms, and 'Alba' is a delightful white.

Pat Hayward

TUSSOCK BELLFLOWER

Latin name: *Campanula carpatica*
Common name: Tussock bellflower
Category: Perennial
Flower color: Blue or white
Plant size: 6"-8" tall x 12"-15" wide
USDA hardiness zone: 4-8
Cultural needs: Full sun to part shade, moderate water

Long flowering and easy to grow, taller bluebells and bellflowers are common perennial-garden plants. There are also many smaller species of bellflower that make excellent railroad-garden plants. Tussock bellflower grows small enough for the railroad, but large enough for human-scale plantings and provides summer-long color in the middle areas of the garden railroad. Emerald-green leaves stay tufted and low until blooming begins in early summer. Sunny locations help keep the plants compact, but the flowers are still abundant in partial shade. When blossoms begin to fade, cut the plant back to the lowest leaves to keep it tight and full.

Pat Hayward

YELLOW PINELEAF PENSTEMON

Latin name: *Penstemon pinifolius* 'Mersea Yellow'
Common name: Yellow pineleaf penstemon
Category: Perennial
Flower color: Yellow
Plant size: 12" tall x 24" wide
USDA hardiness zone: 4-9
Cultural needs: Sunny and dry

For garden railroaders who enjoy color, pineleaf penstemon produces an abundance of small, lemony yellow, tubular blossoms that last for more than a month through early summer. The tiny leaves are narrow, needle-like and evergreen, offering small-scale interest all year long. After blooming, the old flowers should be removed and the plant cut back to about 4" tall. Fresh, new leaves will quickly fill back in. As the branches become woody with age, the plant can be pruned up into interesting forms. This Southwestern-native plant prefers very hot, sunny, and dry conditions.

Pat Hayward

Pat Hayward

AZALEA

Latin name: *Rhododendron* sp.
Common name: Azalea
Category: Shrub and small trees
Leaf color: Green
Plant size: Variable
USDA hardiness zone: 3-10
Cultural needs: Acid soil, part shade, moderate water

Though there are hundreds of varieties of azaleas to choose from, there are some wonderful cultivars that make delightful small-scale trees when properly pruned. Look for those with small leaves, fine branching, and small flowers. For a tree effect like the photo, choose plants with a strong central stem and prune to shape. Azaleas produce showy (though often out-of-scale) blossoms for a few weeks in spring, then are covered with medium-sized green leaves throughout the growing season. Related to rhododendrons (which hold their leaves through winter), azaleas are deciduous (they lose their leaves) and can re-create the effect of a full-size shade tree throughout the seasons.

DWARF BOX-LEAVED HOLLY

Latin name: *Ilex crenata* cultivars
Common name: Dwarf box-leaved holly
Category: Shrubs & small trees
Leaf color: Dark green
Plant size: 1'-2' tall x 1'-2' wide without pruning
USDA hardiness zone: 6-10
Cultural needs: Full sun, moderate water

Specialty growers of miniature and bonsai plants offer several varieties of dwarf box-leaved (or Japanese) holly. With leaves barely ⅛" wide and 3⁄16" long, these evergreen shrubs are perfect for trimming into miniature trees for the garden railroad. Slow growing and easy to care for, these tough little shrubs thrive in the heat of the South as well as in more temperate climates. For single-trunked trees, chose plants with a strong central stem and trim out excess leaves along the main stem. 'Beehive', 'Convexa', 'Dwarf Pagoda', 'Green Dragon', and 'Mariesii' are all excellent varieties to choose from.

Pat Hayward

Pat Hayward

DWARF ENGLISH BOXWOOD

Latin name: *Buxus sempervirens* cultivars
Common name: Dwarf English boxwood
Category: Shrubs and small trees
Plant size: 3'-5' tall x 3'-5' wide
USDA hardiness zone: 4-9, depending on cultivar
Cultural needs: Part shade to full sun, moderate water, well-drained soil

Need a leafy evergreen tree with small leaves for your railroad? Several varieties of dwarf English boxwood exist, and all can be easily pruned to most any shape you want. Rounded, bright-green leaves adorn the branches year round, providing excellent winter color in most areas. For best results, provide plenty of organic matter for acidity and drainage, and keep the plants evenly moist. 'Green Mountain' and 'Green Velvet' are both slow-growing forms that were bred to be particularly cold-hardy. Prune and shape your trees in late spring, just after the new leaves have appeared, but while the stems and leaves are still "soft."

GOLDEN JAPANESE BARBERRY

Pat Hayward

Latin name: *Berberis thunbergii* cvs.
Common name: Golden Japanese barberry
Category: Shrub
Leaf color: Gold to chartreuse
Plant size: 3' x 3' untrimmed
USDA hardiness zone: 4-8
Cultural needs: Moderate sun and water

Nothing lights up a garden like white or golden plants, and these new barberry selections are perfect candidates for many railway gardeners. Several golden varieties, including 'Aurea', 'Bonanza Gold', and 'Sunsation' are now available at local nurseries and garden centers. Slower-growing than their green and red relatives, golden barberries will stay in scale for years to come in most garden railroads. New leaves are golden to lemon yellow, often fading to greenish-yellow as they mature. Like all Japanese barberries, the golden varieties have small, round leaves and tiny, prickly thorns on the stems. Full sun will help brighten color, but too much may cause leaf burn. Fall color is orange.

Water plants

Pat Hayward

VARIEGATED SWEET FLAG

Latin name: *Acorus gramineus* 'Variegatus'
Common name: Variegated sweet flag
Category: Water plant
Leaf color: Green-and-white striped
Plant size: 10"-12" tall x 14"-16" wide
USDA hardiness zone: 5-10
Cultural needs: Part sun, wet soil

Water features, such as ponds and streams, benefit from living plants to help aerate and clean the water for fish and other living organisms. Variegated sweet flag is a beautiful, grass-like plant that's easy to grow and loves wet feet. It can be planted in the shallows of a stream or kept in a pot and set into gravel on a ledge in a pool or container of water. Morning or afternoon sun will keep the slender, variegated leaves bright and colorful, but too much sun may cause them to burn. It may also be grown in a garden setting, but needs access to plenty of moisture.

WATER HYACINTH

Joel Hayward

Latin name: *Eichhornia crassipes*
Common name: Water hyacinth
Category: Water plants
Flower color: Lavender
Plant size: 6"-8" wide x 4"-6" tall
USDA hardiness zone: 10
Cultural needs: Freestanding water, full sun

Any garden-railway pond should have a few water hyacinths floating lazily on the surface. Like most floating plants, water hyacinths are easy to care for. They multiply rapidly and help reduce algae growth by shading the pond's surface. During warm weather, 6"-tall spikes of showy lavender flowers rise above the swollen leaves. Long roots dangle below the leaves, absorbing nutrients directly from the water. Native to tropical South America, this tender plant should be brought indoors during cold weather, or simply be replaced each year. Water hyacinths prefer to live in still or very slow-moving water, but should be kept out of natural ponds or streams because they multiply so rapidly.

SECTION 8

Track maintenance basics

Jim Hudson

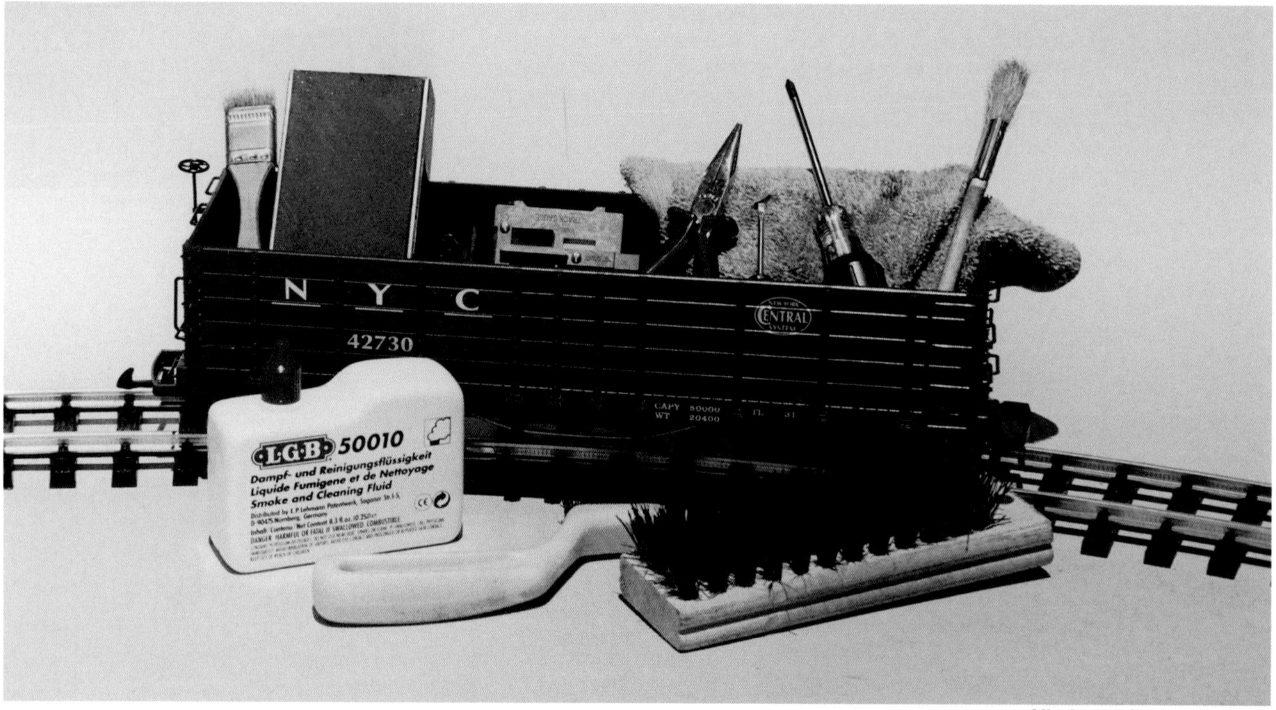

All photos by Jim Hudson

To sum up my feelings on track maintenance, let me paraphrase a popular bumper sticker: "The worst day garden railroading is better than the best day working." Even a seemingly dreary task is still an opportunity to do something with my trains. Fortunately, the track I put down almost 10 years ago is still perfectly serviceable. Only some weed trimming and track cleaning is needed to put things back in operation, even after a couple of months of inactivity.

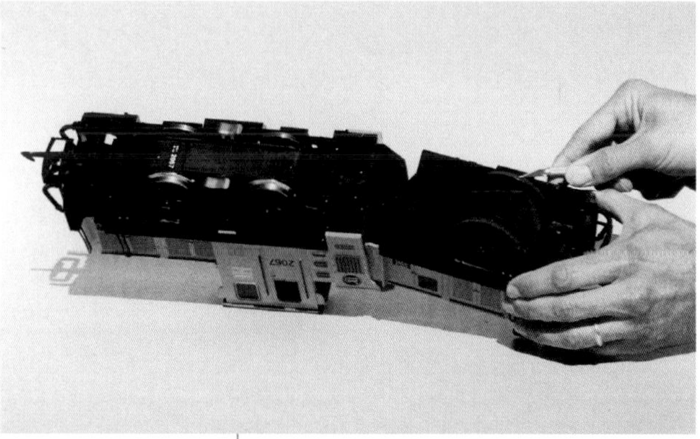

<< A gondola serves as a test car to roll along the track. It's also a convenient carrying tray for basic track-maintenance tools: smoke fluid, track-cleaning block, scrub brush for removing leaves and dirt, small paintbrushes, track gauge, pliers, Phillips and flat-blade screwdrivers, and an old rag.

^ LGB no. 20670 track-cleaning locomotive. The cleaning wheels can be saturated with smoke fluid for easier cleaning.

Ties

I chose LGB track for my railroad and have never regretted it. The brass rails and ultraviolet (UV) stabilized plastic have endured well. A few garden-railroad friends have told me less happy stories, particularly about plastic ties that weren't quite so UV-resistant. Their ties warped, broke, or simply turned to powder after a couple years in the intense Southwestern sun. Ultraviolet damage seems to be the worst, as it weakens the plastic, leaving it susceptible to the other types of damage.

You may find that painting the ties with a plastic-compatible paint helps to protect them from the sun's harmful effects. And while you're down there, take along a track gauge and check the rail spacing. Ties tend to warp upwards at the ends from heat, bringing the rails closer together. If you used screws to fasten the ties to wooden roadbed, the problem is multiplied.

If you handlaid your track, spiking rails to wood ties, you will definitely need to restain or paint those ties occasionally to keep them from disintegrating. As on a full-size railroad, spikes can work loose from the ties due to stress and movement of the rails, so you'll also need to check them and push down any loose ones.

Rails

If you keep your rails clean, you have most of the battle won in keeping your trains running smoothly.

While things like sandpaper, steel wool, and grinding stones will certainly remove dirt and oxidation in short order, they can cause a great deal of damage. Any cleaning substance harder than the rail material itself will leave scratches in the rails. You may barely be able to see the scratches, but they are perfect places for more dirt to build up, meaning you'll be cleaning track again even sooner.

Steel wool has a nasty habit of dropping fine steel fibers that quickly find their way into anything magnetic, like locomotive motors, switch machines, and track contacts. If you've already used steel wool on your track, I suggest finding the largest magnet you can and passing it over the entire length of your track to pick up any fibers. Follow this with a heavy rinse from the garden hose to wash away anything still left behind. Give all your rolling stock the magnet treatment as well, before running any trains on the cleaned track.

Other things to avoid include most chemicals. In my experience, alcohol will clean the track for a while, but after a time it seems to contribute to the formation of a non-conductive oxide on the rail surface.

There are, however, some chemical options that are good for rail cleaning. A product called "RailZip," made by Pacer Technologies, seems to work pretty well, not for actually cleaning the rail but for enhancing conductivity. My favorite cleaning chemical is good old LGB no. 50010 Smoke and Cleaning Fluid. Put a few drops on the rails and wipe them down with a soft cloth. This will remove light oxidation and dirt. Be sure to wipe the rails dry so your locomotives don't spin their wheels.

In the harsh world of the garden railway, you will soon need to move on to stronger cleaning methods. Aristo-Craft offers a track-cleaning car with a rubberized abrasive pad underneath. LGB's no. 50050 track-cleaning attachment uses a spring-loaded cleaning pad for each rail and can be installed on a number of different cars. I've also seen simple blocks of Masonite hardboard mounted under cars, with the rough back side riding on the rails.

All of these options work on the same principle. A very mild abrasive passed over the track many times will help to keep the rails clean.

For heavier dirt and oxidation, you'll need something with a bit more dirtbusting muscle. LGB's no. 50040 track-cleaning block uses a larger pad of the same rubberized abrasive material as the cleaning attachment. Most hobby shops will also carry a Bright Boy, which looks like a big, flat ink eraser. 3M's ScotchBrite dishscrubbing pads are non-metallic and seem pretty safe to use, but you'll need to use a leaf blower or garden hose to get rid of all the tiny fibers left behind.

If you have a larger railroad, or just want a better weapon with which to wage war on dirty track, take a look at LGB's no. 20670 track-cleaning locomotive. This will clean your track more evenly, more rapidly, and more completely than you will ever do in hours of hand scrubbing. There's nothing quite like the sight of a train running smoothly on clean track.

Maintenance of way

Jim Hudson

All photos by Jim Hudson

MOW. While those three letters may well refer to what you need to do to the lawn this weekend, MOW in railroad parlance stands for Maintenance-Of-Way. Full-size railroads employ armies of people and equipment to keep their physical plants in good shape. Your garden railroad may be similar in its needs, if only on a smaller scale. One thing is fairly certain, though—virtually every part of your garden railway system will need some form of maintenance. Locomotives, cars, track, structures, plants—they all need a little attention now and then.

« People from the southeastern part of the U.S. will immediately think of the dreaded, fast-spreading Kudzu plant, which has been rumored to swallow up train tracks. A few months of neglect and some invasive groundcover are the main ingredients needed to re-create the scene on a garden railway.

‹ An LGB container on a flatcar served as the starting point for this creation, a hedge-trimmer car. Model-airplane propellers fastened to locomotive motors do the work. Power is provided by either two or three of the standard, six-cell, rechargeable, nicad battery packs used to power radio-controlled cars.

‹ An LGB two-axle tank car works well as a combination track cleaner and weed-control car. For better track cleaning, the porous, rubberized pads can be saturated with LGB's no. 50010 smoke fluid. The fluid acts as a mild solvent to help loosen dirt and oxidation.

Before we get down to all that work, let me suggest something to you. The drudgery of maintenance is only as bad as you choose to make it. You can actually have fun with a lot of this. Necessity being the mother of invention, a clever modeler was inspired to build a hedge trimmer car, shown above.

While we're on the subject of things that grow along the tracks, here's another idea. LGB tank cars, and perhaps others, have working drain valves. The spigots can be set to allow just a trickle of fluid to dribble out right along the ends of the ties. The tank can be filled with your choice of liquid weed-control solution. Running this car around the railway occasionally will help to keep weeds away from the track, resulting in less work while giving you another reason to run trains.

In the process of constructing your garden railway, you probably put a lot of care and effort into building your track system; not just the track itself, but also the subroadbed, the roadbed, and the bridges that support the track.

Rock ballast will gradually settle and may wash out in spots. Winter weather may move it around a bit, but repair is easy. A weekend of repair will put most railroads back in shape for a whole summer of operation. Just lift the track a touch and spread more ballast to fill in any low spots. It's a good idea to recheck your work with a level just as you did when you first laid the track.

Somehow, it makes the job more enjoyable just knowing that you're doing things in much the same way as the full-size railroads. You can add a little authenticity by running a work train out to the section of track you're maintaining. Use some hopper cars or gondolas to carry ballast and other supplies. You might even make a photo opportunity of the occasion and take some pictures of the work train along the way. Real railroads often employed professional photographers to document things, both for publicity and posterity. It's fun, years later, to go back and look at those photos from earlier days.

If your garden line has wood bridges, trestles, and cribwork, these will certainly need attention. In most climates a fresh coat of a high-quality penetrating stain/sealer/preservative will probably be needed at least every year or two. Keep in mind that you're not dealing with a big piece of lumber, like a fascia board on your house. With something that's maybe only 1/4″ or 1/2″ thick, there's not much material there to spare if a board starts to weather and split. If your scale-size timber is down next to the earth, the problems are compounded. While you're down there brushing on the stain, check for loose nails (or whatever it is that you've used to fasten all those sticks together). Replace any damaged boards, since one weak board tends to result in others being damaged. This may all seem rather tedious, but I think you'll find this task more appealing than the prospect of building new bridges to replace ones that simply fell apart from lack of attention. Who knows—you may even be inspired to invent an automatic trestle-painting machine. In the meantime, keep those trains running!

SECTION 9

Building the Colorado & Pacific, part 1

Marc Horovitz

All photos by Marc Horovitz

One of the wonderful things about our hobby is that there is no absolutely right way of doing things. There are many different methods that work. Granted, some work better than others, and some will work in one climate and not in another, but many paths can lead to the same destination.

Tools required for drawing the site map

- Tape measure for measuring overall dimensions and distances to physical features
- Pencil
- Paper for rough sketch
- Graph paper for scale map
- Ruler for measuring on graph paper

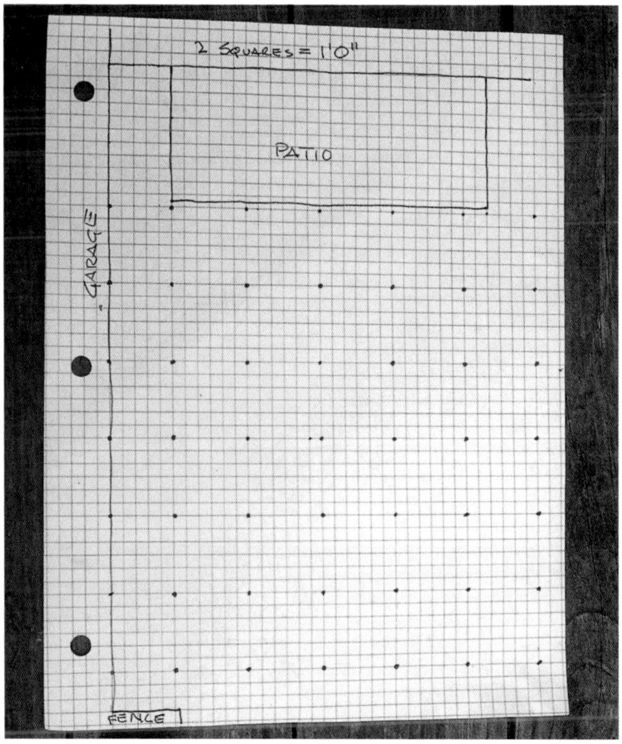

‹ A small passenger train is ready to depart the station on the newly completed Colorado & Pacific. The construction of this line will be fully described over the next chapters of this book.

› The site plan, accurately drawn on graph paper to a scale of ½" = 1'0". Grid lines are noted at 3-foot centers.

When Rod Wentler and I set out to design and build the Colorado & Pacific, we chose methods that should work well in most climates. The methods presented here are certainly not the only ones that can be used in building an outdoor line, but they are good ones, tried and true. The C&P was not built quickly, but it was built to last. Helping us build the railroad were Rod's son Max and my daughter Adriane.

If you use this series as a guide when building your own railroad, examine the techniques described and make your own decisions as to whether or not they are right for you. Consult others in your area to see what they've done and what has worked well for them. I've heard it said that the most difficult step in any project is the first one, so just get in there and make a start. Once you know where you are going, the rest will just flow.

Getting started

The site on which the Colorado & Pacific was to be built is in the Bay Area of California. It is at the far end of a sloping backyard, and over the years it had become overgrown with weeds and blackberries. The first job was to clear the site right down to the ground.

Not wanting to use chemical herbicides, we did this by hand. This was undoubtedly the worst part of the project. We first cut the plants down, just so we could gain access to the area, and hauled them away. We suffered the heat and thorn scratches gallantly. Then, to prevent (or at least inhibit) the weeds from returning, we dug up as many roots as we could. The dirt was hard and full of rocks, making for a long and arduous task.

Once the ground was clear, we were left with an area roughly 12 x 18 feet in which to build our railway. On the south it was bounded by the neighbor's garage, on the east by a fence, on the west by an old concrete half wall, and on the north by the remains of the weed patch, not yet cleared.

The site

The first thing we needed to do was to make an accurate site drawing that showed the overall dimensions, any slope to the land, and other physical features. We first drew a rough sketch of the site and took its measurements: length, width, distance to walls and fences, and so forth, noting them on the sketch. If you have an obstacle that is in the middle of your site, say a tree or a rock, it can be easily "located" (placed accurately on your map) by measuring its distance in two directions from known objects, say the back of your house and the adjoining fence.

1 Measuring from the neighbor's garage wall, I've pounded stakes into the ground at 3-foot centers at the upper end of the site, matching the site-plan grid.

2 A similar row of stakes has been pounded into the lower end of the site.

3 A string, with flags tied on at 3-foot intervals, has been tied to the first stake at the upper and lower ends, thus defining the first line of the grid.

4 The site plan with all dimensions marked on an overlay.

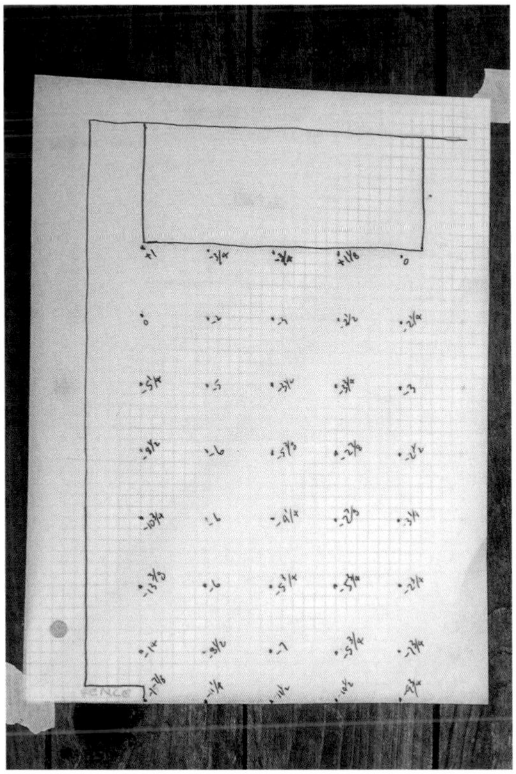

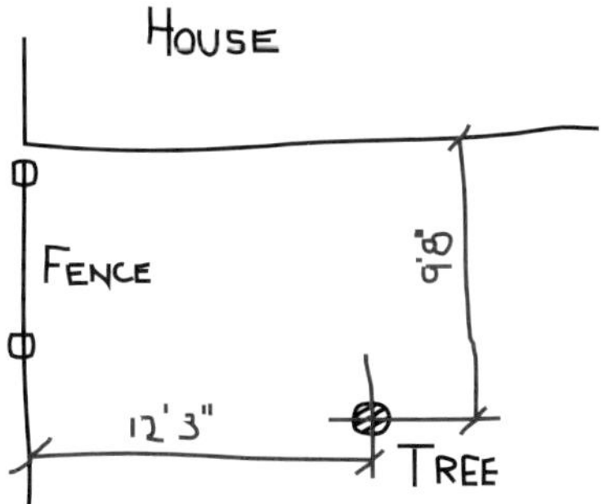

To "locate", or accurately place, an object out in your yard, simply measure its position from two known points, like your house and an adjoining fence. Note these dimensions on your rough plan so you can accurately transfer them to your scale plan.

Locating fixed objects

1 Using the water level. Adriane stays at stake 1 while I move around the yard. Here, the string has been tied to the second set of stakes. I call out dimensions while Adriane notes them on the site plan.

Tools required to grid out the site

- Hammer
- Wooden stakes
- Little cloth flags
- String
- Tape measure
- Site map
- Pencil
- Water level

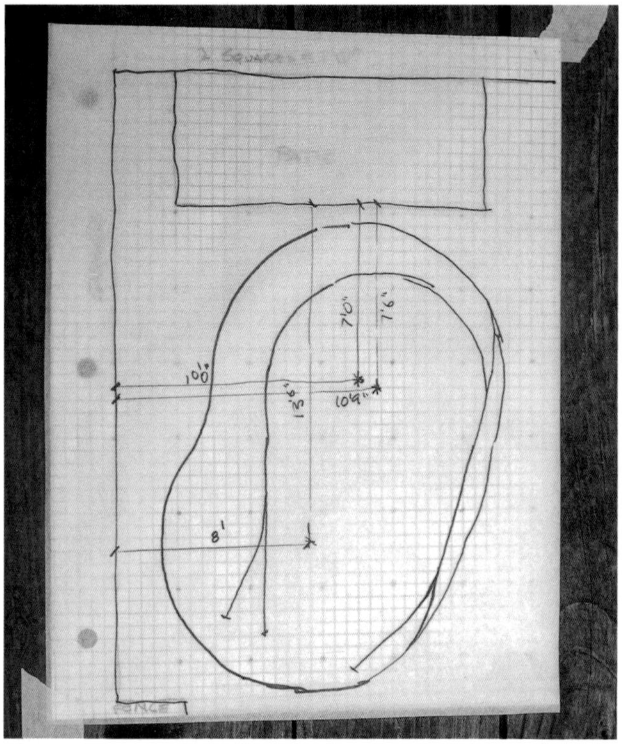

2 Our final rough sketch of the proposed railway. This crude overlay drawing incorporates everything we wanted, roughly placed on the site map.

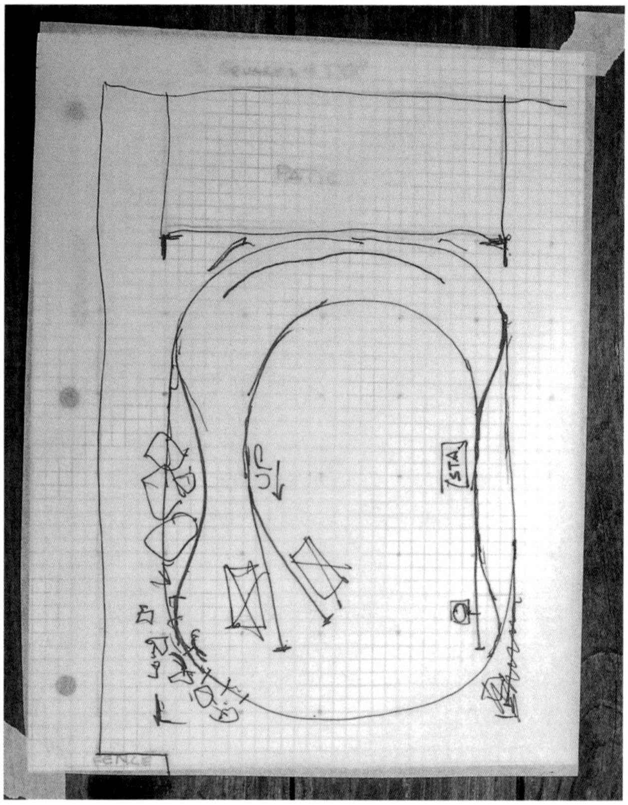

3 The final plan, accurately drawn on the site map. Center points of all curves have been located and can be easily transferred to the ground. The entire plan has been rotated clockwise slightly to add interest, but was later straightened up when we realized that it encroached on the neighbor's property line.

Based on our sketch, we then drew a simple but accurate map of the site on graph paper. Since our site was small, we were able to get it onto an 8″ x 10″ sheet, using a scale of ½″ = 1′0″. This scale map allowed us to better visualize the area we had to work with.

The next step, and an important one, was to figure out the grade of the site. We needed to know how much it sloped and in what directions. This was important, not only because of how the trackplan would be influenced, but also to allow for drainage.

To accurately figure the grade, we first gridded off our site map in 3-foot squares. We then had to grid off the property to match. To do this, we measured from the neighbor's garage at the upper end of the site to the furthest point away on the railway to establish a starting point, and pounded a wooden stake into the ground. This coincided with the same point on the map. Along the line from the garage to the stake, we pounded in additional stakes, 3 feet apart. Next we did the same at the lower end of the site, giving us two parallel lines of stakes.

Then we took a string and tied little flags along it, also at 3-foot intervals. By tying the string to the first stake at the upper end of the site and to the corresponding first stake at the lower end, we quickly established the grid points along the line that coincided with those on our graph paper.

To establish the grade along that line, we used a water level (see sidebar). Adriane stayed at the starting point with one end of the level and a clipboard with our gridded site plan. I moved along the string line with my end of the level, calling out measurements to her at each flag while she noted them at the appropriate points on the grid. When we got to the end of the string, we moved the line over 3 feet to the next set of stakes. Adriane stayed at the starting point while I moved down the string on the second line. This process was repeated until all of the elevations on the grid had been calculated and noted on the graph paper. The first stake was our reference point, so Adriane never moved from there.

When we had finished, Rod and I had a look at our site map. From the elevation measurements we could see that the site sloped away toward the southeast, with a total drop of about 16″. There was an area in the middle that was more level, while

The water level

The water level is one of those wonderfully simple tools that you can make yourself and that will allow you to do surprisingly accurate work. Ours was made with two cheap hardware-store yardsticks and a length of clear plastic tubing. The tubing can be any length, and the larger in diameter the better. It takes water much longer to settle in a thin tube than a fat one.

The ends of the tube are attached to the yardsticks. We put corks in the ends of our tube to prevent the water from coming out when we moved the level around. These were removed when we took readings.

The tube is filled with water up to about halfway up the yardstick. You need enough empty tube at the top for the water to move into as the grade changes. We put a little food coloring into our water, but this is unnecessary. Just make sure there are no bubbles in the tube.

In use, one end of the level stays in one place, while the other end moves around. The end that is stationary becomes the reference point. It doesn't matter where the water starts out on the yardstick because what we are interested in is the difference between the two readings. To double-check the level, place the two yardsticks side by side on an even grade. They should each read the same.

Now, place a 2″ block under one yardstick. Say they both read $13\frac{1}{2}$″ before. Now, the one you raised should read $12\frac{1}{2}$″ while the other one reads $14\frac{1}{2}$″, a difference of 2″. Note that the yardstick with the lower reading is actually at the higher elevation.

To use the water level to measure grade, simply leave one end at one point and move the other around, noting the differences in the readings. It can be moved any distance, since we are only using it to measure vertical dimensions. You'll find that you can easily and accurately measure elevation differences as small as $\frac{1}{8}$″. It is helpful to have someone to work with, but you can work alone if the yardsticks are tied to bricks or something else that will keep them upright by themselves. Put your thumb over the tube when you move around to prevent the water from coming out the top.

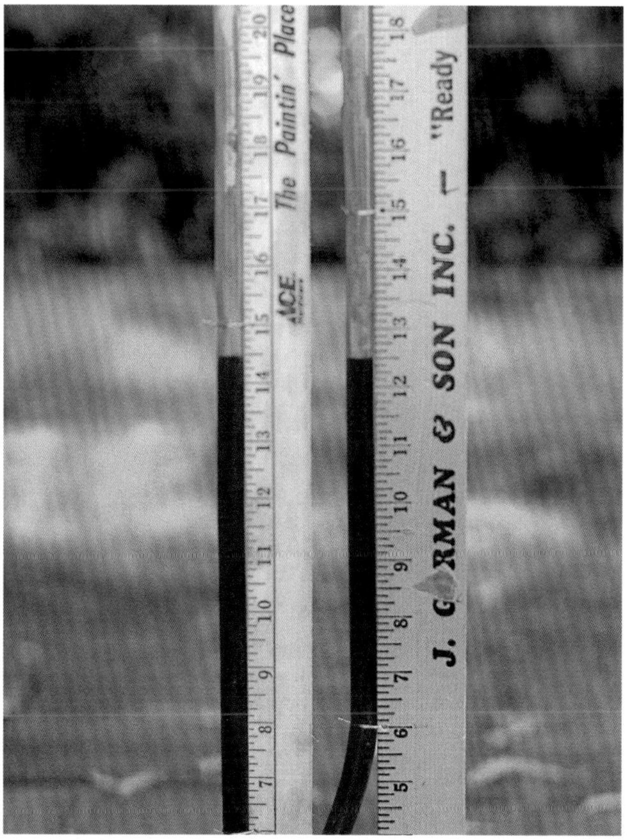

Water level made with clear plastic tubing and cheap yardsticks. When the yardsticks are placed together on even ground, their readings should be identical.

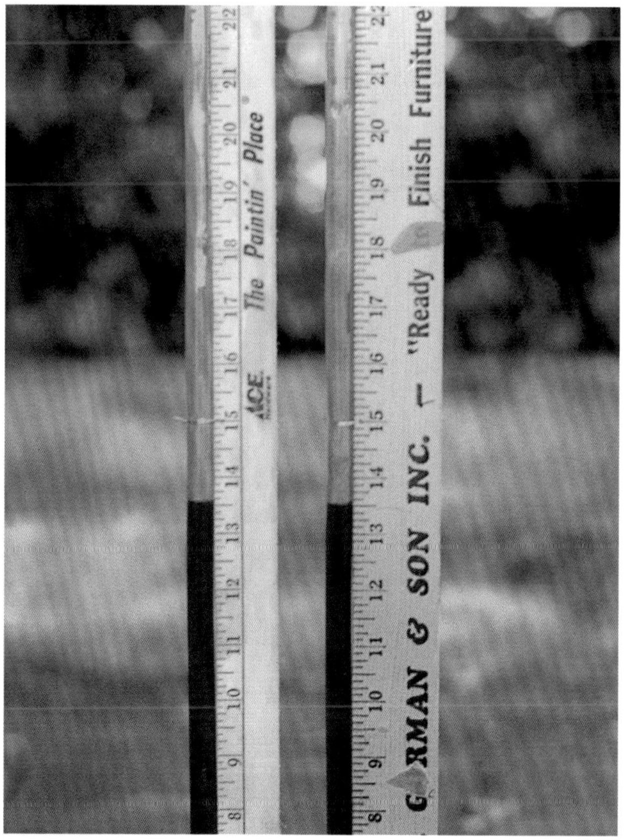

When one stick is raised 2" (in this case, the right-hand one), the difference in the two readings will be 2".

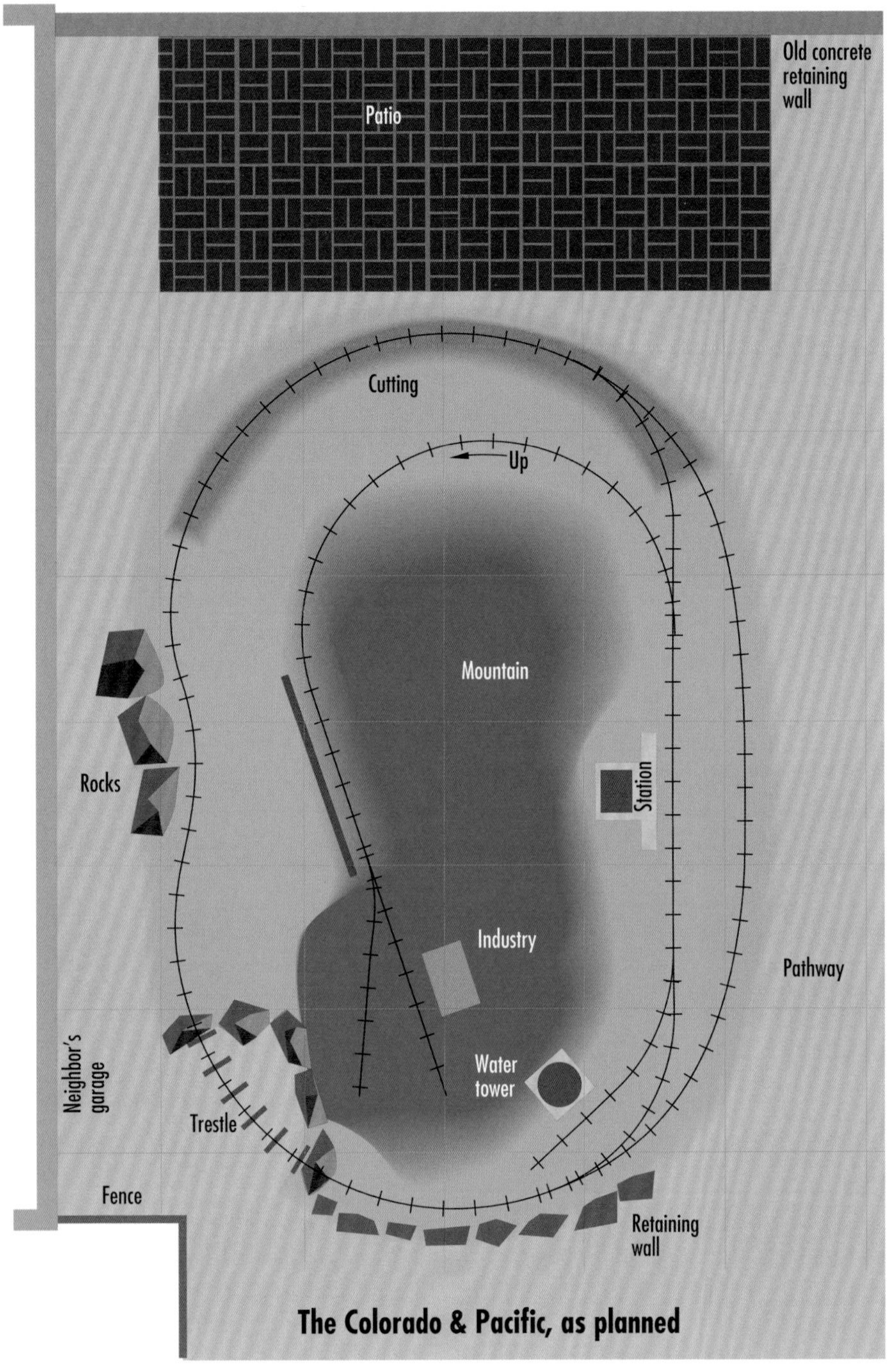

The Colorado & Pacific, as planned

the ground dropped away more steeply toward the garage and the back fence. Now we knew not only how large an area we had to work with, but we had a good idea of its topography as well. It was time to start thinking about our railroad.

Considering the plan

Before we could start building, we needed a track plan. But before we could design our plan, we needed to know what sort of railway we wanted and what was possible. This was an important part of the process and not one to be glossed over. Rod and I sat down and discussed our potential railroad, based both on our wants and on the physical restraints imposed by our site.

We decided that we wanted a general-purpose railroad that offered both freight and passenger service. The era that we chose was early 20th century, say from 1900 to 1930. This gave us quite a bit of flexibility in the type of structures and rolling stock.

Through our discussions, we also decided we wanted a certain amount of operating capability combined with a simple, basic-loop trackplan. Live-steam operation, in addition to track-powered electric, was attractive to us, so a level mainline was desirable. A station with a passing track would give us the potential for two-train operation. We already had a water tower, from Grover Devine's old South Pacific Coast line that we wanted to use, so some sort of engine-servicing facility was in order. A spur line, possibly elevated for interest, serving an industry or two would round out the package.

Our site was on a slope, but we wanted a level mainline, so we knew that we'd have to do some cutting and filling. A flat site, even if sloped, wasn't too interesting, so we decided to build a mountain in the middle, one that would perhaps provide a home for our industry. If the mountain was big enough to obscure the view of the other side of the railway, so much the better. This would add interest and increase the illusion of distance.

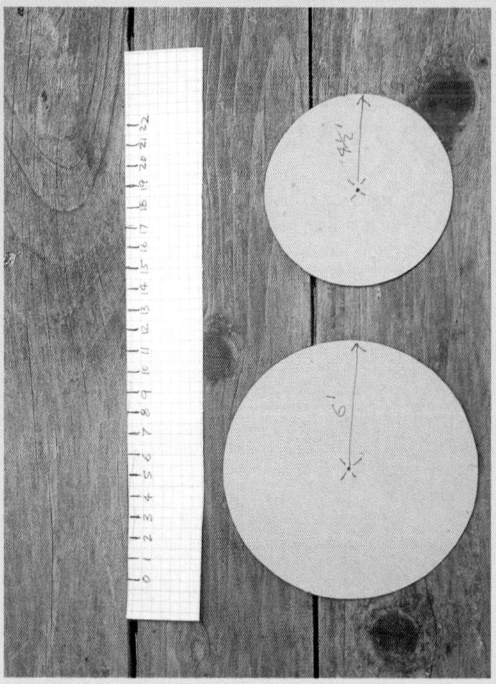

Drawing the plan

We felt it important to have as accurate a drawing of our proposed railroad as possible. To make an accurate drawing, we used tracing-paper overlays over our graph-paper site grid. Since we knew what radii we wanted to use (6 feet for the mainline and 4 feet for the spur), we cut cardboard circles to these radii, drawn with a compass, to the same scale as our site plan. This allowed us to quickly but accurately sketch out the location of the curve to see if it worked.

Once the curves were where we wanted them, we noted their center points on the drawing and figured their locations from adjacent walls and fences. These dimensions would be used later to actually plot the full-size garden railway on the ground, allowing us to place the railway on the site just it was drawn on the map.

Accurately cut cardboard circles and a paper scale help you to draw the final plan.

Our site was pretty small, so track length and radius would be restricted. The rule of thumb is to use the largest-radius track your site will support. Trains, even little ones, don't look natural going around right-angle curves. Even with our small site, we could still have a main loop with 6-foot-radius curves, with a spur line down to, say, 4-foot radius.

Also, because of the limited size of our railroad, large, full-length mainline equipment was out. We opted to go with the smallest equipment we could find to keep the scale of the rolling stock in line with the scale of the railroad itself.

We also discussed mode of power. While we wanted to keep the live steam option, we felt that for instant availability, track power or radio-controlled battery power would be better for day-to-day use. We also wanted to be able to host visiting locomotives, so track power was almost a must.

On the other hand, we didn't want to get into a wiring morass. With a simple-loop plan, we felt we could probably get away with a single set of leads to power the entire line, especially if the rail joints were soldered or if jumper wires were soldered across them. The main power supply would have to be kept in the house, with a line run out to the controller at the railroad, at the far end of the yard.

Drawing the plan

Once we had finally settled on what we wanted for the railway, we sat down to develop and refine the plan. We made lots of rough sketches on tracing-paper over our site map. When finally satisfied, we made an accurate drawing of our proposed line to see if what we wanted would really fit and to check curves and clearances. While we made this drawing as accurately as we could, we kept in mind the fact that things could change somewhat when we finally got down to the site and started construction.

Our final plan showed a kidney-shaped mainline with a cutting at the high end and a retaining wall at the low end. A trestle at the very lowest point would provide drainage for the line. A station with a passing track would be built into the north side. Off the east end of the passing track would would be a short spur to serve as the engine facility, and at the west end a longer spur would ascend the mountain to an industry or two. Large rocks on the south side would provide an obstacle for the train to circumnavigate, adding a little interest, and the hillside would be planted with suitable, scale appropriate plants and miniature trees.

Now we had a plan, something concrete that we could work from, and something that felt good to us and satisfied the requirements that we'd set out. Now it was time to get out the shovels.

Building the Colorado & Pacific, part 2

Marc Horovitz

All photos by Marc Horovitz

In the first part of this project, Rod Wentler, the kids, and I prepared the site, figured its levels, and came up with a trackplan for the railway. We were then ready to begin grading the line. The first thing we had to do was to transfer our design to the ground. This would give us a feeling for how the railroad would actually sit in its site and it would also delineate where the earthwork had to be done.

1 Rod uses a cardboard template to gauge the proper radius of the S-curve while scratching a line on the ground with a stick.

2 When the trackplan was complete in scratched-line form, it was made more visible by going over it with baking flour.

3 Drawing the trackplan on the ground in white gave us our first real taste of what the finished railway might look like.

Tools required for setting out the railway

- Tape measure for locating center points
- Wooden stakes for center points
- String for radii and tangents (straight track)
- Sharp stick for scratching lines
- Cardboard template for making awkward curves
- Chalk, flour, or paint for marking the track line

Transferring the drawing to the ground

To draw our trackplan on the ground essentially amounted to redrawing the plan to a different scale—full size instead of $\frac{1}{2}$″ to the foot. The most important points on the plan were the center points of the curves. Once these points were plotted on the ground the entire plan could be redrawn. Since we located the points using the plan from the edge of the patio and the wall of the neighbor's garage as reference points, it was easy to plot the same points on the ground by taking the measurements from the plan. There were three points that we had to establish: the centers of the two curves that form the ends of the railway and the center of the curve that forms the spur line.

Once these points had been plotted and marked with wooden stakes, we drew in the lines of the track. The main curves were done with a 6-foot-long piece of string (to plot the points for a 6-foot radius) with a loop in each end. One loop was placed over the center stake while the other was looped over a sharp stick. The curve at each end was then simply scratched in the dirt. The process was repeated with the spur track, but using a string that was 4$\frac{1}{2}$ feet long.

The straight passing siding was drawn in by scratching a line down a piece of string held taut from the points where the switches departed from and rejoined the mainline. The slightly bowed mainline adjacent to the passing siding was eyeballed in until it looked good.

We wanted a smooth and accurate S-curve on the opposite side of the railway—the "inside" of the kidney, as it were. We couldn't plot the center point of

The finished trestle rests in its future position on the railway.

The trestle

Our simple, single-tier trestle had no diagonal bracing on the bents themselves, only between the bents to give the structure strength. The trestle was made of old redwood cut up on a table saw.

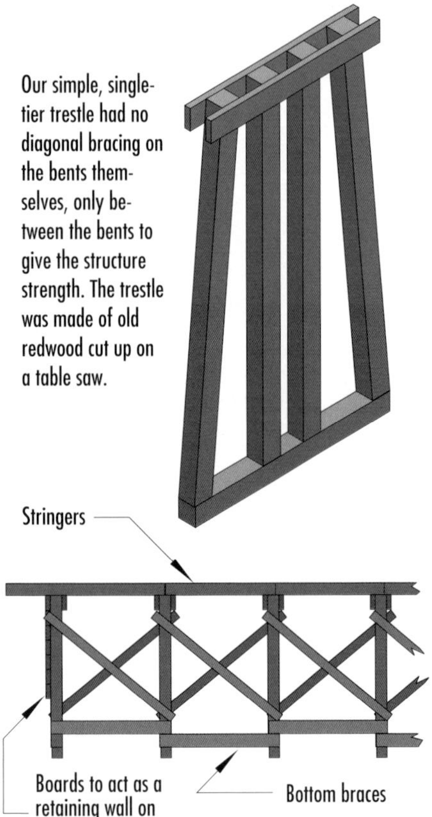

The trestle

We didn't have a trestle when we started, so we had to make one. Rod had an antique table saw in the garage, so we dragged it out onto the driveway, only to discover that it wouldn't start. The starting capacitor was dead. However, we reasoned, that capacitor was only there to get the motor up to speed. If we could somehow rev up the motor, it should then continue on by itself and we could cut some wood for the trestle. We pondered this conundrum for a while before arriving at the expedient of simply wrapping a rope around the motor's pulley and giving it a tug, like starting a lawnmower. It worked. Through careful planning and a stiff dose of dumb luck we were able to cut all the wood necessary for our trestle in one session on our rope-started table saw.

The trestle was short in length and not very tall. We made up a simple jig for the bents and nailed together half a dozen of them. Since the trestle would be on a curve, we drew the line of the curve on a piece of paper and used this as a guide when assembling the structure. The first two bents were the hardest to stick together, since there was nothing to hold either one of them upright except us. We eventually held them in place with bricks while nailing on the top stringers and side braces. The other four bents went on more easily.

To the outside two bents we nailed boards to act as retainers. These would help prevent the earth from filling in around the trestle. The finished trestle was fairly sturdy and would become more so when placed in the ground.

that curve because the neighbor's garage was in the way and we weren't up to doing a lot of fancy geometry. Instead, we took a large piece of cardboard and cut one edge to a 6-foot-radius curve. That became a template that we aligned with the ends of the approach curves, and then scratched a line along it.

Our railway was now complete in the form of rough lines scratched in the dirt. The only problem was that it was hard to see. We got some baking flour from the kitchen and poured it on the ground along the lines of the railway (we could also have used chalk or spray paint intended for ground work). The result was magical. All of a sudden, there was our railway, fully laid out on its site just as it was on the paper plan. Viewing it like this really brought it to life. We could see where we had to make cuts, where our retaining wall would have to go, and where the mountain could be built.

Rough earthwork

A fair amount of rough earthwork had to be done, even on this tiny railway. We had to cut and fill so the mainline would be level, build a retaining wall to hold the fill in place, carve away the area where the trestle would go, place the big boulders near the S-curve, and, of course, build our mountain in the middle.

We started with the cutting at the top end. First, we marked where we reckoned it had to be, based on our elevation readings and the track line on the ground. Then we started digging. The ground was very hard and progress was slow, but we kept at it. Fortunately, the weather smiled on us. All of the removed dirt was hauled in a wheelbarrow and dumped at the lower end of the line as fill.

When the cutting was as deep as we wanted (checked with the water level), we started on the fill. We had a fairly substantial pile of rocks that had been dug up, so we decided to use them for the retaining wall. We located the base of the wall a foot or so from the track line and sloped it up toward the track. The wall defined both the curve and the lower end of the railway.

Then we were ready to build the mountain. Before we started, we removed the stakes for the center points of our

<^ Rod begins to dig the cutting at the high end of the line. Dirt removed from the cut was taken to the low end to act as fill.

^^ Raw material. The pile closest to the camera is rock found while clearing the site. That farthest away is concrete rubble from an old patio that we used as landfill to form the mountain.

^ The retaining wall at the low end as seen from the top side. Earth backfill has been tamped to level the ground and prevent subsidence.

curves and replaced them with much longer ones, so they wouldn't get buried when we started building the mountain. We'd need them in the future to restore the track line to the ground.

We started building the mountain by piling up concrete rubble that we had from an old patio. This formed the rough shape of the mountain. On top of that came dirt—lots of dirt. We had to have a deep enough layer of dirt on top of the

‹ ^ The retaining wall from its face. It is a low wall, only three or so courses high. The trestle sits on the ground in the place where it will ultimately be installed.

‹ Mountain building begins. The short center-point stakes have been replaced with long ones. Concrete rubble, which formed the base for the mountain, is covered with dirt.

^ A gorge for the trestle to span was dug and retained with large rock. When the trestle is in place on a bed of ballast, the hole will be filled in to grade.

Building a retaining wall

The area to be retained must first be cleared away and a shallow trench dug, sloping a little to the inside, to receive the first course (layer) of stones. These stones are then laid in. Try to match the ends of the stones to their neighbors so there aren't huge gaps between them. Flat stones generally work better for walls. Use the largest stones on the bottom courses to give the wall stability, always sloping them back into the hill a little. This is so that rainwater will flow back into the hill where it can do some good, and not just run away.

When the first course is laid, the area behind it must be backfilled and tamped (packed down). This is the hard work in building a stone wall, not moving the stones. Fill in the dirt up to the level of the first course. Tamp the dirt with a tamper or a 4″ x 4″ post to minimize settling. If necessary, add another layer of dirt until the tamped soil is level with the top of the course.

The second course can then be laid on top of the first (and set slightly back from it), always sloping the stones back. When the second is in place, backfill and tamp again. Keep adding courses and backfilling until you are finished. You'll find that the higher you go, the more backfilling is required for each course.

When adding a course, try to overlap the stones so that one stone covers the joint between the two below it. This not only strengthens the wall, but it looks nicer, too.

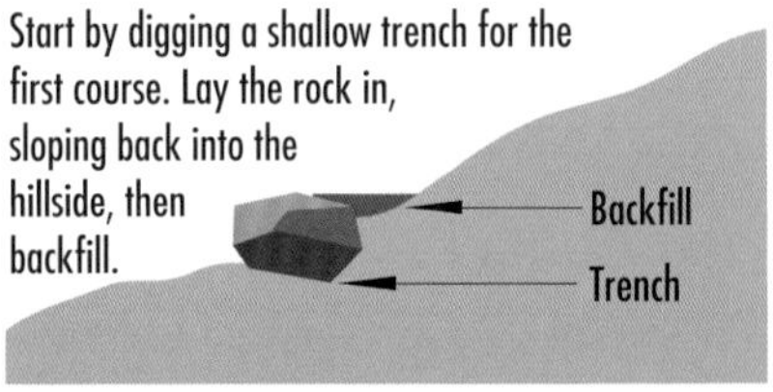

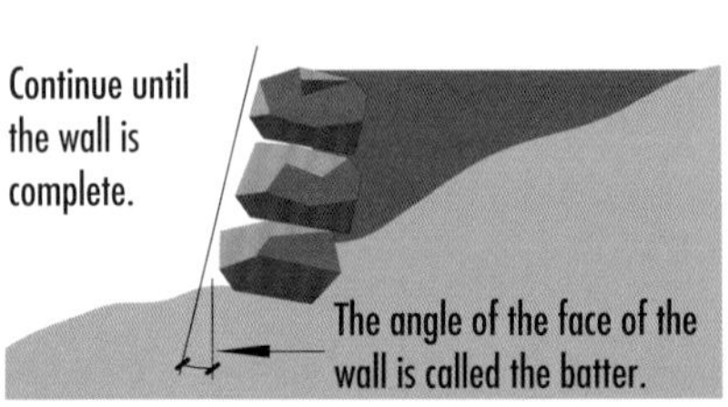

rubble that, when we started planting things, we wouldn't run into concrete. Consulting our plan, we shaped the mountain as we went, keeping it away from the station area at the base.

When we finally achieved the pinnacle of alpine perfection, we created some natural stone outcroppings at the top with some leftover rocks.

Once the mountain was reasonably finished, we dug out the place for the trestle. We did this by eye, using our plan and the actual trestle as a guide. One face of the gorge in which the trestle was to sit backed up into the mountainside, so it had to be retained with some large rocks. We didn't actually install the trestle at this point because our final grade had not been established, but we carved the land around it to the point that we knew the trestle would fit well when the time came.

At this point, we were nearly finished with the rough earthwork. Our track line on the ground had long since vanished, so we put it back to see how the railway would look in its brand new landscape. This was an easy job (especially when compared with building the mountain) and in 15 minutes or so the track line was back on the ground. Time to deal with the site of the S-curve.

We had some fairly large rocks on hand, so we used them to make a rock formation near the garage wall. This was a contrivance to justify our S-curve, which evolved like this:

"Let's have an S-curve in the railway."

"Why?"

"Because the train will look cool going through it. It's less boring than a straightaway."

"But we can't just have an S-curve sitting out there in the middle of nowhere. That would look pointless."

"Well, OK, let's stick something there for the curve to go around."

"Like what?"

"Well, how about a rock formation, something too big to blast into oblivion, so the railroad had to go around it?"

So that's how we ended up breaking our backs constructing a natural rock formation that looked like it'd been there since the dawn of time, something that a railroad absolutely had to go around. But, when the project was finished, it looked pretty neat and we were glad we did it. The train not only looked good going through the S-curve, but it looked just right coming through the rocks.

< ^ These rocks will form the rock outcropping that made the S-curve "necessary."

^ Cribbing that retains the earth along the spur line up the mountain was made from garden stakes (see page 57).

The spur line was to climb the back side of the mountain to reach the banjo factory that was inexplicably built at the top. We had to retain the grade going up the mountainside, so we built some cribbing and installed it adjacent to the route of the spur line. This involved building the crib as a single, solid unit, digging the dirt away so it could be properly placed, then backfilling up to grade. Cribbing adds an interesting man-made feature to a garden line, and miniature plants can grow between the stringers.

Once all of the earthwork was finally done, the track line was restored one last time in preparation for trackwork.

Building the Colorado & Pacific, part 3

Marc Horovitz

All photos by Marc Horovitz

Finally—track! I confess to being something of a track fanatic. I love track. To me, the railway is the track. Track can make or break a line. No matter how beautiful or well thought out the rest of the railroad is, poor trackwork can ruin it. On the other hand, really good trackwork can make a railway a joy to operate.

1

2

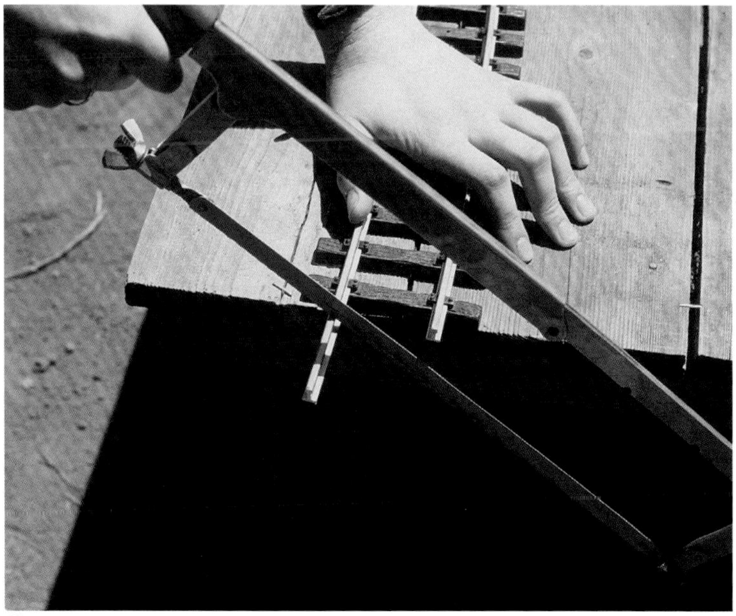

3

Adriane curves the rail in a bench-mounted rail bender.

She tests the curvature of the rail against the chalk line on the ground.

On curved track, the ends of the inside rail must be trimmed to length with a hacksaw, then smoothed with a small flat file.

Because of the limitations of sectional track, Rod and I decided to use LGB flex track for the Colorado & Pacific. This track, like other large scale flex track, is supplied with the rails and plastic tie strips separate. You must slide the tie strips onto the rails to complete a section.

However, before you can do that, the rails must be bent to their proper curvature. The term "flex track" is something of a misnomer, especially in the larger rail sizes like the code-332 rail we are using. The track is, in fact, not very flexible at all. In the small scales—HO for instance—you can take a stick of flex track and bend it into place as you lay it. Not so in the larger scales. If you try it, the track, in its contrary way, will spend all of its time trying to unbend and will eventually succeed. To counteract this problem, we prebend the rails.

To bend a rail smoothly and accurately, a rail bender can't be beat. These are available from people who make track or from aftermarket suppliers. We mounted our rail bender to an old workbench we'd set up near the railway. Since we were basically just using two different radii (not counting the very broad radius on one side), we made some cardboard templates to those radii, against which we could match the bent rail.

The trackwork has been made and placed in its final position on the ground.

▲ Each joint was marked so the track could be reassembled in the same place. Then the track was removed.

◀ Rod digs trenches for the ballast. The finished track will be right at grade (ground level).

Rail-bender suppliers

Rail benders are available from a variety of sources, some of which are listed here. Make sure you know the size rail you are working with, as benders will usually only work well with one size, and find out if your supplier offers a bender for that size rail.

Sunset Valley Railroad
13428 209th SE
Issaquah WA 98027
425-255-2453
E-mail: svrrted@sprynet.com

Llagas Creek Railways
Available from:
California & Oregon Coast Railway
POBox 57
Rogue River OR 95737
800-866-8635

Istra Metalcraft
6089 Lee Ann Lane
Naples FL 34109
941-597-6445

The track up to the banjo factory is in its final position, awaiting connection to the mainline and top ballasting.

Rail codes

You will hear rail referred to by code number. For example, LGB, Aristo-Craft, and others is code 332. Llagas Creek and Sunset Valley offer code-250 rail. Though this is a code, it isn't a secret. The "code number" simply refers to the height of the rail in thousandths of an inch. So, code-332 rail is .332″ tall. Code 250 rail is .250″ tall, or 1/4″. That's all there is to it.

A rail bender has three wheels that bear against the rail—two on one side and one on the other. The position of the single wheel is adjustable, usually by a screw, and it is this adjustment that allows you to vary the curvature of the rail. Bending rail accurately takes a little bit of practice, but you soon get the hang of it. The beauty of it all is that if you bend it too far (and who hasn't?), you can turn the rail around and unbend it. In fact, you can perfectly straighten it out again.

We purchased the switches that our plan called for and placed them out on our chalk-line railway. They didn't match the printed lines exactly, but that was OK. They gave us some solid benchmarks to work to, and we'd just adjust the track to fit properly as we went along.

We began making up the track. I bent the rails and Rod assembled the track sections. The bent rails didn't have to be spot on, but they had to be close to the correct curvature. Small corrections could be made later by hand. When making a section of curved track, the ends of the inner rail stick out farther than those of the outer. We trimmed these with a hacksaw, cleaning up the rough cut with a flat file. Then rail joiners were added so the track could be joined to its neighbor, making a continuous line.

Track alternatives

There are basically three ways to go with track: sectional, flex, and handlaid.

Sectional track is just that—track that comes in predetermined lengths and radii. It is good for getting something up and running quickly or for portable or temporary tracks that need to be assembled and taken apart repeatedly. Its main drawback (and this is huge) is its inflexibility. Your railroad pretty much has to go where the sectional track can go and you are limited to whatever radii are available for curves.

Flex track is a much better option for a permanent garden line. It can be bent (with a rail bender) to whatever curvature is necessary to get the railway where it needs to go, in much the same way full-size railroads are built.

Perhaps the ultimate in trackwork is handlaid track. This is where the rails are hand-spiked to individual wooden ties. There are several reasons why people handlay track. These include the desire for a specific look, dislike of plastic, the need for some type of specialized trackwork that isn't commercially available, or just the feeling of satisfaction that comes from actually building the railroad the same way that a full-size railroad is built.

Some track, including some of the commercial flex tracks in the smaller rail sizes, is too light to float by itself in ballast. It needs to be anchored to something.

One system that works well is to attach the track to battens, or long wooden stringers. A parallel pair of these under the track does several things. They increase the track's weight and depth, and significantly increase the surface area that comes in contact with the ballast. All of these factors combine to hold the track much more firmly in place.

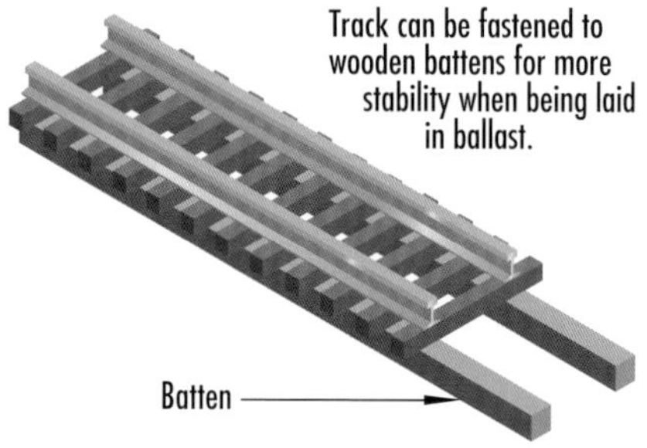

Attaching track to battens

Track problems to be aware of

When laying track, there are several potential problems to be aware of.

Too-tight radius both looks unsightly and can cause your trains difficulty. Plan your railway with the largest radius your space will allow (7- to 10-foot is good) and bend and lay your track carefully to ensure a curve's consistency.

Doglegs occur at joints where one curve doesn't exactly match the next, creating a kink. This is a potential source of derailments.

Vertical kinks can happen when a track changes elevation. These transitions should be smooth and gradual for good operation.

S-curves can be an attractive feature to a track plan, but care must be taken in their design. If you are using a very wide radius, a simple "S" is possible. However, with tighter radii, an S-curve poses potential danger of derailments, especially when backing or when using very long equipment, like mainline passenger cars. To help alleviate the problem, add a straight section of at least one car length in the middle of the S.

Straight track that isn't truly straight is more of a visual problem than anything. A railroad just looks nicer with straight sections that are truly straight.

Levelness in the track (or lack thereof) can affect operation as well as look bad. Track that leans the wrong way on curves can dump the train. Unlevel track can cause derailments and coupling problems, too.

Dogleg

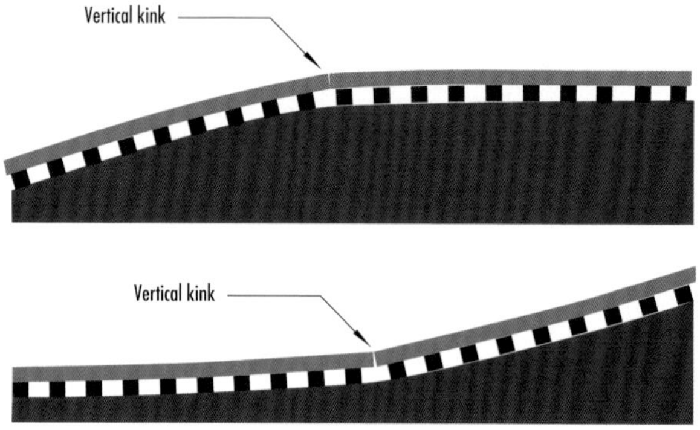

Vertical kinks are not just unsightly. They can be a cause of derailments, especially with larger equipment.

Vertical kinks on inclines

Ballast

The purpose of ballast is to hold the track firmly in place while, at the same time, allowing it to move a little with climatic changes. The type of ballast to look for is crushed rock, often mixed with rock dust. The dust is good because it helps the ballast to set up, almost like cement, but still allows it to be easily broken apart again.

Non-dusty ballast, like chicken grit (available from feed stores), is also good, as it, too, is a crushed stone. A crushed rock has sharp corners and edges, or "tooth," that help it lock with its neighbors, forming a firm but porous base for track.

Crushed rock can usually be found at rock yards and landscape suppliers. It is used for garden paths, mulch, and other things. It is known by a variety of different names, including crusher fines, rock fines, quarry waste, and quarter minus (meaning 1/4" rock and less). Your rock yard might call it something different, but it's all the same stuff.

Important: Don't use pea gravel, squeegee, or other rock like this. These are basically river rocks or stones that have had their edges and corners worn away by being tossed about in water for centuries or through glaciation. These rounded stones will never interact with each other in the way that we want. They are solitary beings that want nothing more than to roll away from everything else. If you step on track laid in pea gravel, it will feel squashy, not firm. A heavy downpour, or even the garden sprinkler, can easily wash away pea-gravel ballast. Pea gravel will neither anchor your track nor keep it level. It's just not nice stuff.

The right stuff. The ballast on the right is what we call "crusher fines," though it has other names around the country. It is composed of crushed rock, usually ¼" or smaller, and rock dust. This is the stuff to use for ballast. It tamps well and holds the track in place. On the left is squeegee, a rounded river rock that will never hold your track in place.

When each section of track was finished, we put it in place on our chalk line. It was fun seeing the actual railway finally coming together like this. Slight adjustments were made as we went along. Since we knew that the chalk line was pretty accurate, we adhered to it as well as we could. We found that it was not difficult to stick closely to the line.

A tricky part came when it was time to close the loop. The last piece of track would be a non-standard length. We had to measure and cut it carefully to ensure a good fit. Also, we had to follow the same procedure to get the straight passing siding to fit properly.

Once all the track was in place we were able to stand back, admire our work, and congratulate one another on our good sense and aesthetic taste, before moving on to the next hard job—ballasting.

Ballasting

LGB track is heavy enough to float by itself in ballast, just like full-size railroad track. The ballast not only provides a good, solid base for the track, it keeps the track away from the soil and provides good drainage.

Before we could begin ballasting, we had to remove our carefully made and placed track. We first scratched lines in the dirt on either side of the track. Then, to ensure that it went back together the same way, we labeled each track joint so we could easily match it with its neighbor later. Then we carefully lifted it, section by section, and stacked it out of the way.

We then dug a trench 1″ to 2″ deep along the entire roadbed to accept the ballast. Full-size railroads don't put their track in trenches, they build the ballast up. Unfortunately, this doesn't work so well on little railroads. Our ballast doesn't have the

‹ ^ ^ The trestle was set in ballast as a unit, like the track, and brought up to track level. A layer of earth covers the ballast below.

‹ ^ After the initial ballast was put in place, not all the track was level. There were high spots and low ones like this, which had to be filled in with more ballast.

^ Rod checks side-to-side levelness of the track prior to tamping the top layer of ballast. Adjustments can be made at this time. The broom is used to help evenly spread the ballast.

< Ballast has been poured in the trench and Adriane tamps it smooth and hard.

v The 3 percent grade up to the banjo factory is fine tuned with the aid of a step block and level.

mass of the larger stuff and tends to subside, erode, and generally go away, leaving the track high, dry, and usually uneven. So we put it in a trench, which retains it.

Once the arduous task of digging the trench was finished and we all had something tall and cold to drink, we went off to get some ballast. We found what we needed at a local landscape supplier and filled the back of our pickup with it. When we got home, the kids very kindly brought it around back in many wheelbarrow loads. They dumped it on a tarp that we'd spread on the lawn nearby.

We then began filling the trench with ballast. It was filled more or less to the top, then tamped with a tamper. You can also use a 4″ x 4″. Tamping the ballast is extremely important. If it isn't thoroughly tamped, it would settle erratically, negating all the work required to get it level.

When the whole trench was filled and tamped, the track was replaced in it. Our trusty water level was brought out again and the mainline was checked for levelness. Of course, it wasn't level at all, so we had to go back in and add more ballast in places and remove ballast from other places. Gradually the line became level.

Since we had now established the final level of the track, the trestle was also installed at this time. It was sunk in ballast much the same way the track was, bringing it up to the level of the track above. The trestle was tamped in so that it actually supported the track. The track was attached to the trestle by Jack Verducci's method of drilling holes through the web of the rails and literally tying the rails to the top stringers of the trestle with copper wire (*Garden Railways,* December 1998, p. 118). This method is surprisingly unobtrusive when the ends of the wires are clipped.

The road up

Our spur line takes the high road up the side of the mountain. We'd calculated a 3 percent grade, which shouldn't overtax our little engine too badly, and roughed it in accordingly. However, now we wanted to make sure that the grade was smooth and accurate all the way up, not steep here and shallow there, just averaging out to 3 percent.

To easily measure our grade, we adopted the step-block method. This involved using a level of a set length with one end set up on a block of known height (see the sidebar). Using the level and step block, we measured the angle of the track all the way up, smoothing where necessary, until we reached the top and the track became level again.

< This track has been properly ballasted, then watered down.

v Trackwork is finished and the railway looks just fine sitting snugly in its new bed of ballast. The roadbed at this point is easily strong enough to walk on without disturbing the track.

Final ballasting

Once the track was level, final ballasting could begin. We poured loose ballast over the track and brushed it down between the ties with a broom. Then we took tamping sticks—sticks that were narrow enough to fit between the ties—and we began to go around the track, using our sticks to force the ballast into all crevices, compacting and settling it. We could feel the ballast firm up under the stick. In some places the ballast was very loose, and more was required to maintain the level, which we added as we went along.

This was fairly hard work, but it was important. Track in firmly tamped ballast stays put. In harsher climates, where frost heave occurs, well-ballasted track requires much less reballasting and releveling in the springtime than loosely ballasted track or track with no ballast at all.

The level was checked one last time and a very few minor adjustments were made. Finally, we took a hose with a fine-spray nozzle and watered in the track. This helps the rock dust to settle in and bond the track with the earth. Well-ballasted track looks like it is of the earth, not sitting on top of it. When we finished, we walked on the track. It felt firm and stable underfoot—no give at all, which is what we wanted.

There's a psychological element at work here, too. The more effort expended on a project, the greater the sense of pride and accomplishment once the job is finished. When we finally completed the job of tamping, we stood gazing at our work, feeling like something really good had been done.

Using a step block to measure grade

Each 1/8" step is 1/2% of incline (you could use 1/4" steps if you prefer to measure by full percentage points)

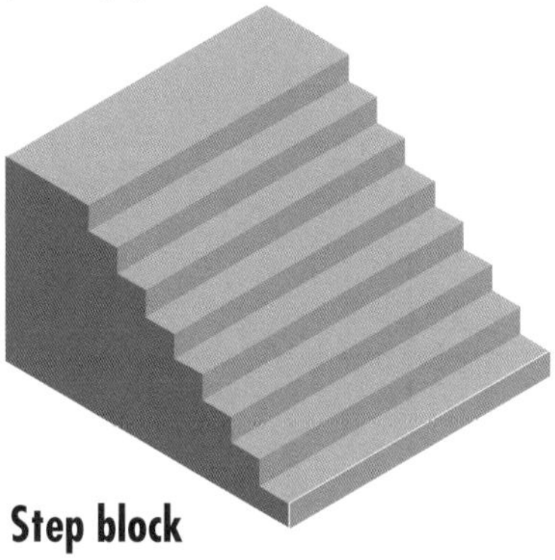

Step block

By placing a level on a 25"-long board, then elevating one end of the board on the step block, the percentage of a grade can be determined.

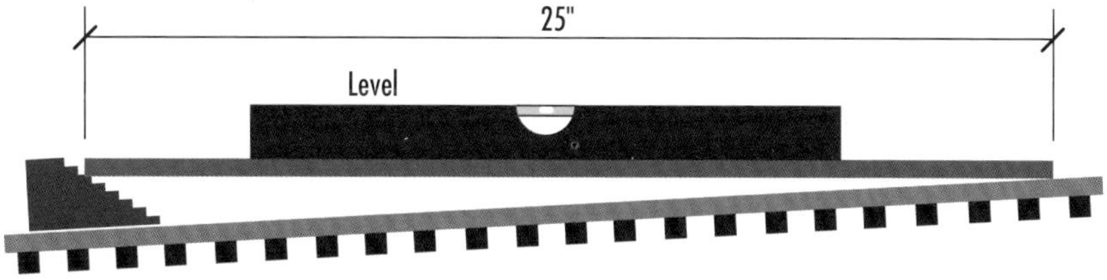

Using the step block

Grade is measured by percentages. A 3 percent grade means that the track will rise 3″ over 100″ of forward travel. Generally, three or four percent is as steep as a railroad should be; use less if possible.

The percentage of elevation of a grade can be easily measured using a simple homemade tool. You'll need a level (a line level or a carpenter's level is fine), a board a couple inches wide by 25″ long, and a step block. The step block (see drawing) needs to have ⅛″ steps in it, each step representing ½ percent of incline (you can use ¼″ steps to measure in full percentages, if you prefer).

To measure an existing grade, simply set the end of the board, with the level on top, at the high end, and elevate the lower end on the step block until it is level. Then just read off the elevation on the block. To plot a specific grade, fix the end of the board to the block at the desired percentage, then grade your line so that it reads level.

Building the Colorado & Pacific, part 4

Marc Horovitz

All photos by Marc Horovitz

With our trackwork complete, we could now turn our thoughts toward wiring the Colorado & Pacific. Since ours was a small railroad, wiring would be simple. There were two ways we could set up the wiring. Despite the railway's size, we could actually wire it in blocks for two-train operation. The mainline could be one block and the spur up the mountain another. This way, we could operate, say, a passenger train around the continuous loop while a small freight train took goods up and down the hill on what amounted to a separate point-to-point track. However, since we had only one electric locomotive, we decided to wire it up as a single block.

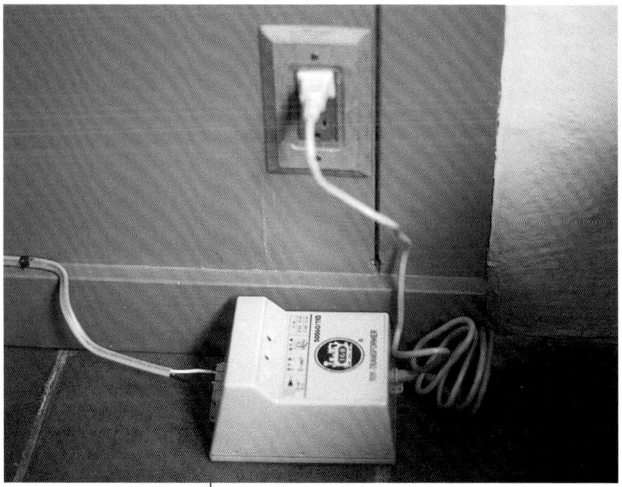

One of the biggest problems with a track-powered railway is maintaining electrical continuity across the joints, between the track sections. There are a couple good ways to remedy this problem. One is to solder jumper wires across each joint. Another is to solder the joint up solid. Since this was a small railway in a fair climate, we opted for the latter. On a larger railway, or on one subject to frost heave, soldering jumper wires across the joints will give the railroad more flexibility to move around as it needs to.

Soldering the joints

Soldering rail joints is a relatively simple matter with a small, hand-held butane torch. The rail ends must be clean. Since all of our track was new, this wasn't a problem. We used a liquid flux to ensure that the solder would flow properly. We covered the plastic ties adjacent to the joints with wet paper towels to minimize melting. You could also use wet ballast.

The secret to soldering is getting a lot of heat to the joint quickly, flowing the solder, and getting out. The heavy brass rails tend to suck up the heat, so this sometimes took a little longer than we expected. A few of the ties suffered a little damage, but when the ballast had been smoothed around the joints again, the melted ties were hard to see. We used jumper wires at the switches in case a switch went bad and had to be replaced. In that instance, jumper wires could be easily cut and the switch removed, whereas a soldered joint would be more difficult to undo.

Once the soldering was finished, we had a sort of monolithic electrical block. Because our track length was minimal, a single set of leads would accommodate the entire line. We soldered these leads to the rails near the upper end of the line at the patio, where our control station would be. We buried the line in the ground, with the ends of the wires sticking out where the controls would later be located.

Electricity

We wanted to keep the primary transformer in the house, out of the weather, and just run the low-voltage line down to the railway. An out-of-the-way place near an unused electrical outlet was found inside where the transformer could be permanently installed.

Unfortunately, the railway, at the bottom of the yard, was 40 or 50 feet away from the house, and there was no convenient way of permanently running an above-ground line down to it. On a trip to the hardware store we found some cable that was intended to be buried in the earth. This was heavy stuff that looked like it would last forever, so we bought enough for our job.

Upon returning home, we hooked the cable to the transformer and ran it through a small hole in the wall, which was later caulked. Most of the distance from the house to the railway was covered by lawn. Burying the cable was a relatively simple matter of inserting a shovel about 6″ into the turf, spreading the grass apart, laying the cable into the bottom of the split, then closing it up again. Even immediately after the cable was placed in the ground, its route was nearly invisible. We noted on our map the position of the cable for future reference.

« The construction of the Colorado & Pacific has reached the end, or is it the beginning? Plants are in, buildings are placed, and trains are running, but there's always lots to do on a garden railway.

^ Electrical leads, once they have been soldered to the rails, become nearly invisible.

^ The power supply lives indoors. Only the low-voltage line goes outside.

At the railway, we dug a hole in the ground and set a 4″ x 4″ post in it. This would support our control platform. Since all of our controls amounted to simply an LGB no. 5012 speed controller, nothing too fancy or elaborate was called for. Simple is good in garden railroading. We attached a plain wooden platform to the top of the post, which was set at a comfortable height for operating from a lawn chair while holding a hot dog in the one hand, and our controller was mounted to it. The simple expedient of a plastic bag over the lot when not in use would protect it from the weather.

We ran the cable underground from the house to the post, along with the lead from the track. We brought the cable and leads up the side of the post and anchored them neatly and securely so they wouldn't accidentally get snagged when we got up for another hot dog. Connections were now complete and it was time for our first test run, which was actually pretty exciting, given the amount of work we'd put into the project so far.

Electrical cable is easily buried in the turf by splitting the ground with a shovel.

This column supports our control center. Leads have been neatly attached to it.

Some hints on planting

When planting your railway garden, try to keep several things in mind. You want the garden to look natural and to reflect a full-size landscape. You are not creating a model of a landscape, but an actual landscape in miniature.

When planting a forest, plant the trees in groups or drifts, not evenly spotted over the landscape. Likewise, when planting the rest of the garden. Plants of the same type tend to grow together. A miniature landscape will have many examples of the same plant, as opposed to one each of a vast variety of individual plants.

Railway gardens are often planted in "zones." Zone One is the closest to the trains, track, structures, and other miniature man-made features. It is this zone that requires the most care, as you want these plants to be closest to scale and to relate to the miniatures in a plausible manner.

Zone Two is a sort of mid-ground. Larger plants can be planted in Zone Two, but these should still have small-scale elements—little leaves, fine twig structure, and so forth. Zone-Two plants can be used to fill larger areas away from the track.

Zone-Three plants can be just about anything. These larger plants form a backdrop to the whole scene and are, in a way, invisible. They are far enough away that their size does not appear incongruous to the small goings on in the foreground.

Before planting, arrange your plants around the railway and try to visualize what they will look like when they are in the ground and fully mature in two or three years. If you have the time and resources, you can plant densely at the beginning, then thin them out as they grow and fill the space. Otherwise, place your plants based on their growth habits, leaving them the space to fill in as they get bigger. Your railway will look bare and spotty the first year or so, but you'll be surprised at how it changes over time. Take some pictures right after you plant for reference. When you live with it on a daily basis it's sometimes hard to measure progress.

A variety of plants have been chosen to populate the railway. Some came from the nursery, some from friends, and some from other parts of the garden.

Max digs a hole in which he will plant a miniature tree.

The trains

As mentioned in the first installment, since we had a little railroad, small equipment was called for. The smaller the equipment, we reasoned, the greater the illusion of distance traveled.

So, we opted for the smallest equipment we could find, which was an LGB 0-4-2 Chloe; some of the little, open Grizzly Flats coaches for our passengers; and some of the four-wheel industrial freight stock that LGB offered. By using this diminutive equipment, we could still run trains of reasonable length—say six to eight cars—without having them look out of place on our minuscule railroad, especially if they were run at low scale speeds. Model railroading in all forms has to do with illusion. We model railroaders deal with the illusions of size, speed, time, and distance traveled, and we need to do everything we can to enhance those illusions.

With our new engine on our new track, we notched up our new controller and—it ran! Everything was as it was intended to be. We spent the next 30 or 40 minutes just running the engine around, up the mountain and back, and congratulating one another on what brilliant fellows we were. But we were far from being finished. We still had the garden and some final details to attend to.

The garden

While building the railroad we casually discussed plant material. What would look good here, what kind of effect were we trying to create there, how should we plant this rock formation? So, when it

finally came down to it, we had a rough idea about what we wanted.

The next step was a visit to the garden center with Rod's wife, Petria, our resident railway gardener. While we knew what we wanted as far as the look, Petria provided the necessary expertise to translate our nebulous and ill-expressed desires into reality. We discussed groundcovers, woody plants, miniature trees, and more. It was fun, walking around the nursery, seeing what was available, determining what would be right for specific areas of the line, and deciding if certain plants would be right for our microclimate.

We purchased a fair selection of plants of many different types and varieties and returned home, ready to plant. Because our dirt was so thin and dry, we also bought some planting soil to amend our own and help give the plants a good start.

The smallest, more in-scale plants we kept for sites near the track and to use in conjunction with our few structures. We reserved most of the miniature trees, the tallest plants, for the mountainside. These vertical elements would help to draw the

Plants of the same variety are arranged in drifts. While the area looks new and spotty here, once the trees grow up and the groundcover matures, it will fill in nicely.

The station, resplendent on its concrete platform, sits in a newly planted area of the railway. Smaller-scale plants are used close to track and structures.

Plant list for the Colorado & Pacific

Berkeley, California
USDA hardiness zone 10a
Plant list compiled by Petria MacDonnell

Dwarf Conifers

Chamaecyparis thyoides cv.
Dwarf red cedar
Juniperus procumbens 'Nana'
Japanese garden juniper
Tsuga mertensiana
Mountain hemlock

Small Shrubs and Perennials

Dianthus gratianopolitanus 'Tiny Rubies'
Tiny rubies dianthus
Hebe cupressoides 'Nana'
Dwarf cypress hebe
Rhododendron radicans
Miniature rhododendron
Rhodohypoxis baurii 'Pictus'
Red star
Sisyrinchium bellum 'Dwarf Blue'
Dwarf blue-eyed grass
Veronica x 'Waterperry Blue'
Waterperry blue veronica

Groundcovers

Cotula sp.
Brass buttons
Cymbalaria aequitriloba
Creeping cymbalaria
Herniaria glabra
Green carpet
Laurentia fluviatilis
Blue star creeper
Mentha requienii
Corsican mint
Raoulia australis
Silver raoulia
Sedum album
White sedum
Sedum spathulifolium 'Cape Blanco'
Cape Blanco sedum
Sedum sp.
Baby tears sedum
Sempervivum arachnoideum
Cobweb houseleek
Soleirolia soleirolii
Baby tears
Thymus pseudolanuginosus
Wooly thyme
Thymus serpyllym 'Reiter'
Reiters thyme

Annuals

Gypsophila muralis 'Gypsy'
Gypsy baby's breath
Nemesia caerulea 'Compact Innocence'
Dwarf nemesia
Verbena cv.
Verbena

eye up and make the mountain seem taller. Other intermediate-sized plants would be arranged in drifts and groups to fill in the surrounding areas.

To get an idea of how the whole thing would look, we simply placed the plants, in their pots, around the railway. We talked about them and we moved them around several times until we had what we wanted.

Then it was time to plant. With four of us working, this went quickly. For each plant, we dug a hole and added some amendment. We popped the plant out of its plastic pot, spread the roots a little, and plopped it into a hole. We packed in dirt around it to firmly hold it in place and gave it a drink of water to help it get started.

When we were done we admired our handiwork. It was a remarkable transformation. What had been before a dry, barren pile of dirt with a railroad around it suddenly became a miniature landscape, alive and green. Yes, it did look a little spotty, but that would change in time as the plants grew in and matured. We also knew that if, later, we didn't like something, we could easily change it.

Final details

Our railway was nearly finished, or at least as finished as a model railroad ever is. (There's always something else to do, change, or set right.) The final thing was the placement of the structures. Since we had limited land area to work with, we didn't want to fill it with buildings. Suggesting a town or human habitation would be better than trying to squeeze a whole town into our tiny space. Viewers could imagine that a town existed somewhere and that they could see only part of it from their vantage point.

After much discussion, we settled on just three structures, each integral to the functioning of the railroad. We had our old water tower from Grover Devine, a scratchbuilt structure that just exuded character; a passenger train needs a place to stop, so we had to have a station; and a freight train needs a source of freight, so we needed a structure for our banjo factory, high atop the mountain. That was it. Plastic kits sufficed for the latter two, most likely to be replaced at some later date by more attractive scratchbuilt structures.

A pet peeve shared by Rod and me was that, all too often, model buildings—particularly those in garden settings—suffer from two faults. They either don't stand exactly perpendicular to the earth or they don't actually meet the ground all the way

The railway with all its initial plantings in place. It is the plant material that brings the railway alive. It will always be changing. Some will die, others will thrive, new plants will be added, and maybe some will be moved to more appropriate locations.

Inset: The rock wall has been planted with sedums, hens-and-chicks, and other rock-garden plants.

Concrete foundations

A concrete foundation under a building is a fine thing. It is easy to make, cheap, and durable. If you should bring your buildings indoors, the foundation can stay outside to hold its place. Here's how we made the foundation and platform for our station.

We first marked on the ground the size and shape of the platform. This was important, since the whole concrete area was larger than the station building itself. For our other structures, we simply took their measurements.

Then we made a frame, or form, of 1″ x 2″ wood for the cement. The curved edge was actually the back of an old chair.

Next we dug away the ground where the foundation was to go, so the finished foundation would be at grade.

The area was leveled with ballast and the form placed in position next to the track.

Next, metal mesh, in this case some that we had on hand, was cut to size and tried in the form for fit.

The mesh was removed, we mixed our cement, and carefully poured it into the form, filling it about halfway. The mesh was placed over the wet cement and more cement was placed on top. Using homemade tools, the cement was smoothed and left to cure.

After the concrete had hardened, the form was carefully removed, leaving a beautiful new foundation and station platform. The earth around it was backfilled, leaving the foundation sticking up just a little. When the area and been planted and the station put in place, everything looked just right.

1 The formwork for the foundation has been made and its location marked on the ground.

2 A hole has been dug, the bottom filled with ballast and leveled, and the form placed in it. The wire mesh is being tried on for size.

3 The finished station platform. Backfilling around the edge remains to be finished.

around, or both. We reasoned that a full-size building sits on a foundation to prevent problems such as these, so why should a miniature building be any different? So, we provided each of our three structures with a real concrete foundation. These made a world of difference. They provided each building with both a firm footing and a sense of place. Our buildings looked to us as though they were really meant to be where they were placed.

So, we have arrived at the end of our journey—or have we arrived at its beginning? We have a fully functional garden railway, attractively planted, with some structures to give it humanity and purpose. What's left? Well, two of the buildings cry out to be replaced with more charismatic scratchbuilt ones. The trains look bright, shiny, and new. Some painting and weathering, perhaps in our own Colorado & Pacific livery would be nice.

The garden will need attention as time goes on. Plants will die and need to be replaced. The ones that thrive will need pruning. Trees, as they grow, can be trimmed to resemble gnarly old mountain pines. New areas can be developed.

And already there is some discussion of a branch line to another part of the yard. A garden railroad is not something you have, it is something you do—a journey, not a destination. Building the Colorado & Pacific has been a lot of hard work, but great fun as well, as we saw our dreams and ideas come to fruition by our own sweat and labor. What could be more satisfying?

Grover Devine's old Camp Teller water tower represents the engine-servicing facilities on the C&P.

GLOSSARY

Basic garden railroading terms

Kevin Strong

All photos by Kevin Strong

East Broad Top no. 11 dodges the sunlight as it winds its way along the right-of-way. Ballast covers the ties past the bridge. Moss provides lush groundcover.

Before venturing too far into the backyard, it would probably behoove us to update our vocabulary a little. Like any new venture, garden railroading has its own lingo. Knowing the terminology will allow you to better communicate and understand the advice you get from others. What follows is a basic glossary of some of the terms you will encounter as you begin your journey outdoors.

Note: Some concepts have different terms, depending upon which side of the Atlantic Ocean you live. Where there is a difference, the British nomenclature is in parentheses.

Alternating current—AC. This is a form of electrical power in which the current goes first one direction, then the other. Our household electricity is 120 volts

AC. This type of power is fine for running light bulbs and some garden-railroad accessories (after the voltage is reduced to a manageable and safe level), but is not intended for the trains. See "transformer."

Ballast. Material put down around the track to provide support and allow for drainage. In garden-railway circles, this is usually in the form of crusher fines or some other small stone. (Chicken grit is a popular choice.)

Control panel. A central location where all the controls for the railroad are located. There is often a graphic representation of the railroad on the panel showing locations of turnouts and sidings, and electrical switches for turning power to particular sections of the railroad on and off. If there is a fixed throttle for the railroad, it is usually located here as well.

Coupler. The device used to connect the cars in a train.

Crossing. The place where two tracks cross one another, or where a road crosses the track.

Current. The flow of elections through a wire or rail that provides power for electrical devices.

Curve radius. A measure of how tight a curve is. While most of our trains are designed to operate around a 2-foot radius, it's advisable to use the widest possible radius that will fit the available space. The radius of a curve is measured from the center point of the circle of which the curve is a part.

Cut (or cutting). A slice through a hill or mountain through which a railroad runs.

Dogbone. A type of trackplan in

< ^ ^ Turnouts are a necessary part of a railroad if you want track that go in different directions.

< ^ Woodland Railway no. 18 leaves the tunnel and enters the cutting as it starts its downhill ride to Woodland Junction. When a hill got too tall for a cut, a tunnel was bored.

^ The engineer keeps a sharp eye out. A trestle is often the focal point of a garden railroad, and it is worth the time and effort it takes to build one. They are not, however, indestructible, as can be seen by the broken cross brace at the bottom.

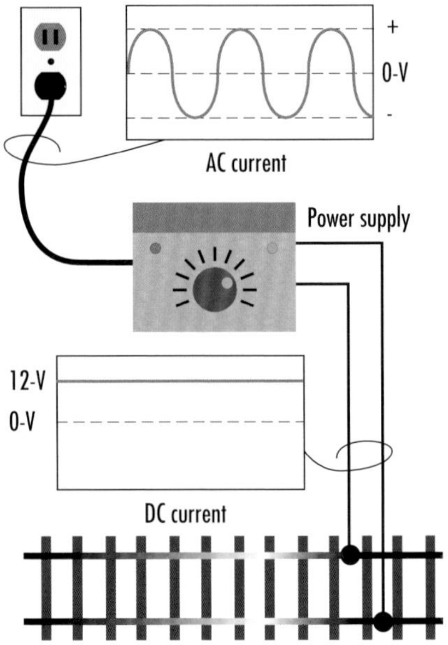

Electricity

Railroad yards can be either stub-end yards or through yards like this one on the author's railroad.

which there is a loop at either end of a long, narrow section of double track.

Direct current—DC. A form of electrical power in which the current flows only in one direction. This can come either from batteries or from AC power that has been rectified and filtered (electrical terms that mean it cleans up the AC power and makes it useful for us). Most of our trains operate on between 12 and 24 volts DC. See "power supply."

Drainage ditch. A channel designed to carry water run-off. For our purposes, it can either mean a model of one along the right-of-way, or a full-size one intended to divert water away from or around the garden railroad.

Embankment. The side of a hill or fill. A typical angle for an embankment is around 40 degrees from the horizontal. Much steeper, and the material used in the embankment will tend to wash away.

Fill. An area where the ground is built up to support the track.

Frog. The center part of a turnout where the rails converge. In model-railroad terms, a frog can be either "live" or "dead." A live frog carries electricity to the trains, whereas a dead one doesn't. Most commercially available turnouts have dead frogs.

Gauge. The distance between the insides of the rails on the track. The most common gauge for outdoor modeling in the U.S. is no. 1 gauge (45mm).

Grade. A measure of the steepness of a hill or incline, most often measured in terms of a percentage. A 3 percent grade has 3″ of rise for every 100″ of length. It is advisable to keep grades as flat as possible in the garden. The steepest practical grade for outdoor railroads is around 4 percent. You can build them steeper if you want, but your usable train length will be significantly shortened and you will put undue stress on the motor of your locomotive.

Groundcover. Low-growing plants that grow along the right-of-way and elsewhere in the garden. These plants often have very small leaves, the idea being that they represent grass and other low plants that would occur naturally next to a railroad.

Ground throw. A low device (as opposed to a switchstand) used to manu-

‹ ^ Woodland Railway no. 3 (upper right) enters the passing siding at Strongton.

^ Scale is simply the ratio of the size of the prototype to the size of the model. The caboose in the picture is 1/22 the size of the prototype that runs on the full-size rails.

‹ Groundcovers provide a scenic function as well as the practical one of holding the soil in place. Mosses make great, low-lying groundcovers.

ally throw the points of a turnout one way or another.

Irrigation. A method of getting water to the plants on the railroad. This can be as simple as a lawn sprinkler or as complex as a full, drip-irrigation system. Your local nursery will be able to give you information about those, should you elect to go that route.

Live steam. A term used to describe locomotives in the garden scales that run on real steam. They have a small boiler and a burner that heats the water to create steam. This is perhaps as close to "the real thing" as you can get in this scale when it comes to running a locomotive.

Locomotive. The moving force on a train, normally located at the front.

Mainline. The primary route of travel of a railroad.

Motor. (1) The electrical device that provides the force necessary to move the locomotive. This force is transferred to the wheels through a set of gears or pulleys. (2) A small, self-propelled rail vehicle with a gasoline engine (railcar, maintenance car, etc.). Short for "rail motor."

Points. The moving rails of a turnout that determine which way the train will go through. These are moved by a ground throw or switchstand.

Power supply. A device that supplies the necessary power for the railroad and its accessories. it usually consists of a transformer to change the voltage to 24V and rectifier to convert the AC power to DC. It may also contain a throttle, which varies the voltage going to the trains.

Prototype. A term applied to full-size trains, structures, or other things upon which our models are based.

Rail. The metal bars that support the weight of the train. When these are attached to the ties, they form the track. The most common metals for rails in the garden are brass, aluminum, nickel silver, and stainless steel.

Rail joiner. This is the mechanical device that holds the sections of rail together and in alignment. Usually, these are sheets of brass or steel bent in the shape of the base of a rail, but can take other forms such, as clamps or strips of metal bolted to the rail.

Retaining wall. A structure, usually made of stone or wood, anchored firmly in the ground, that holds back the earth behind it. It is usually used in places

Retaining walls are often used to elevate a railroad to a more comfortable level. Here, Dave Goodson of Seattle, Washington, has used large rocks to build up the peninsula in the middle of his railroad.

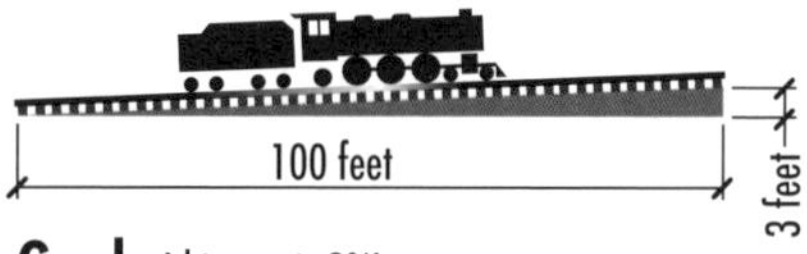

Grade (this one is 3%)

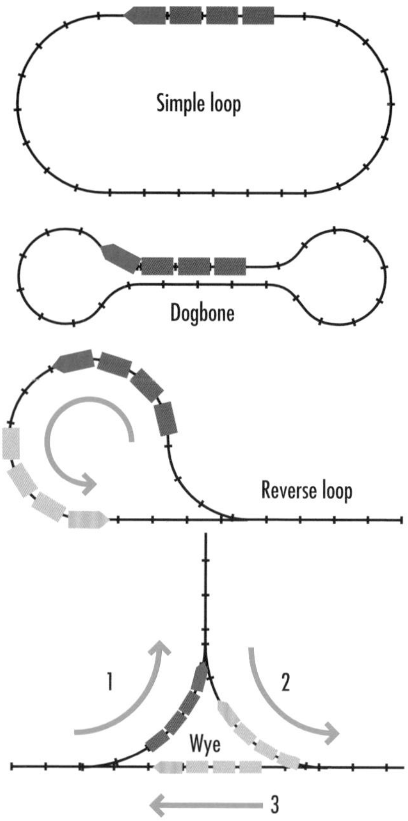

Trackplans

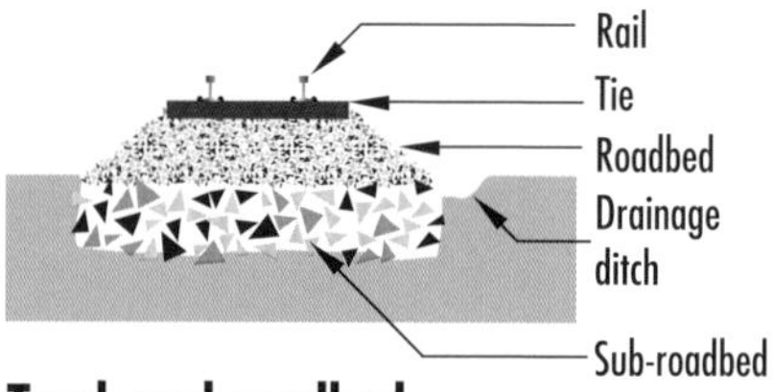

Track and roadbed

where physical space limitations prohibit the use of an embankment. In the garden, we use both full-size and miniature retaining walls in our landscaping.

Reverse loop. The most common method for turning trains around on a railroad in which the track loops around, connecting with itself to form a teardrop. Electrical considerations must be made when using reverse loops, as the power going to the train will otherwise short-circuit.

Right-of-way (permanent way). The physical space that a track occupies.

Rolling stock. The cars that make up the trains on a railroad.

Roadbed. The ground support on which the track is laid.

Scale. A ratio showing the size relationship between a model and its prototype. A 1:20-scale locomotive is 1/6 the size of the prototype upon which it was based.

Siding. A stretch of track alongside the mainline on which a train can sit, safely out of the way of another train passing on the mainline.

Sound system. An electronic means of making model trains sound like full-size trains. Today's systems use digital recordings and can be quite realistic, adding to the atmosphere in the garden.

Spike. A small, specialized nail used to hold the rail to the tie. The head of the nail is offset to one side, allowing it to overlap the base of the rail and hold it in place.

Spur. A branch line off of the mainline of the railroad. A spur generally runs to a specific town or industry that the railroad serves.

Sub-roadbed. The foundation below the roadbed. This often takes the form of a trench filled with stone or treated lumber. The particular construction method is usually dictated by the climate in which you live.

Switch. (1) An electrical device that allows us to either turn power on or off, or change the direction of current on a given section of the railroad. (2) A piece of track (called points in Britain) that allows the railroad to head off in two separate directions. (in model-railroad circles, we often refer to these as "turnouts," to avoid confusion with the first definition.)

Switchstand. A (usually) waist level, mechanical device (as opposed to a ground throw) used to move the points on a switch. A switchstand usually bears a "target" at the top, a device that indicates to an engineer which way the switch is set.

Terminal. The beginning or end of a railroad mainline. A terminal usually has a yard for storing rolling stock and locomotive-servicing facilities.

Throttle. The device used to control the speed (and direction) of a locomotive.

Tie (sleeper). A piece of wood or other material used to support the rails on a stretch of track and keep them in gauge.

Trackplan. A drawing or map of where the tracks in a model railroad actually go and how they are connected to one another. This can also show the locations of towns, buildings, and other physical and landscape features associated with the railroad.

Transformer. An electrical device that takes household power and lowers its voltage to a safe level for use in the garden.

Trestle. A long wooden (or steel) bridge used to traverse expanses where a fill is not possible or desirable.

Truck (bogie). The swiveling four- or six-wheel carriage beneath the railroad car. Two of these support the car.

Turnout. Term given to a "railroad switch" by model railroaders to avoid confusion with the electrical switch used to supply power to various parts of a model railroad.

USDA Plant Hardiness Zone. A climate scale devised by the U.S. Department of Agriculture, based on average minimum temperatures in the U.S. This scale is used to determine which plants are able to survive in your specific geographic region. The lower the number on the scale, the colder it gets in the winter.

Wiring. The electrical switches and lengths of wire used to get the power from the power supply to the model railroad. The more complex the railroad, the more complex the wiring.

Wye. A method used by prototype railroads to turn trains around. These generally aren't too popular in the garden, as they tend to take up a lot of space and require a lot of special wiring. Reverse loops are the generally accepted substitute.

Yard. An array of tracks used to store trains when not running on the mainline. These are usually found in small or large towns along the way and at the major terminals of a railroad.

Suppliers and organizations

When writing for information, be sure to include a self-addressed, stamped envelope. Some firms offer free catalogs or literature; others charge for their catalogs. Some large railroad suppliers will sell directly to consumers; others sell only to hobby shops. Always check with your local hobby shop before attempting to order direct from a manufacturer or importer. If you don't have a hobby shop in your area, there are a number of firms that sell large scale equipment by mail order.

Aristo-Craft
698 S. 21st St.
Irvington, NJ 07111
Gauge 1 track plus a complete line of 1:29 scale locomotives, cars, and accessories

Bachmann Industries, Inc.
1400 East Erie Ave.
Philadelphia, PA 19124
Complete line of Gn3 products, including locomotives, cars, track, power packs, train sets, and accessories

Coronado Scale Models
1544 E. Cypress St.
Phoenix, AZ 85006
Mail order source for ½" scale kits and parts for scratchbuilding

Depot G Hobbies
371 Florida Ln.
Winfield, IL 60190
Structure kits and freight car loads

Eastern Railways
RD 1, Box 254
Beech Creek, PA 16822
Importer of handcrafted brass locomotives and cars in No. 1 scale

***Finescale Railroader* Magazine**
1574 Kerryglen St.
Westlake, CA 91361
Bimonthly magazine devoted to large scale railroading outdoors

***Garden Railways* Magazine**
21027 Crossroads Circle
P.O. Box 1612
Waukesha, WI 53187
Bimonthly magazine serving the hobby of garden railroading. See the latest issue of *Garden Railways* magazine for up-to-date information on garden railway clubs.

Garich Light Transport
13428 209th St. S.E.
Issaqua, WA 98027
Gauge 1 track, turnout kits, rail, spikes, tie plates, dual-gauge track (0 and 1)

Grandt Line Products Inc.
1040 Shary Ct.
Concord, CA 94518
Manufacturer of ½" plastic scale windows, doors, and other parts for scratchbuilding structures

Kadee Quality Products Co.
673 Ave. C
White City, OR 97503
Knuckle couplers for large scale that can be uncoupled over magnetic uncoupling ramps

LGB of America
6444 Nancy Ridge Dr.
San Diego, CA 92121
U.S. office of German firm Ernst Paul Lehmann, which invented G scale in 1968. Company offers a complete line of Gn3 equipment, including locomotives, cars, track, figures, power packs, and accessories

LGB Model Railroad Club, Inc.
1854 Erin Dr.
Altoona, PA 16602
Association of LGB fans publishes a magazine and sponsors an annual convention

Lionel Corporation
50625 Richard W. Blvd.
Chesterfield, MI 48051-2493
Manufacturer of No. 1 scale locomotives, cars, and track

Micro Engineering Company
1120 Eagle Rd.
Fenton, MO 63026
Gauge 1 track and turnouts sold under the G-TRAK brand name

Mini Forest by Sky
P.O. Box 1156
Mulino, OR 97042
Source for miniature trees and groundcovers suitable for garden railroads

Miniature Plant Kingdom
4125 Harrison Grade Rd.
Sebastopol, CA 95472
Source for miniature trees and flowers suitable for garden railroads

Model Die Casting, Inc.
5070 Sigstrom Ave.
Carson City, NV 89701
Gn3 locomotives and freight cars, 1:32 scale freight cars

***Model Railroader* Magazine**
21027 Crossroads Circle
P.O. Box 1612
Waukesha, WI 53187
Leading model railroad magazine, serving all scales

Model Rectifier Corp. (MRC)
200 Carter Dr.
P.O. Box 267
Edison, NJ 08818
Power packs

National Model Railroad Association (NMRA)
4121 Cromwell Rd.
Chattanooga, TN 37421
International association of model railroad hobbyists. Organization sets industry standards, publishes a monthly magazine, and sponsors local meets and regional and national conventions. Write for current annual membership fee.

Nicholas Smith Trains
2343 West Chester Pike
Broomall, PA 19008
Mail-order source for large scale trains

NorthWest Short Line
Box 423
Seattle, WA 98111
Motors, gears, special tools, gauge 1 power packs

Ozark Miniatures
P.O. Box 107
DeSoto, MO 63020
G scale logging equipment and detail parts

Playmobil USA Inc.
P.O. Box 877
Dayton, NJ 08810
Toy manufacturer whose line includes large scale trains, sets, and accessories for young children (LGB compatible)

Pola
Am Bahndamm 59
D-8734 Rothhausen
Germany
Manufacturer of G scale structures

Preiser
Steinfield Postfach 12-33
D-8803 Rothenburg o.d.T.
Germany
Extensive line of G scale and some No. 1 scale (1:32) figures of people and animals, plus detail items

St. Aubin Station
11100 Rt. 176
Woodstock, IL 60098
Source for large scale trains and plant items

San-Val Trains
2444 Valjean Ave.
Van Nuys, CA 91406
Mail order source for large scale trains. Manufactures gauge 1 wheelsets, track-cleaning devices, and screw-on rail joiners

Sidestreet Bannerworks
P.O. Box 460222
Denver, CO 80224
Videotapes on garden railroading, gauge 3 freight car trucks, and small scale live-steam locomotives

***Steam in the Garden* Magazine**
P.O. Box 335
Newark Valley, NY 13811
Publication dedicated exclusively to small scale live-steam locomotives operated on garden railways

USA Trains
P.O. Box 100
Malden, MA 02148
Manufacturer of a line of Gn3 freight cars

Watts' Train Shop
9180 Hunt Club Rd.
Zionsville, IN 46007
Mail order source for G scale trains

West Lawn Locomotive Works
P.O. Box 570
Madison, WI 53701
Source for gauge 1 live-steam locomotives

William K. Walthers, Inc.
P.O. Box 3039
Milwaukee, WI 53201-3039
Manufacturer and distributor of model railroad products in all scales. Publishes a catalog and reference manual, *The World of Large Scale Trains*, which lists most products offered.